The
SECOND COMING
of SATURN

*"...returns old Saturn's reign, with a
new breed of men sent down from heaven."*

The
SECOND COMING
of SATURN

*The Great Conjunction, America's Temple,
and the Return of the Watchers*

DEREK P. GILBERT

DEFENDER
CRANE, MO

The Second Coming of Saturn: The Great Conjunction, America's Temple, and the Return of the Watchers
By Derek P. Gilbert

All rights reserved. Published 2021. Printed in the United States of America.

ISBN: 978-1948014519

A CIP catalog record of this book is available from the Library of Congress.

Cover illustration and design by Jeffrey Mardis.

All Scripture quotations from the English Standard Version unless otherwise noted.

CONTENTS

PREFACE

Before you go any further, please read this.

In our previous books, Sharon and I have attempted to sketch the history of the long supernatural war between God and the gods. We've found that the three-letter word *G-O-D* is a stumbling block to some, so I'd like to explain how and why I use it.

Modern Christians have been taught and conditioned to believe that there is only one God in all of creation. That is true. However, as the Hebrew prophets, the first-century apostles, and the early Church Fathers knew, there are many gods.

We English-speakers tend to use that three-letter word as a proper name: "God," meaning the Creator, the God of Abraham, Isaac, and Jacob; the Trinity, composed of Father, Son, and Holy Spirit. But "God" is not the name by which He revealed Himself to Moses. The name God shared with Moses was I AM, or YHWH, which is usually transliterated into English as "Yahweh." (And before that, He was known to Abraham, Isaac, and Jacob as *El Shaddai*, usually rendered in English as "God Almighty.")

The bottom line is this: The English word "god," with a lower-case *g*, refers to a spirit being, a denizen of the spirit realm, often worshiped by pagans as a deity. If this sounds like polytheism, please put that thought out of your mind. God—that is, Yahweh—calls these beings "gods" multiple times in the Old Testament. This is solid theological ground. These entities are not imaginary; God Himself decreed judgment against the gods of Egypt in Exodus 12:12, issued a death sentence to the unjust gods of the nations in Psalm 82, and made His will clear to Moses when He issued the first of the Ten Commandments, "Thou shalt have no other gods before Me."

Jesus equated Satan with Baal[1] and Zeus (the Greek form of Baal),[2] and I think we can agree that Satan exists. If Satan exists, then Baal/Zeus is real; and if Baal is real, then why not Astarte (Aphrodite/Venus), Chemosh (Ares/Mars), and the rest of the pagan pantheon? As we've shown in previous books, the pagan gods are there if we dig beneath the English translations. Words like "plague," "hail," "pestilence," and "terror" were gods and demons well-known to the prophets and apostles named Resheph (Apollo to the Greeks and Romans), Barad, Deber, and Pachad.

The use of the plural "gods" in Exodus 12, Psalm 82, and other Bible verses is significant. Contrary to what most of us were taught in church, our supernatural enemy is not just "the" devil. Satan is important, yes, but an entire army of fallen angels and demons—"gods"—is preparing for a final war against our Creator.

But deep in the earth, in an unimaginably dark prison, an old and powerful entity has been in chains for millennia. In this book, I call him a god because that's how he was known to the ancient world. That's how he and his brothers were known to our Lord. He plans to return to the earth as a god. And not just as "a" god—he schemes to become "the" god, replacing Yahweh as supreme in the cosmos.

He is in chains, but his role in the long rebellion of the gods is not yet ended.

This is his story.

---

1. Matthew 12:22–26.

2. Revelation 2:13. Pergamum was the home of "Satan's seat," the Great Altar of Zeus.

FOREWORD
by Pastor Carl Gallups

Following are just a few delectable excerpts from Derek Gilbert's *Saturn's Reign*, hopefully giving you a taste of what you're about to experience.

> The movement of the planets and the stars across the sky do not have any influence on our lives whatsoever. But *important people believe they do*, so it's worth paying attention. We want to understand what the enemy—by which I mean fallen angels and demons who have been worshiped by pagans for thousands of years—wants them, and us, to think.
>
> If this sounds to you like a fanciful conflation of the Bible with a hodgepodge of ancient myths and legends, you would have been among a small minority in the early church. Christians during the first few centuries after the Resurrection knew that the gods of their pagan neighbors were fallen angels and demons....
>
> The goal of this book is to shed some light on a powerful, supernatural rebel who continues to influence the world today. We'll examine what the ancients believed about this entity and share some surprising examples of how he is still venerated.

Interested yet? Just wait!

Before you begin reading Derek's newest offering to the world of biblical enlightenment, let me first share a few tidbits of personal insight about the man himself.

I have known and worked with Derek for a number of years. His mind is like an effervescent encyclopedia of knowledge. His impeccable research skills are a thing to behold. And his insatiable thirst for digging deeper into the buried mysteries of God's Word is academically enviable. Within the context of our numerous theological conversations and the countless hours spent together in broadcasting and conference settings, I have learned a lot from Derek about several intricate and often over-looked biblical concepts that directly connect to what we're watching unfold around us in our rapidly changing world.

But what impresses me most is that within the vast collection of his amazing and God-given skill sets, he's simply a down-to-earth, humble, and amazing person who genuinely loves the Lord Jesus Christ and His Word. And, to top it all off, he's a blast to hang out with! If you've ever had the pleasure of meeting him in person, you know exactly what I mean.

The unique combination of all these attributes, wrapped up in one great person, make for a very rare package indeed. To me, this is another reason that Derek's books are so enjoyable to read. You can feel his enthusiasm for what he's discovered within every page he writes. As you can tell, I'm not only a big fan of the man, but I'm also an aficionado of the stunning truths he's consistently mining out of God's Word and the annals of ancient history.

As you embark upon this stunning journey of a biblical, theological, and historical treasure trove of thought-provoking propositions, make certain that you have a highlighter pen handy! This is a book you'll want to keep in your library, refer back to, and share with others many times over.

When you've completed your reading of *The Second Coming of Saturn*, you'll be left anxiously awaiting his next book. Knowing Derek as I do, I'd be shocked if that subsequent work isn't coming relatively soon. In fact, he's probably researching it right now!

But until the next one appears, *you have this one*! Prepare yourself for a biblical excursion like you've probably never before experienced.

I assure you—you'll be glad you took the voyage.

THE GREAT CONJUNCTION

I t's fitting that this book is coming together now. It's been percolating in my head for a while, but other projects took priority and pushed this one back until recently, when it suddenly became obvious that the timing was ideal to buckle down and finish it.

The year 2020 is drawing to a close as I write this. It was a year few of us will remember fondly. We've been locked down, compelled to wear masks in public, seen friends and family members grow ill and, in some cases, die of a disease that didn't even exist eighteen months ago, as far as we know. Wealthy elites openly campaign to use the COVID-19 pandemic to justify a fundamental transformation of our world. This is the Great Reset initiative promoted by the World Economic Forum, which they tell us would create a utopia in which most of us will own nothing and be happy. Whether they truly believe that or just say they do to sell you and me on the idea is an open question.

Meanwhile, the evening skies above our home featured a rare sight as the two outermost planets visible to the naked eye, Jupiter and Saturn, came within a tenth of a degree of each other on the winter solstice, December 21, 2020. This was the closest conjunction between the two since 1623, and the closest *observable* conjunction since 1226.[3] Famed astronomer Johannes Kepler thought that this astronomical event might have been the Star of Bethlehem that guided the Magi to the Christ child, although the nearest Jupiter-Saturn conjunction to the birth of Jesus was in 7 BC, too early for the other historical clues in Scripture.[4]

That hasn't stopped the media from dubbing the Great Conjunction "the Christmas Star," even though the actual event was much less impressive than the Star of Bethlehem depicted on greeting cards. The link between Christmas and the winter solstice, which has been accepted by some well-meaning but misinformed Christians, is certainly more palatable to our secular culture than a connection to God made flesh. Certainly, the principalities and powers behind the scenes prefer that we identify the season with Saturnalia, and the dark god behind it, rather than with Jesus Christ.

We'll deal with that in the book, but for the record: The selection of December 25 as the date to celebrate the birth of Christ had nothing to do with Saturnalia or the winter solstice. Besides, Saturnalia wasn't always celebrated in December, and it wasn't even originally named for Saturn.

We Christians understand that our lives are not dictated by the movements of the planets. Astrology, defined as looking to the stars to

3. Deborah Byrd and Bruce McClure, "Jupiter and Saturn's Great Conjunction Is Today!" *EarthSky*, Dec. 21, 2020. https://earthsky.org/astronomy-essentials/great-jupiter-saturn-conjunction-dec-21-2020, retrieved 12/28/20.

4. The Star of Bethlehem was more likely a series of conjunctions in 3 BC that culminated on September 11 of that year when Jupiter and Regulus came together, representing the king of the Roman pantheon and the "king star" in Leo. See E. L. Martin's *The Star That Astonished the World*, available to read free online: http://www.askelm.com/star/index.asp, retrieved 12/28/20.

foretell the future, is forbidden in Scripture,[5] and it's junk science besides. Still, it's significant that the Great Conjunction fell exactly one month before the World Economic Forum met to unveil its Great Reset. Why? Because even in our technologically advanced age, astrology still guides the actions and decisions of many otherwise intelligent, productive people. In fact, it's experiencing something of a boom in recent years. A study by Pew Research found that about a third of Americans between ages eighteen and forty-nine believe in astrology,[6] part of a growing "psychic services" industry that takes in more than $2 billion a year in the United States.[7]

Astrologers call the Great Conjunction of 2020 the "Great Mutation." Saturn and Jupiter met at 0° of Aquarius, signifying the end of a transition from "earth" signs to "air." (Yes, more than half a century after the Fifth Dimension released its iconic song, we have, finally, fully entered the Age of Aquarius.) Astrologers claim this signals a shift to a world that's less materialistic and more decentralized—a transformation into the World Economic Forum's new socialist order.

In short, it looks like some very powerful people believe the Great Mutation is the trigger for the Great Reset, and they're working very hard to make it so.

What does Saturn have to do with geopolitics or economic policy? Those who believe our lives are ruled by the stars will tell you that Saturn means a return to reality. Rules, structure, hard work, and the old ways

5. Deuteronomy 18:10; Isaiah 47:13–14.

6. Claire Gecewicz, "'New Age' Beliefs Common among Both Religious and Nonreligious Americans." *FactTank*, Oct. 1, 2018. https://www.pewresearch.org/fact-tank/2018/10/01/new-age-beliefs-common-among-both-religious-and-nonreligious-americans/, retrieved 12/28/20.

7. "Psychic Services Industry in the US." *IBISworld*, Dec. 1, 2019. https://www.ibisworld.com/united-states/market-research-reports/psychic-services-industry/, retrieved 12/28/20.

of doing things are ascribed to Saturn. Jupiter, on the other hand, represents spiritual insight and innovation. The conflict between those two is reminiscent of their history in the religions of Greece, Rome, Anatolia (ancient Turkey), Canaan, and Mesopotamia, as revealed in the myths of Zeus and Kronos, Teshub and Kumarbi, Baal and El, and Marduk and Enlil.

To emphasize the point, I will repeat: The movement of the planets and the stars across the sky do not have any influence on our lives whatsoever. But *important people believe they do*, and so it's worth paying attention. We want to understand what the enemy—by which I mean fallen angels and demons—wants us to think.

Saturn has been known by many names over the years. In Greece, he was Kronos, king of the Titans. To the Phoenicians, he was known as Baal Hammon. The Hittites and Hurrians, who lived in what is today Turkey and the Kurdish regions of northern Syria and Iraq, called him Kumarbi. Canaanites called him El, while their Amorite cousins farther east knew him as Dagan (Dagon of the Philistines). He was Assur, chief god of the Assyrians, and in Akkad and Sumer, he was Enlil.

I'll piece together evidence to show you that this entity was also Milcom, chief god of the Ammonites, whose name was twisted by the Hebrew prophets into Molech—the abomination who demanded that his followers sacrifice their children in fire, and who convinced Solomon to build a high place on the Mount of Olives that looked down on the Temple of Yahweh.

I will make the case that the ancient world knew him as Shemihazah, leader of a rebellious faction of powerful angels who plotted to corrupt humanity and steal dominion of the earth for their own race of hybrid offspring, the gigantic Nephilim. I'll show that the cult of the dead Sharon and I documented in our 2019 book *Veneration* was inspired by this entity, and, thanks to recent archaeological discoveries, we can pinpoint the cult's historic roots on the Ararat Plain—the land below the mountains where the ark of Noah came to rest.

And I will argue that parallel Scriptures in Isaiah 14 and Ezekiel 28 are condemnations of this entity, and not the serpent in the Garden of Eden.

In other words, Lucifer is not Satan—it's Shemihazah.

If this sounds to you like a fanciful conflation of the Bible with a hodgepodge of ancient myths and legends, you would have been among a small minority in the early church. Christians during the first few centuries after the Resurrection knew that the gods of their pagan neighbors were fallen angels and demons. Paul, for one, was explicit on that point. Further, the early Church Fathers identified the heroes and demigods of Greece and Rome as the Rephaim of Canaan, who were understood to be the demonic spirits of the Nephilim destroyed in the Flood.

The Bible tells us that Saturn/Shemihazah and his co-conspirators are chained in a place of impenetrable darkness, where they will remain until the time of the end. Less than a hundred years after John wrote the book of Revelation, one of the most important early Christian theologians, Irenaeus of Lyon, speculated that the prophesied Antichrist might be called "Teitan," a variant of "Titan" that numerologically equals 666. Jewish religious scholars who translated the Hebrew Scriptures into Greek about three centuries before the birth of Jesus made the connection obvious by translating the Hebrew word *rephaim* into *titanes* and *gigantes*—"Titans" and "giants."

The goal of this book is to shed some light on a powerful supernatural rebel who still influences the world today. We'll examine what the ancients believed about this entity and share some surprising examples of how he is still venerated. Technocrats and secret societies are working to bring to life what they believe is a prophecy more than two thousand years old, composed by the Roman poet Virgil just after the reign of Julius Caesar, less than half a century before the birth of Jesus.

The poet looked ahead to the return of a Golden Age, ushered in by a savior—a boy who would "receive the life of gods" and grow to rule a world at peace. In later years, some Christians tried to interpret the poem as a prophecy of Jesus Christ, but the piece is clearly pagan. Virgil longed for "a new breed of men sent down from heaven" and "heroes with gods commingling," concepts that are not exactly Christian. They are, however, entirely consistent with the pluralistic, transhuman future envisioned by the globalists at the World Economic Forum.

The relevance of Virgil's classic work is this: The pagan poet prophesied that this glorious future would arrive when "the majestic roll of circling centuries begins anew." Astrologers, New Agers, occultists, and some of the world's wealthiest and most powerful people believe this cosmic Great Reset began with the Great Conjunction of December 21, 2020, an event that marked a new beginning; a blessed change from the harsh, iron rule of Jupiter—and the return of old Saturn's reign.

Chapter One

SHEMIHAZAH

Let's start with a bit of explanation about where this book is going. It's my belief that the entity known to us as the Roman god Saturn or his Greek equivalent Kronos has gone by many names over the centuries. We can trace his origins much farther in history, however, than the classical era—farther even than Greece's Archaic period, which began around the time that Isaiah was called to prophesy in the middle of the eighth century BC.

In this book, when you see any of these names: Saturn, Kronos, Baal Hammon, El, Milcom (and its variant, Molech), Dagan, Assur, Enlil, Kumarbi, and Shemihazah, please remember that they all refer to the same entity. It's the same god who's used different identities as times, places, and people changed.

I believe this entity has two other names, but I'll withhold those for now to build dramatic tension.

The characteristics of this entity—his personality, if you will—has changed over the years, or at least has been perceived differently by various cultures. He was often seen as cunning, cruel, and vindictive, especially where humans were concerned; at other times, he was believed to be kindly, wise, and the ruler of a better time when the world was at peace and blessed with plenty.

All of his aspects, however, are linked to the netherworld. Clues embedded in the myths and rituals of the cultures that occupied the lands of the Bible lead to fascinating conclusions about the nature of this character.

Most significant, he led a rebellion against God that was remembered by Jews of the Second Temple period, the time that includes the ministries of Jesus and the apostles. This uprising, believed to be one of the reasons the world is in its fallen state, is referenced in the New Testament, most prominently by Peter and Jude. This rebellion not only violated a taboo against species propagating outside of their own kind, but Saturn and his colleagues were also condemned for teaching humanity things we weren't supposed to know.

For this rebellion, he and his associates were banished to Tartarus. This is an important piece of information that's not obvious to English-speakers because the Greek word *tartarōsas* in 2 Peter 2:4 is rendered "hell" in most English-language Bibles.

However, even though his rebellion took place before the Flood of Noah and was probably the reason for it, this fallen angel still affects our world today, and not in a good way. How is that possible? We can only speculate, but I'll try to offer some plausible reasons.

We'll begin with his oldest incarnation and work our way forward in time. This takes us back to the first book of the Bible, where the first four verses of the sixth chapter of Genesis describe, very briefly, an event that's had a far-reaching impact on humanity.

When man began to multiply on the face of the land and daughters were born to them, the sons of God saw that the daughters of man were attractive. And they took as their wives any they chose. Then the Lord said, "My Spirit shall not abide in man forever, for he is flesh: his days shall be 120 years." The Nephilim were on the earth in those days, and also afterward, when the sons of God came in to the daughters of man and they bore children to them. These were the mighty men who were of old, the men of renown. (Genesis 6:1–4)

Those four verses are among the most controversial in the Bible. The early church understood their meaning. So did the apostles. In short, the "sons of God" were supernatural beings who came to earth and mated with human women. These unions produced monstrous offspring with disastrous consequences.

This is not the majority view of Christian theologians today. Most seminaries teach that the *bene ha'elohim* of Genesis 6 were righteous male descendants of Seth, the third son of Adam and Eve. The Nephilim were created by their unions with the wicked female descendants of Cain. This interpretation was brought into the mainstream of Christian theology in the early fifth century AD by Augustine, the bishop of Hippo, who popularized a view put forward about a hundred years earlier by Julius Africanus.[8]

We've dealt with this elsewhere, especially in *Veneration* and *Giants, Gods & Dragons*, the books I coauthored with my best friend (my wife Sharon), so I won't recapitulate the arguments here. The bottom line is that Genesis 6:1–4 means exactly what it says: Angels mated with humans. This had disastrous consequences for humanity, and it earned the angels a terrible punishment as a result.

The noncanonical Book of 1 Enoch, written between the late fourth century BC and about the time of Jesus' birth,[9] describes this event in more detail. What's more, it names the leader of the rebellion—the entity we identify as Saturn of the Romans.

When the sons of men had multiplied, in those days, beautiful and comely daughters were born to them. And the watchers, the sons of heaven, saw them and desired them. And they said to one another, "Come, let us choose for ourselves wives from the

8. Jaap Doedens, *The Sons of God in Genesis 6:1–4* (Leiden: Brill, 2019), pp. 250–252.

9. 1 Enoch 6:1–7. George W. E. Nickelsburg and James C. VanderKam, *1 Enoch: The Hermeneia Translation* (Minneapolis: Fortress Press, 2012).

daughters of men, and let us beget children for ourselves." And
Shemihazah, their chief, said to them, "I fear that you will not
want to do this deed, and I alone shall be guilty of a great sin."
And they all answered him and said, "Let us all swear an oath,
and let us all bind one another with a curse, that none of us turn
back from this counsel until we fulfill it and do this deed." Then
they all swore together and bound one another with a curse.
And they were, all of them, two hundred, who descended in
the days of Jared onto the peak of Mount Hermon. And they
called the mountain "Hermon" because they swore and bound
one another with a curse on it. And these are the names of their
chiefs: Shemihazah—this one was their leader.[10]

Shemihazah, sometimes transliterated Shemyaza or Samjaza, likely
means "the Name has seen" (or "My Name has seen"), a reference to
Yahweh. That's ironic, because of course God *did* see, and He did not
approve. But we're getting ahead of ourselves.

You may be surprised to learn that the Watchers are mentioned in
the Bible—just once, in the fourth chapter of Daniel, where the Chaldean king Nebuchadnezzar relates his dream:

I saw in the visions of my head as I lay in bed, and behold, a watcher,
a holy one, came down from heaven.... Let his mind be changed
from a man's, and let a beast's mind be given to him; and let seven
periods of time pass over him. The sentence is by the decree of the
watchers, the decision by the word of the holy ones, to the end that
the living may know that the Most High rules the kingdom of men
and gives it to whom he will and sets over it the lowliest of men.
(Daniel 4:13, 16–17)

---

10. Ibid.

Since the punishment of Nebuchadnezzar, the earth's most powerful king in his day, was decided and decreed by the Watchers, they clearly have some authority over the administration of God's creation. Obviously, this was not the same group who rebelled in the days of Jared and Enoch, so the term "watcher" (Hebrew `*iyr*) appears to define a class of powerful angel, not all of whom were loyal.

That disloyalty shouldn't surprise us. We know that the rebel in Eden, Satan, is called a "guardian cherub" in Ezekiel 28, and, like the sons of God in Genesis 6, he chose to reject God's authority and do his own thing. So, it's evident in the Bible that angels were created with free will, just like we humans. God did not create the entities in the spirit realm or those of us occupying the natural realm as automatons, unable to think and act for ourselves. And, just like us humans, a fair number of angels decided to go their own way with predictable consequences.

Peter specifically identifies the place of incarceration for the rebel faction as Tartarus. That bit of information is obscured by our English Bibles, most of which translate the word *tartarōsas* as "hell." That's an error. The word refers to Tartarus, not Hades.

That may seem like splitting hairs, but it's not. To the Greeks, Tartarus was separate and distinct from Hades, the final destination for human dead, and it was believed to be as far below the earth as the earth is below the sky. Some texts even put Tartarus as far below Hades as the earth is below the sky. It was a place of impenetrable darkness reserved specially for supernatural threats to the divine order—rebellious gods.

Second Peter 2:4 is the only place in the New Testament where *tartarōsas* is used, which means we need to sit up and pay attention. Why did Peter choose that word instead of "Hades" or "Gehenna"? It's clear from the multiple uses of those terms that they both refer to a place of punishment in the afterlife, usually by fire.[11] The only difference is

---

11. For example, see Matthew 18:9; Mark 9:43; James 3:6; and Luke 16:19–24.

that those being punished in Peter's account are angels. Apparently, the place reserved for sinful humans in the afterlife—Gehenna, Hades, or hell—is not where disobedient angels are sent.

What's even more interesting about his account is that Peter makes it clear that the sin of the angels thrust down to Tartarus was sexual. The second chapter of 2 Peter refers to Sodom and Gomorrah, "sensual conduct of the wicked," and "the lust of defiling passion."[12] Jude is even more direct in his brief epistle, specifically accusing the imprisoned angels of sexual immorality.[13] The only example of sexual immorality by angels in the Bible is Genesis 6:1–4.

Back to our question: Why did Peter choose the word *tartarōsas*? Given that he wrote under the inspiration of the Holy Spirit, the choice was deliberate and inspired. At the time he wrote, Judea had been under the influence of Greek culture and language for more than three hundred years. Peter understood what Tartarus was, how and why it was different from Hades, and who was imprisoned there.

The Jewish religious scholars who translated the Tanakh (what we Christians call the Old Testament) from Hebrew into Greek about three hundred years before the birth of Jesus understood the connection between the old gods of the pagans and the giants of Genesis 6. In the Old Testament, there are verses where the translators chose *titanes* (Titans) and *gigantes* (giants) for the Hebrew word *rephaim*. As we explained in chapters 1 through 3 of our book *Veneration*, the Rephaim were the spirits of the Nephilim destroyed in the Flood, but the pagan cultures around ancient Israel believed they were the spirits of their deified royal ancestors—in other words, "the mighty men who were of old."[14]

---

12. 2 Peter 2:6–10.

13. Jude 6–7.

14. Sharon K. Gilbert and Derek P. Gilbert, *Veneration* (Crane, MO: Defender Publishing, 2019), pp. 9–37.

There was a clear connection between the Nephilim of the Hebrews and the demigods of Greece and Rome. As the hybrid offspring of gods and humans, heroes like Herakles and Perseus were by definition Nephilim. Even though that was understood by the Jews of Jesus' day and the early Christian church, it wasn't until 1999 that Estonian scholar Amar Annus made the connection for us in the modern world. Annus showed that the term used by the Greek poets Hesiod and Homer to describe the men who lived during the Golden Age when the Titan king Kronos ruled the world, *meropes anthrôpoi*, was derived from the same Semitic root, ʾrp, behind the Hebrew word *Rephaim*.[15] He went a step farther, showing that the name of the old gods of the Greeks, the Titans, came from an ancient Amorite tribe, the Tidanu,[16] about which we'll have more later.

The extrabiblical Book of 1 Enoch expands on the account in the Bible, especially 1 Enoch chapters 6–11, part of what scholars call the Book of Watchers (chapters 1–36 of 1 Enoch). As noted above, it records that two hundred Watchers descended to the summit of Mount Hermon in the days of Jared, the great-great-grandfather of Noah, and swore a mutual oath to carry out their plan to satisfy their desire for mortal women. Hermon sits on the border between Israel, Syria, and Lebanon, and it's the highest peak in the Levant. When the Hebrews arrived in Canaan, the native Amorites called the mountain "Sirion" or "Senir,"[17] although there is evidence that an older name for the mountain was something like "Harnam." The Amorite *Story of Aqhat*, dated to the time of the judges in Israel, calls Aqhat's father Daniel the "man of Rapiu" (the singular form of "Rephaim"), "the hero," and the "Harnamite," which is probably a reference to

15. Amar Annus, "Are There Greek Rephaim? On the Etymology of Greek *Meropes* and *Titanes*." *Ugarit-Forschungen* 31 (1999).

16. Ibid.

17. Deuteronomy 3:9.

the mountain.[18] "Hermon" appears to be a deliberate twisting of the Amorite name to connect the mountain to the Hebrew word *kherem*, which means "ban"—as in "devoted to destruction," a term applied to people and things declared off-limits by God.

The Book of Watchers makes the case for God's punishment of the rebellious angels. The offspring of their forbidden unions with human women drove creation to the brink of destruction. First Enoch 7:2–5 describes three generations of monstrous descendants—first "great giants," then Nephilim, and then *Elioud*, a Greek word that means "gods of glory." Apparently, the author of Enoch understood the terms in Genesis 6—Nephilim (or "giants"), *gibborim* ("mighty men"), and *anshei hashem* ("men of renown" or, more accurately, "men of the Name")—to refer to three successive generations of giants rather than the same group.[19]

Whether our pre-Flood ancestors contended with one generation of giants or three, the effect was the same: It was believed that the half-divine monsters nearly drove humanity to extinction. The Book of Watchers describes the giants as insatiable, devouring first the product of human labor, then humans, and then birds, beasts, and fish. When even that didn't satisfy their hunger, they turned on each other. And if posing a threat to the existence of all life on earth wasn't bad enough, Enoch underscores the wickedness of the giants by noting that they "drank the blood," presumably of the creatures they consumed.[20] This was taboo. God told Noah and Moses that this was forbidden because the blood was the life,[21] a prohibition that was part of the Law given to Moses at Sinai.[22]

---

18. Klaas Spronk, *Beatific Afterlife in Ancient Israel and in the Ancient Near East* (Kevelaer: Butzon & Bercker, 1986), pp. 168–169.

19. George W. E. Nickelsburg, *1 Enoch 1: A Commentary on the Book of 1 Enoch*, Chapters 1–36; 81–108 (Minneapolis: Fortress, 2001), p. 184.

20. 1 Enoch 7:2–5.

21. Genesis 9:4.

22. Leviticus 7:26–27, 17:10–14, 19:26; Deuteronomy 12:16, 23; 15:23; 1 Samuel 14:33–34. See also Acts 15:28–29.

But the transgression of the Watchers was more than just violating a taboo against interspecies sex and burdening mankind with the threat of destruction at the hands of their monstrous offspring. The text of Enoch, which influenced Jewish thought about the rebellious Watchers down to the time of Jesus and the apostles, makes clear that the other half of their plot was the dissemination of forbidden knowledge—deadly secrets that humanity was not meant to know.

Chapter Two

SECRETS AND SPIRITS

The story in the Book of 1 Enoch would make a compelling supernatural thriller. It has two main villains—Watcher-class angels named Shemihazah and Asael (sometimes rendered Azazel).

Shemihazah, as noted in the previous section, is the leader of the rebel faction—their king, if you will. Afraid that he'd be left holding the bag, he convinced the rest of the two hundred who followed him to Mount Hermon to swear and bind one another with an oath and a curse. Chapters 6 and 7 of 1 Enoch focus on Shemihazah and the mixing of human and angelic bloodlines.

The sins of Asael form another narrative that's worth our attention. While Shemihazah is called the chief of the rebellious Watchers, chapter 8 of 1 Enoch blames Asael for myriad sins:

> Asael taught men to make swords of iron and weapons and shields and breastplates and every instrument of war. He showed them metals of the earth and how they should work gold to fashion it suitably, and concerning silver, to fashion it for bracelets and ornaments for women. And he showed them concerning antimony and eye paint and all manner of precious stones and dyes. And the sons of men made them for themselves and

for their daughters, and they transgressed and led the holy ones astray. And there was much godlessness on the earth, and they made their ways desolate....

You see what Asael has done, who has taught all iniquity on the earth, and has revealed the eternal mysteries that are in heaven, <which the sons of men were striving to learn.>...

[A]ll the earth was made desolate by the deeds of the teaching of Asael, and over him write all the sins. (1 Enoch 8:1; 9:6; 10:8, Hermeneia Translation)

In a nutshell, Shemihazah was blamed for the cohabitation of angels and women while Asael was responsible for teaching humans forbidden knowledge. Unlike the Shemihazah story, the role of Asael in 1 Enoch has no parallel in Genesis 6, which only deals with the creation of the Nephilim. Likewise, Peter and Jude only mention the sexual aspect of the Watchers' sins. However, this transfer of secrets from the divine realm to humanity influenced Jewish religious thought in the pre-Christian era.

Since 1999, Amar Annus has produced invaluable work showing the links between Jewish theology and the religions of their Mesopotamian forebears and the later Greeks and Romans. Added to earlier landmark works such as Martin L. West's 1997 book *The East Face of Helicon* and Michael C. Astour's *Hellenosemitica*, published in 1965, it is now clear that the origins of the so-called myths of classical Greece and Rome can be traced back through the Semitic people of the Levant to ancient Babylon, Akkad, and Sumer.

The research of Annus and others has revealed that the Watchers of Hebrew theology were known in ancient Mesopotamia by the Akkadian name *apkallu* (Sumerian *abgal*), which roughly translates as "big water man."[23] This refers to their home, which was believed to be the fresh-

---

23. Sjur Cappelan Papazian, "Abgal or Apkallu." *Cradle of Civilization*, April 5, 2015. https://aratta.wordpress.com/2015/04/05/abgal-or-apkallu/, retrieved 5/16/21.

water ocean beneath the earth, the *Apsû* or *abzu*, from which we get the English word "abyss." This was the domain of Enki, the clever god who alone among the Sumerian deities was always favorably disposed toward humanity. (The others you could never be sure about.) The *apkallu* were divine sages, on the earth before a great flood swept over the land of Sumer, who brought the gifts of civilization from Enki to humanity.

There were three types of *apkallu*: A bearded man with wings, a hawk-headed humanoid with wings, and a man who appeared to wear a fish cloak. The fish-garbed *apkallu* has been incorrectly identified as the god Dagon or one of his priests, thanks to Alexander Hislop's 1858 book *The Two Babylons*. Hislop meant well, but he was mistaken. As we'll see later in this book, Dagon (originally spelled "Dagan") was a grain-god, not a fish-god.

The three forms of *apkallu* in Mesopotamia[24]

---

24. Stephanie Dalley, "Apkallu." In: Eggler J./Uehlinger Ch., eds., *Iconography of Deities and Demons in the Ancient Near East*, http://www. religionswissenschaft.uzh.ch/idd/prepublications/e_idd_illustrations_apkallu. pdf, retrieved 6/26/21.

While the *apkallu* were believed to be the source of all Mesopotamian priestly knowledge, they were also connected to sorcery and were occasionally considered dangerous, demonic beings. They were invoked as protective spirits in Mesopotamia, but were viewed as the origin of evil by the later Hebrews. Interestingly, the Babylonian *Epic of Erra* records that the *apkallu* had been banished forever to the *Apsû* by the chief god Marduk as a consequence of the great flood, just as the sinning angels had been thrust down to Tartarus by God.[25]

The Apostle Paul wrote to the church at Rome that "sin came into the world through one man,"[26] that being Adam. That is true, but unlike Christians, who blame the fallen state of the world on Adam's sin, Jews in Jesus' day also pointed to the incidents of Genesis 6 and 11, the Mount Hermon rebellion and the Tower of Babel. I've gone into detail on the consequences of Babel elsewhere, especially chapter 3 of my book *The Great Inception*, so I won't repeat that here. To summarize: Babel was humanity's attempt to build an artificial mountain as an abode for the gods. I believe this was the ancient temple at Eridu, the cult center of Enki. Nimrod tried to build this divine abode right on top of the *Apsû*, the "abyss." As punishment, God delegated supervision of the earth to another group of "sons of God."[27] They rebelled, too, and so God decreed their deaths. You'll find that in Psalm 82, which reads like a courtroom scene in heaven:

God has taken his place in the divine council;
in the midst of the gods he holds judgment:
"How long will you judge unjustly
and show partiality to the wicked? *Selah*" [...]

---

25. 2 Peter 2:4.

26. Romans 5:12.

27. Deuteronomy 32:8: "When the Most High gave to the nations their inheritance, when he divided mankind, he fixed the borders of the peoples according to the number of the sons of God."

I said, "You are gods,
sons of the Most High, all of you;
nevertheless, like men you shall die,
and fall like any prince." (Psalm 82:1–2, 6–7)

Those "sons of the Most High" are the pagan gods of the neighbors of the ancient Israelites—from Baal, Asherah, Astarte, and Chemosh to Zeus, Apollo, Artemis, and Ares.

The entities we're concerned with belonged to an earlier age. These were the deities later called the "old gods" or "former gods" by the pagans. The Hebrews referred to them as Watchers. The Mesopotamians called them *apkallu*, although there is another tradition in the religion of Sumer, Akkad, and Babylon that the gods who formerly ruled the heavens, the Anunnaki, had become judges of the underworld by the time of the Old Testament patriarchs.

The Old Babylonian copy of the *Epic of Gilgamesh* connects the mountain of the Watchers' oath to the old gods of Sumer, describing the cedar forest around Mount Hermon as the "secret dwelling of the Anunnaki."[28] Hermon overlooks the land of Bashan, which was considered the literal entrance to the netherworld by the Canaanite neighbors of ancient Israel. The tale of Gilgamesh thus links the rebellion of the Watchers to the old Sumerian gods who, at some point in history, were demoted from the heavens to the underworld—like the Titans of the Greeks.

Since Shemihazah was the chief of the group that descended to Hermon, it's a good guess that he can be identified as Kronos, the youngest of the twelve Titans believed to have been born to Gaia by the sky-god, Ouranos. (We can assume that stories of gods born to older gods were created for human consumption by the rebel angels. According to Jesus,

---

28. Edward Lipiński, "El's Abode: Mythological Traditions Related to Mount Hermon and to the Mountains of Armenia," *Orientalia Lovaniensa Periodica* II (1971), pp. 18–19.

angels in heaven "neither marry nor are given in marriage,"[29] probably because eternal spirit beings don't need to procreate.) Asael was singled out for the sin of revealing hidden knowledge to humanity. The character in Greek myth that most fits his story is the Titan Prometheus, who was sentenced to eternal torture in Tartarus by Zeus for stealing fire from Olympus and giving it to humanity. For his crime, Prometheus was chained to a rock, helpless, while an eagle ate his liver. Every night, the liver grew back, so the gruesome process would repeat the following day, and the day after that, *ad infinitum.*

Chapter 10 of 1 Enoch describes how Asael, who was obviously more deserving of punishment than Prometheus, was bound by the archangel Raphael, dropped into a hole in the desert onto jagged rocks, and covered with darkness where he will remain until Judgment Day. This is strikingly similar to Peter and Jude's description of the sentence meted out to the angels who sinned.

The punishment of Shemihazah was assigned to Michael, who was commanded to bind him and the other Watchers who had "defiled" themselves with women for seventy generations in the "valleys of the earth."[30] Note that "seventy" in the ancient Near East was not a literal number, but a symbol that represented "all of them." In other words, Shemihazah and his colleagues are imprisoned in the netherworld until the end of the age, the time of the final Judgment.

We'll go into more discussion of the parallels between the Watchers of Enoch and the Titans of Greece in a later chapter. The other important consequence of the sin of the Watchers that we need to discuss here is the creation of demons.

It is explicit in 1 Enoch that the giants after death became "evil spirits," condemned to wander the earth until the Judgment. The mixing of human and divine was forbidden, so the spiritual part of the giants were to remain on earth, suffering hunger and thirst but unable to satisfy

---

29. Matthew 22:30.
30. 1 Enoch 10:11–12.

those wants, afflicting and oppressing humankind until the great Judgment.[31] This is the textbook definition of a demon.

The oldest sections of the Book of 1 Enoch, which includes the Book of the Watchers, were probably written no earlier than the Greek period of Israel's history, after Alexander the Great conquered the Levant in the late fourth century BC. This means that the Hebrew Scriptures of the Tanakh, the Christian Old Testament, are older than 1 Enoch. And there are very few references to demons in the Old Testament; in fact, the word "demon" is only used three times. In Leviticus 17:7, Hebrew *se'irim* is rendered "goat demon," which is especially interesting in this context. Leviticus 16 records the instructions given by God to Moses and Aaron for the Day of Atonement, during which they were to cast lots over two male goats. One was sacrificed as a sin offering to God, but Aaron was to take the other, place his hands on its head and transfer the sins of Israel onto the goat, then send it "into the wilderness for Azazel."[32] This wasn't an offering to Azazel/Asael; the goat carried the sins of the people out of the camp, which was ground sacred to Yahweh, and into the wilderness, which was Asael's jurisdiction.

This is consistent with other Jewish writings from the Second Temple period that depict the desert wilderness as a place occupied by demons. This gives a different flavor to the verse from Isaiah quoted by John the Baptist: "A voice cries: 'In the wilderness prepare the way of the LORD; make straight in the desert a highway for our God.'"[33] The herald boldly calling for God's people to prepare for His arrival was in enemy territory!

In Deuteronomy 32:17 and Psalm 106:37, "demon" is used for the Hebrew word *shedim*. This is probably based on the Akkadian *shadu*, which means "mountain" and may be the word behind El Shaddai ("God of the Mountain"). The Akkadian *shadu* were protective spirits also called *lamassu*. They were typically depicted as winged creatures

---

31. 1 Enoch 15:8–16:1.

32. See Leviticus 16:1–22.

33. Isaiah 40:3.

with the bodies of lions or bulls and human faces. The famous *lamassu* at the British Museum, which once stood guard outside the palace of the Assyrian kings at Nineveh, are winged, human-headed bulls with the feet of lions.

Author with *lamassu* at the British Museum

You no doubt noticed that the *lamassu* possesses the four aspects of the biblical cherubim—human (face), lion (paws), ox (body), and eagle (wings). This is not a coincidence. The *shedim*, then, were lesser supernatural beings, possibly fallen cherubim, who were venerated by the pagans.

However, there is nothing at all in the Old Testament about the differences between fallen *elohim*, like the "sons of God" in Genesis 6 and Psalm 82, and the demonic spirits described in 1 Enoch. You won't find anything about the origins of demons, either. That doctrine comes into focus sometime around 300 BC with the Book of 1 Enoch.

We could ignore what Enoch has to say about demons if the section of 1 Enoch we're discussing, the chapters called the Book of the Watchers, hadn't been referenced by Peter and Jude. But it's pretty clear that their knowledge of the transgressing angels, especially their punishment, came from 1 Enoch. So, while most of the Christian church doesn't consider it inspired Scripture, 1 Enoch is useful insofar as it helps us understand Genesis 6 and the sin of the angels mentioned by Peter and Jude.

The early church clearly accepted the origin story of demons that's straight out of chapters 7 and 15 of 1 Enoch. Christian theologians for the first four hundred years after the Resurrection were almost universally agreed that demons are the spirits of the Nephilim destroyed in the Flood, and that the Nephilim were the children born from the infernal unions of rebellious Watchers and human women.

That is the legacy of Shemihazah, chief of the Watchers who descended to Mount Hermon in the distant past. By leading his two hundred colleagues to violate the species barrier and produce children with human wives, he set in motion a chain of events that continues to impact the world to this day. Shemihazah essentially created a supernatural army—one that deceived Israel into offering sacrifices to the dead before Joshua led the people into Canaan.

Chapter Three

SACRIFICES FOR THE DEAD

The people of the ancient Near East, which is roughly defined as the lands of the Bible during the Old Testament period, never really said goodbye to their ancestors. The dead hung around, always near, part of everyday life. In fact, they required the care and attention of their descendants, and through the rituals of the living, those who passed on remained an active part of family, tribe, and community. The Amorites of the second millennium BC, who dominated the culture that produced Abraham, Isaac, and Jacob, had relationships with family and tribe, both living and dead, that were very similar to ancestor veneration cults and traditions found today in many parts of the world.

Mesopotamians four thousand years ago believed the netherworld was a dark, dreary place. The only food and drink available to the dead was what was provided by one's descendants. The living were duty-bound to summon the ancestors to a ritual meal called the *kispum* on the thirtieth day of each month. This was the night of no moon, the darkest night, when the veil between the world of the living and the land of the dead was believed to be thinnest. This is likely why one text in Sumerian and Akkadian from the time of Abraham described the last day of the month as "the evil day," "dangerous day," "the day of the *kispum*," "day of the disappearance," and "the day of 'purification'."[34]

Kispum was literally a necromancy ritual at which the family summoned deceased ancestors by name. Failure to perform the rite condemned the ancestors to a gloomy existence of dull, constant hunger. The rite probably originated with the Amorites, as the first written references to it date from the early second millennium BC when control of Mesopotamia shifted from the Akkadians and Sumerians to the Amorites.[35] The ritual was comprised of three elements: a communal meal, *šuma zakāru* ("remembering the name"), and *mē naqû* ("pouring the water"), while the departed ancestors were represented by statues call *en-en-ku-ku* ("lords who are sleeping").[36] These statues are probably what the Bible calls teraphim, the household gods stolen by Rachel when Jacob fled from his father-in-law, Laban (see Genesis 31).

It's difficult for us in the modern world to grasp how crucial these monthly rites were. Participation in the afterlife depended on one's descendants faithfully performing the ritual every new moon.[37] This not only nourished the dead, it kept them pacified. This was important because, long before Hollywood's recent fascination with zombies, it was believed that the unquiet dead could be dangerous![38] To guarantee that the heir, usually the eldest son, did right by the expired ancestors, inheriting the family estate was tied to the performance of the *kispum*.

---

34. Renata MacDougal, *Remembrance and the Dead in Second Millennium BC Mesopotamia* (University of Leicester: Doctoral dissertation, 2014) pp. 58–59.

35. Ibid., p. 26.

36. Nicolas Wyatt, "After Death Has Us Parted," in *The Perfumes of Seven Tamarisks* (Munster: Ugarit-Verlag, 2014) p. 261.

37. Jo Ann Scurlock, "Death and the Afterlife in Ancient Mesopotamian Thought," in *Civilizations of the Ancient Near East*, ed. Jack M. Sasson (New York: Scribner, 1995) p. 1884.

38. Wyatt, op. cit., p. 264.

Receiving one's birthright was conditional on performing the monthly rites.[39] Disobedient children could be punished by being denied access to the gods and the recently deceased in a parent's will.[40] Being cut off from the family gods was traumatic, which explains Laban's desperation to catch Jacob and recover his teraphim.

The month of Abu in the Babylonian calendar (the Hebrew month of Ab, or July/August) seems to have been especially important in the annual cycle of the *kispum*. It appears that Abu was believed to be a good time of the year to consult dead relatives for supernatural advice—and ask them to leave the living in peace.[41]

Not coincidentally, the name of the month may derive from the Semitic term *ab*, meaning "entrance to the netherworld."[42] In Hebrew, *ab* also means "father," but in the broader sense of honored ancestors (or deities). Many of the gods worshiped in Mesopotamia were called "father," such as the creator-god of Canaan, El, the "father of mankind," and the war-god Chemosh, who is described as the father of the Moabites.[43] This is especially relevant to this study because another word based on *ab*, the Hebrew *Abarim* ("Travelers"), is another name for Nebo, the mountain from which Moses got his only look at the Promised Land.[44]

The 1889 *Encyclopedia Biblica* defined *abarim* as "literally, 'Those-on-the-other-side'—*i.e.*, of the Jordan,"[45] a reference to the mountains

39. Ibid., p. 265.

40. MacDougal, op. cit., p. 25.

41. Scurlock, op. cit, p. 1889.

42. Wyatt, op. cit., p. 261.

43. Numbers 21:29.

44. Numbers 27:12; Deuteronomy 32:49.

45. *Encyclopaedia Biblica: A Critical Dictionary of the Literary, Political and Religion History, the Archeology, Geography and Natural History of the Bible, Vol I: A to D*, edited by Thomas Kelly Cheyne and J. Sutherland Black (London: Adam and Charles Black, 1899), p. 9.

of the present-day country of Jordan east of the Dead Sea. More recent research reveals that the encyclopedia's editors, Cheyne and Black, were *almost* right. The *abarim* weren't the mountains of Moab across the Jordan from Jericho, they were the dead—spirits who were "on the other side," in the same way we use the phrase today to refer to those who've passed on.

The tragedy suffered by the Israelites as they camped on the plains of Moab, across the Jordan from Jericho, confirms this reading of Abarim. Chapter 25 of the book of Numbers tells of how Israel was lured into the worship of Baal-Peor. Aaron's grandson, Phinehas, was so outraged that he speared an Israelite prince and Midianite princess who appear to have been engaged in a fertility rite in view of the entire camp, and possibly inside the Tent of Meeting itself.[46]

That such an act would take place, especially "in the sight of the whole congregation of the people of Israel," is shocking, but that's not what provoked the Lord to punish Israel with a plague that killed twenty-four thousand. In our book *Veneration*, Sharon and I showed that the name of that mysterious deity was derived from a Hebrew root meaning "cleft," "gap," or "opening,"[47] thus making Baal-Peor "lord of the opening to the netherworld,"[48] a name we're tempted to translate "Lord of the Gates of Hell."

Writing four hundred years or more after the event, the psalmist confirms our suspicion:

Then they yoked themselves to the Baal of Peor,
and ate sacrifices offered to the dead;

---

46. Numbers 25:1–9.

47. Klaas Spronk, "Baal of Peor." In K. van der Toorn, B. Becking, & P. W. van der Horst (Eds.), *Dictionary of Deities and Demons in the Bible* (2nd extensively rev. ed.) (Leiden; Boston; Köln; Grand Rapids, MI; Cambridge: Brill; Eerdmans, 1999), p. 147.

48. Gilbert & Gilbert (2019), op. cit., p. 50.

they provoked the LORD to anger with their deeds,
and a plague broke out among them.
Then Phinehas stood up and intervened,
and the plague was stayed. (Psalm 106:28–30, emphasis added)

The sense of "those on the other side" is captured by another term that's only recently been discovered by scholars. It was found among a group of three texts from the site of ancient Ugarit, an Amorite city in northern Syria destroyed around 1200 BC, about two hundred years after Moses and the Israelites fell into worship of Baal-Peor. These tablets, designated by scholars KTU 1.20–1.22 and called the Rephaim Texts, were translated for the first time around 1980. Scholars have been debating their precise meaning ever since, but the consensus has gradually shifted to interpreting them as a ritual summoning spirits of deified ancient warriors—in other words, a rite very much like the *kispum*.

There are three very important details that connect the Rephaim Texts, and thus the Rephaim of the Bible, to the Abarim of Moses' day and the demons of the previous chapter. First, they are described as divinized, supernatural chariot warriors. This description is similar to the Bible's depiction of the Nephilim, the "mighty men who were of old," especially when Genesis 6:1–4 is considered alongside passages like Isaiah 14:9–19 and 26:13–14, where the word translated "shades" is the Hebrew *rephaim*; and Ezekiel 32:20–28, a polemic against the Pharaoh that compares the Egyptian king unfavorably with the "mighty chiefs" (literally, "chiefs of the *gibborim*") in Sheol. The Jewish translators of the Septuagint understood the thrust of Ezekiel's argument, as they rendered verse 27 this way: "And they slept with the giants, who had fallen from eternity, who descended into Hades with weapons of war."[49]

---

49. Ezekiel 32:27, *The Lexham English Septuagint* (Second Edition), (Bellingham, WA: Lexham Press, 2020).

Second, the Rephaim are called "vagabonds," "travelers," or "those who came over"[50] in one of the Ugaritic Rephaim Texts.[51] The Ugaritic word *'brm*, which is behind those English terms, is a cognate (same word in a different language) to the Hebrew *'ōbĕrîm*, which is rendered "Travelers" and "can be interpreted as a divine name in Ezek[iel] 39:11, 14, which may have also been preserved in the geographical name Abarim."[52]

Remember that the Mountain of the Abarim ("Travelers"), Mount Nebo, is just across the Jordan River from Jericho, overlooking the plains of Moab where the Israelites provoked God's wrath by eating sacrifices offered to the dead. The geographical picture here is the Jordan River serving as a barrier between the land of the living and the realm of the dead, like the Styx in Greek mythology. The Travelers are the spirits of the Rephaim who "travel" or "cross over" from the netherworld to interact with the living.

Third, and most important, is that the Rephaim in the Ugaritic ritual texts are summoned to the tabernacle or threshing floor of the Canaanite creator-god El, which can only mean the summit of his sacred mountain, Hermon. This is where the two hundred Watchers led by Shemihazah, their chief, swore a mutual oath to go forward with their rebellion, which resulted in the creation of the demonic spirits who were venerated as honored dead and divinized kings of old by the Amorites and Canaanites at least from the time of Abraham, and probably much earlier.

This impacted the Israelites and the early church far more deeply

---

50. Klaas Spronk, *Beatific Afterlife in Ancient Israel and in the Ancient Near East* (Kevelaer: Butzon & Bercker, Neukirchen-Vluyn, 1986), p. 172.

51. KTU 1.22.

52. Klaas Spronk, "Travellers." In K. van der Toorn, B. Becking, & P. W. van der Horst (Eds.), *Dictionary of Deities and Demons in the Bible* (2nd extensively rev. ed.). (Leiden; Boston; Köln; Grand Rapids, MI; Cambridge: Brill; Eerdmans, 1999) p. 876.

than we've been taught. Once you know what to look for, you see that this pagan practice must have been all around the ancient Hebrews. There are hints throughout the Old Testament. For example, Abraham's distress at being without a blood descendant is easier to understand when you realize that he probably believed he and Sarah would have to depend on someone from outside the family to "say their names," offer them bread, and pour drink offerings to sustain them in the afterlife. Odd sections of Scripture like Isaiah 57 suddenly make sense when you understand the context of the drink offerings and grain offerings condemned by the prophet:

> You who burn with lust among the oaks,
> under every green tree,
> who slaughter your children in the valleys,
> under the clefts of the rocks?
> Among the smooth stones of the valley is your portion;
> they, they, are your lot;
> **to them you have poured out a drink offering,**
> **you have brought a grain offering.**
> Shall I relent for these things? (Isaiah 57:5–6, emphasis added)

The dead in ancient Israel were often buried on the slopes of valleys or along the banks of wadis (dry riverbeds). And the Hebrew words translated "smooth stones" in 57:6 can also mean "the dead," which makes it obvious that Isaiah's anger was directed at those who still venerated demonic spirits more than seven hundred years after God destroyed twenty-four thousand Israelites for that sin on the plains of Moab.

This is the legacy of Shemihazah and his co-conspirators. We can only speculate on this point, but it's worth asking: Did the Watchers sire their hybrid children to create a superhuman, semi-divine army for the War of the Ages? The Ugaritic ritual texts refer to the *rapi'uma*

(Rephaim) as "warriors of Baal";[53] is that because they were remembered as mighty heroes of a bygone era, or because they were created to steal the inheritance God allotted for humanity?

This is an important question. As we noted above, "Traveler" is a divine name in Ezekiel 39, meaning it identifies a type of supernatural entity. The Rephaim Texts identify the "Travelers" as the Rephaim, which means these "warriors of Baal" have a role to play in the final battle of the age:

> On that day I will give to Gog a place for burial in Israel, the Valley of the Travelers, east of the sea. **It will block the travelers**, for there Gog and all his multitude will be buried. It will be called the Valley of Hamon-gog. (Ezekiel 39:11, emphasis added)

The Hebrew word translated "block," *ḥōsemet*, is only used one other place in the Bible:

> You shall not **muzzle** an ox when it is treading out the grain. (Deuteronomy 25:4, emphasis added)

So, what does it mean to "block" or "muzzle" these Travelers? We'll get to that later in this book, but since we're dealing with demonic spirits, it's safe to conclude that Ezekiel did not prophesy a traffic tie-up for sightseers on the King's Highway in Jordan.

To summarize this section of the book: An entity named Shemihazah was identified by the author of 1 Enoch as the "chief" of the two hundred Watchers who descended to Mount Hermon in the distant past. Based on the few clues in the Bible, we can conclude that the Watchers are a powerful class or rank of supernatural being. They decreed Nebuchadnezzar's punishment for his unwarranted pride,[54] which implies that

---

53. Spronk (1986), op. cit., p. 171.
54. Daniel 4:17.

God has delegated some degree of authority to them. But Shemihazah and his colleagues overstepped the limits of their authority and paid a heavy price for their rebellion. Peter and Jude were apparently aware of their fate as described in 1 Enoch, where the patriarch was told that the angels who'd sinned were confined in a dark and terrible place until the judgment.[55]

Even though the Watchers are confined now, their actions have had serious consequences for humanity through the ages. Although most churches don't teach on demonic possession these days, it is biblical. There is no scriptural reason to believe that demons ceased interfering in human activity at the end of the apostolic age, and there is plenty of evidence to suggest that demonic activity is, if anything, increasing.

The question that remains is this: Does Shemihazah, who led a rebellion to steal the birthright of Adam and Eve for his hybrid children and those of his divine brothers, still influence the world from his prison in the depths of the abyss?

The answer is unquestionably yes.

---

55. 2 Peter 2:4; Jude 6; 1 Enoch 21:1–6.

Chapter Four

KUMARBI

The first identity of this rebellious Watcher to appear in the historical record is not Saturn or his Greek analogue, Kronos. The Titan king and his Phoenician equivalent, Baal Hammon, don't appear until the first millennium BC. Enlil of Akkad and Sumer appears in the written record around the end of the Uruk period, roughly 3200–2800 BC.[56] But there is another identity worn by Saturn in ancient times that pre-dates even Enlil.

Kumarbi was the primordial creator-god of the Hurrians, a people who lived in eastern Anatolia and northern Mesopotamia. For nearly two thousand years, between the middle of the fourth millennium BC and about the end of the fourteenth century BC, the Hurrians controlled an area more or less occupied today by the Kurds in Iraq, Syria, and Turkey. At its peak, during the time of the Mitanni kingdom (1600–1350 BC), the Hurrians extended their power well into what is now Turkey, Syria, and northwest Iran, and there are some scholars who believe that the powerful Minoan civilization on the island of Crete may have been Hurrian, or at least dominated by a Hurrian elite for a time.

---

56. Xinhua Wang, *The Metamorphosis of Enlil in Early Mesopotamia* (Münster: Ugarit-Verlag, 2011), p. 245.

Scholars are still debating the origins of the Hurrians. Their language was neither Semitic nor Indo-European, but an isolate like Sumerian and Elamite—unrelated to anything else, as strange as that seems. However, recent research has led a few to suggest that Hurrian is, in fact, a Proto-Indo-European (PIE) tongue that branched off before the Anatolian languages such as Hittite, Luwian, and Lydian.

Kumarbi's story parallels those of several other entities we'll discuss in this book, and that is precisely the point. When you compare the broad outlines of the tales told about the old god, you'll see that they describe the same entity who has been called by other names around the world over the centuries.

Most of what we know about Kumarbi comes from Hittite texts, based on older Hurrian originals, excavated from the ruins of Hattusa, the capital of the kingdom of the Hatti near what is now Boğazkale, Turkey. The Hittites were heavily influenced by Hurrian religion, and they seemed to go to great lengths to please the gods of their neighbors. The Hittites apparently believed you could never have too much divine protection.

Just as the stories of the storm-god of the West Semitic people, Hadad (Baal in the Bible), have been preserved in what's called the *Baal Cycle*, scholars dubbed the collection of texts about the Hurrian creator-god the *Kumarbi Cycle*, which has been more accurately renamed the *Kingship in Heaven Cycle*. The most important of these texts is the *Song of Kumarbi*, now more commonly called the *Song of Going Forth*. It describes the cosmic transfer of power from the sky-god, Anu, to Kumarbi, and from Kumarbi to the storm-god, Teshub.

If you're familiar with Greek mythology and the background of Zeus' rise to the top of the pantheon, the conflict between Anu, Kumarbi, and Teshub will be familiar. Here's the outline of the story:

- The primordial god Alalu reigned in heaven for nine years, after which his cupbearer, the sky-god Anu, rebelled and took his place. Alalu escaped by fleeing into "the dark earth."

- Nine years later, Anu was overthrown by *his* cupbearer, Kumarbi. Anu tried to get away to the sky, but Kumarbi grabbed his legs and pulled him back to earth—and then castrated Anu by biting off his genitals.
- This act had unintended consequences. Anu warned Kumarbi not to celebrate, because he was now impregnated with Anu's children: the storm-god Teshub, the Tigris River, and two unnamed "terrible gods."
- Sure enough, after some discussion between characters about where these gods were to be born, probably due to the obviously inappropriate physiology of the male deity, the storm-god emerged through "the good place." The text (perhaps mercifully) never explains what "the good place" was, but it may have been Kumarbi's skull.
- At some point after this, Teshub, the storm-god, became powerful and replaced Kumarbi as the king of the Hurrian pantheon.

The *Song of Going Forth* is difficult to translate in detail because it's been compiled from tablets that are heavily damaged. This isn't surprising, considering their age. There are other details that are hard to explain because of the fragmentary nature of the source material, but one section seems to depict Kumarbi demanding that the god of wisdom, Ea (called Enki by the Sumerians), hand over the newborn storm-god so that Kumarbi can eat him. It appears that Kumarbi was given a stone instead, which causes the god great pain when he tries to bite it. Then there is the mention of a *kunkunuzzi*-stone, and something (presumably that stone) that's to be venerated through sacrifices.

A separate tale, the *Song of Ullikummi*, tells of Kumarbi's attempt to regain the throne by creating a giant stone monster to depose the storm-god. At first, it appeared that Ullikummi would prevail, despite the collective efforts of the gods. Teshub fled to ask the help of Ea, the one god who hadn't joined the battle. The clever god realized that Ullikummi drew his strength from standing on the shoulder of the dreaming mountain-god Upelluri, who, like Atlas in Greek myths, held up the earth and sky. Ea went to the "former gods," obtained the cutting tool used to separate earth and sky, and severed Ullikummi from Upelluri, destroying the giant's power. The end of the story is lost, but it's safe to assume that Teshub was restored to the kingship in heaven—hence the name of the epic.

There are a number of parallels between these Hurrian tales and later stories of the Greek gods:

- Kumarbi, like Kronos, king of the Titans, was the son of the sky-god. Like Kronos, he deposed and castrated his father—although Kronos used a sickle rather than his teeth to remove the member of Ouranos.
- Anu warned Kumarbi that he would regret what he'd done; likewise, Ouranos warned Kronos and the Titans that they would pay for their rebellion.
- Kumarbi and Kronos both carried a number of deities in their stomachs for a time, although for different reasons.
- Both gods were overthrown by their son, the storm-god—Kumarbi by Teshub and Kronos by Zeus.
- Kumarbi and Kronos were both given a stone to swallow in lieu of the storm-god, which was later venerated as a sacred object. (The stone given to Kronos as a substitute for Zeus was set up at Delphi as the omphalos, the world-navel. It was believed that Delphi, home of the famous oracle, was the center of the world.)
- Even the detail of Kumarbi giving birth to Teshub through his skull has an echo in the Greek myth of Athena's birth through the forehead of Zeus.

Further, the storm-gods in both pantheons had to survive challenges to their reign after taking the throne. The struggle between Teshub and Ullikummi is accepted by many scholars as foreshadowing the Greek story of the battle between Zeus and the chaos-monster Typhon.

There are other connections between the epics, but the bottom line is this: The early Greek poet Hesiod, from whom we have learned much of what we know about Greek religion in the classical era, was clearly familiar with Hittite texts that preserved the older Hurrian religion. In geographic terms, the stories moved from east to west, traveling from the Hurrian heartland to the Aegean, either through Anatolia or the Levant. The time frame was roughly between the Exodus, around 1400 BC, and the ministry of the prophet Isaiah in the late eighth/early seventh century BC, which is probably when Hesiod lived and wrote. So, over a period of about seven hundred years, the origin story of the Hurrian pantheon was transmitted to the Hittites, and either westward through Anatolia or southward through the Neo-Hittite kingdoms of northern Syria to what eventually became the Greek civilization of the Archaic period.

Modern archaeology is shedding light on the question of how these stories migrated from Mesopotamia to Greece. Archaeologists digging in the Amuq River valley in southern Turkey since the early 2000s have discovered evidence of a powerful early Iron Age state called Palistin (or Walistin) based at a city called Kunalua about fifteen miles southeast of Antioch. This may be the Calneh or Calno mentioned twice in the Bible (Amos 6:2 and Isaiah 10:9).[57] Palistin emerged after the Bronze Age collapse around 1200 BC, when the Hittite Empire in Anatolia was destroyed along with most of the kingdoms in the eastern Mediterranean. This new state survived from the eleventh century BC down to about 700 BC, roughly from the time of Samuel and Saul to the time of Isaiah and Hezekiah (and Hesiod).

---

57. "Calneh" in Genesis 10:10 may be a mistranslation of a Hebrew word meaning "all of them," resulting in the translation "all of them in the land of Shinar" (RSV). See W. A. Elwell & B. J. Beitzel, "Calneh." *Baker Encyclopedia of the Bible Vol. 1* (Grand Rapids, MI: Baker Book House, 1988), p. 405.

Archaeologists first assumed that eleventh century BC pottery found at Kunalua was Aegean, produced by the remnant of the Mycenaean Greek civilization that had waged the long war with Troy. However, that theory has been reconsidered. It's now believed that the pots were local copies of styles "not of Greece but rather of Cyprus and south-west Asia Minor."[58] That means these people weren't invaders, but descendants of the survivors of the chaos and destruction scholars call the "Bronze Age collapse."

You've surely noticed the similarity between "Palistin," "Philistine," and "Palestine." Scholars are fairly certain it's the same name. Since the Philistines of the Bible occupied the coastal area around Gaza, it's fair to ask how these people moved an entire kingdom from the modern border between Turkey and Syria down to the area between Israel and Egypt.

Egyptian records document several battles with the invading hordes they called the Sea Peoples between about 1200 and 1150 BC. This coalition included groups the Egyptians named the Ekwesh, Denyen, Sherden (probably Sardinians), Weshesh, Tjekker, and the Peleset, who were almost certainly the Philistines. It's been assumed that these battles took place near the Egyptian homeland, and that afterward the defeated Philistine invaders were settled along the coast in Canaan in the cities that became infamous in the Old Testament—Gaza, Gath, Ashdod, Ekron, and Ashkelon. But some scholars have proposed a different scenario, placing those battles in what is now Syria rather than in Egypt:

1. The land battles between Egypt and the "Sea Peoples" occurred along the northern frontiers of the Egyptian empire in the Levant.
2. The naval clashes were most likely raids on the prosperous Egyptian cities of the Nile Delta.

---

58. Shirly Ben-Dor Evian, "Ramesses III and the 'Sea-Peoples': Towards a New Philistine Paradigm." *Oxford Journal of Archaeology* 36(3) (2017), p. 278.

3. The "Sea-Peoples" were essentially north Levantine (including western Anatolian) populations known as former allies of the Hittites.
4. There is no textual or archaeological evidence that Philistines were ever settled by the Egyptians in Canaan. There is, however, evidence of their settlement in Egypt and in Syria soon after the battles.
5. Some of those "Sea Peoples" established the kingdom of Palistin in the 'Amuq Plain. Others reached Philistia, probably by sea, as Egyptian rule over the Levant deteriorated.[59]

Most relevant for our study here, this not only explains how the Philistines moved from northern Syria to the coastal plain bordering Egypt, it also identifies the kingdom of Palistin as the mostly likely place where the Hittite and Hurrian myths of Kumarbi were transmitted to Cyprus and western Asia Minor, where, over the course of several hundred years, they were transformed into stories of the Greek Titan, Kronos.[60]

An additional piece of evidence may be found in the deity's name. "Kumarbi," meaning "he of Kumar," may refer to a north Syrian site identified with modern Kīmār about twenty-five miles northwest of Aleppo.[61] This was part of the territory controlled by Palistin at its peak, during the reign of one King Taita, who is known from an inscription found in the temple of the storm-god at Aleppo.

The Hurrian myth also locates Kumarbi in the western part of the Khabur River triangle, along the border between Turkey and Syria, and at the ancient city of Tuttul, near modern Raqqa. Tuttul was a major

---

59. Ibid.
60. Jenny Strauss Clay & Amir Gilan, "The Hittite 'Song of Emergence' and the Theogony." *Philologus* 58 (2014), pp. 1–9.
61. Michael C. Astour, "Semitic Elements in the Kumarbi Myth." *Journal of Near Eastern Studies*, Vol. 27, No. 3 (July, 1968), p. 172.

cult center of Dagan,[62] another name and identity used by this spirit that we'll discuss in an upcoming chapter. However, according to texts found at Hattusa, a city farther east in Syria called Urkesh was believed to be the home of Kumarbi. That makes the story of this "former god" absolutely critical to understanding the long supernatural war for the souls of humanity.

---

62. Lluis Feliu, *The God Dagan in Bronze Age Syria* (Leiden; Boston: Brill, 2003), p. 212.

Chapter Five

URKESH

In 1984, a husband and wife team of archaeologists in far northeastern Syria began work at a site that should be far better known than it is. Their discoveries could be the link between the earliest post-Flood civilizations, the mysterious "sons of God" mentioned in Genesis chapter 6, and the myths of Greece and Rome.

Tell Mozan is an archaeological site that rises about seventy feet above the surrounding plain in northeastern Syria, very close to the border with Turkey. Its location in the southern foothills of the Taurus Mountains was strategically located on a trade route that brought valuable raw materials like stone, timber, copper, and silver through the Mardin Pass to the cities of southern Mesopotamia.

In ancient times, the city was called Urkesh. It was occupied from at least 3500 BC until the rise of the Assyrian kingdom toward the end of the Bronze Age, around 1200 BC. What makes the city so fascinating and relevant to our topic is the spiritual significance of Urkesh. About the time the city was founded, a raised terrace was constructed and a building with a niched exterior wall, a style common in Sumerian cities of the day, was built on top of the terrace. Like buildings of similar style in Uruk, it was almost certainly a temple.[63]

---

63. Marilyn Kelly-Buccellatti, "Urkesh: The Morphology and Cultural Landscape of the Hurrian Sacred." in P. Matthiae and M. D'Andrea (eds.),

What's unique about Urkesh is that, unlike nearby neighbors in northern Mesopotamia, it never fell under the political or cultural control of Uruk. For example, Nagar (modern Tell Brak), about thirty miles south of Urkesh, had grown into a major city during the fourth millennium BC with megalithic buildings dated to as far back as 3800 BC. Contrary to what was believed after the spectacular discoveries of cities like Ur and Uruk a century ago, recent research at sites like Tell Brak and Tell Mozan has led scholars to conclude that northern Mesopotamia was where the earliest large-scale urban civilization developed in the ancient Near East. Not surprisingly, with growth comes competition; mass graves found in 2010 suggest that many of Nagar's citizens met violent ends in four separate events between 3800 and 3600 BC. This may be evidence of failed insurrections by local residents, but it's also possible that they were victims of the expansionist policies of Uruk; it's known from pottery finds that an Urukean colony was established in the city around 3600 BC.

The Bible tells us that Erech ("Uruk" by a different spelling), Babel, and Accad were the power base of history's first would-be empire builder, Nimrod:

> The beginning of his kingdom was Babel, Erech, Accad, and Calneh, in the land of Shinar. From that land he went into Assyria and built Nineveh, Rehoboth-Ir, Calah, and Resen between Nineveh and Calah; that is the great city. (Genesis 10:10–12)

Based on the mass graves at Nagar, it appears that the kings of Uruk did not tolerate dissent. Historically speaking, the Uruk period, between about 3800 BC and 3100 BC, is the logical time frame for Nimrod's reign. Genesis 10:8–12 gives an accurate capsule summary of his career.

Accad, usually spelled "Akkad" outside of the Bible, was the city from

---

Ebla e la Siria dall'età del Bronzo all'età del Ferro, (Accademia Nazionale dei Lincei: Atti dei convegni Lincei 304, Roma: Bardi Edizioni), pp. 109–110.

which Sargon the Great conquered all of Mesopotamia around 2334 BC, making him the first Semitic ruler of the ancient Near East. That city hasn't been found, but it's believed to have been on the Tigris River near modern Baghdad, and may be hidden beneath Baghdad itself.[64] Sargon is also credited with being the world's first empire-builder, but that's because historians generally don't believe that Nimrod was a historic character. (Sargon is one of the candidates put forward as the basis of the Nimrod "legend.")

Calneh likewise hasn't been found, but the name may be a misreading of a Hebrew phrase that simply means "all of them." So, the original sentence might have read, "the beginning of his kingdom was Babel, Erech, and Accad, *all of them* in the land of Shinar."[65]

From there, we're told Nimrod went to Assyria, or northern Mesopotamia, and built Nineveh, Rehoboth-Ir, Calah, and Resen. While those cities may not have been founded by Nimrod (for example, archaeologists believe Nineveh was occupied as early as 6000 BC), the Genesis account does fit the general story of an empire-builder from Sumer who expanded his kingdom along the Tigris and Euphrates rivers, which is exactly what's revealed by the archaeology of the fourth millennium BC. Armies traveled north and west from Sumer to impose Uruk's will on the cities of what is now northern Iraq, northeastern Syria, and southeastern Turkey. Although not confirmed, the mass graves at Tell Brak could be evidence of this, but the destruction of nearby Hamoukar was definitely the work of Uruk's military. Archaeologists call the battle of Hamoukar the "earliest evidence for large scale organized warfare in the Mesopotamian world."[66]

---

64. Christophe Wall-Romana, "An Areal Location of Agade." *Journal of Near Eastern Studies*, Vol. 49, No. 3 (1990), pp. 205–245.

65. William F. Albright, "The End of 'Calneh in Shinar.'" *Journal of Near Eastern Studies* 3, no. 4 (1944), pp. 254–255.

66. Owen Jarus, "New Discoveries Hint at 5,500 Year Old Fratricide at Hamoukar, Syria." *The Independent*, Oct. 23, 2011. https://www.

The attack was brutal. Using clay bullets and "cannonballs" fired from slings, thousands of which have been uncovered at the dig,[67] the Urukean army breached the ten-foot-thick walls of Hamoukar, overwhelmed the city's defenders, and burned the prosperous city to the ground.[68] It appears that Hamoukar was quickly rebuilt and settled by colonists from Uruk, possibly to take over the city's profitable obsidian trade, which is indicated by the workshops for fabricating obsidian tools just outside the city walls.[69]

This is consistent with what little we know of the character of Nimrod. However, the point of this brief rabbit trail is not to document Nimrod's political and military exploits, but to highlight the remarkable fact that Urkesh, a thriving religious and economic center just thirty miles north of Nagar, at the time of the violence there and the destruction of Hamoukar, remained independent and untouched by the military might of Uruk.

So, it appears that copper, a strategically important metal, was either brought through Urkesh, with the Hurrians there acting as middlemen between miners in the Taurus Mountains and the powerful Uruk state, or the rulers of Uruk opted to bring copper down the Euphrates via a longer route that meandered through Turkey and Syria to the west of the Khabur Triangle. The question is: Why?

---

independent.co.uk/life-style/history/new-discoveries-hint-5-500-year-old-fratricide-hamoukar-syria-2088467.html, retrieved 2/11/21.
67. William Harms, "Evidence of Battle at Hamoukar Points to Early Urban Development." *University of Chicago Chronicle*, Jan. 18, 2007. http://chronicle.uchicago.edu/070118/hamoukar.shtml, retrieved 2/12/21.
68. Ibid.
69. Richard E. J. Burke, "Uruk's Monstrous Crime at Hamoukar." *Raising Up Pharaoh*, Oct. 10, 2015. http://www.raisinguppharaoh.com/2015/10/24/65-uruks-monstrous-crime-at-hamoukar/, retrieved 2/11/21.

We can only speculate. We do know that every city in the ancient Near East had a patron deity. In Uruk, it was originally Anu, the sky-god—the one who was deposed and castrated by Kumarbi. According to the Sumerian poem *Enmerkar and the Lord of Aratta*, Enmerkar, the second king of Uruk after "the flood swept over," whom I have argued elsewhere was the biblical Nimrod,[70] built a magnificent temple in his city for the goddess Inanna. She's better known to us as Ishtar, the biblical Astarte, and Aphrodite and Venus of the Greco-Roman world. Enmerkar's apparent motive was to show his rival, the lord of Aratta, that he and his city were Inanna's favorites. In the tale, which preserves the broad outlines of the Tower of Babel story, Enmerkar pressures Aratta into providing the materials needed to build the *E-ana* ("House of Heaven") for Inanna and, most relevant to our study, to expand the temple of the god Enki at Eridu, the *E-abzu* ("House of the Abyss"). Following Egyptologist David Rohl,[71] I believe the *E-abzu* at Eridu was the historic Tower of Babel.[72]

Scholars don't agree on the location of Aratta, with guesses ranging from Afghanistan to India to Armenia. On the basis of the name alone, Armenia makes the most sense; the ancient kingdom of Urartu, centered on Lake Van and the nearby mountains of Ararat, seems to fit both the general description of Aratta and the presence of Urukean outposts in the region to access raw materials. However, other geographic clues in the texts, such as placing Anshan in southern Elam (western Iran) between Uruk and Aratta, confuse the issue, so the matter of Aratta will not be settled soon.

The point is this: The powerful kingdom of Uruk, presumably at its peak under Nimrod/Enmerkar between 3500 and 3100 BC, extended

---

70. Sharon K. Gilbert and Derek P. Gilbert, *Giants, Gods & Dragons* (Crane, MO: Defender, 2020), pp. 37–58.

71. David Rohl, *Legend: The Genesis of Civilisation* (London: Century, 1998).

72. Gilbert & Gilbert (2020), op. cit.

its control well into Anatolia to the north and west of Urkesh, and even set up an outpost just thirty miles south at Nagar, but it never tried to move against Urkesh itself or establish control over the key Mardin Pass just twelve miles north of the city.

Likewise, when Sargon of Akkad established himself as the first Semitic ruler of a pan-Mesopotamian kingdom nearly a thousand years after the end of the Uruk period, neither he nor his successors led a force against Urkesh, even though Sargon or one of his successors found it necessary to conquer nearby Nagar.[73] Instead of conquest, the Akkadians opted for alliance; cylinder seals at Urkesh reveal that Tar'am-Agade, a previously unknown daughter of Sargon's grandson Narām-Sîn, was married to the *endan* (Hurrian for "king" or "ruler") of Urkesh in the late twenty-third century BC.[74] In fact, a new palace for the reigning *endan* named Tupkish was built next to the city's temple around 2250 BC,[75] at the very height of the Akkadian Empire.

The armies of Akkad reached Anatolia to the northwest, overwhelming the powerful Syrian states of Mari and Ebla on the way. Akkad sent expeditions as far south as modern Bahrain and Oman. It seems probable that the Akkadians could have taken Urkesh if they'd wanted to, but, for some reason, they didn't want to. Was it because of cultural and ethnic links between the rulers of Urkesh and the miners who controlled the supply of copper and silver in the Taurus Mountains? In other words, did Sargon and his successors, like Nimrod before them, figure it was easier to cut a deal with the Hurrian rulers of Urkesh than to risk alienating their kin in the mountains and losing a key source of those metals?

Since writing hadn't been invented yet in the fourth millennium BC, we'll never know for sure. Based on the archaeological sites scat-

---

73. Federico Buccellati, *Three-dimensional Volumetric Analysis in an Archaeological Context: The Palace of Tupkish at Urkesh and its Representation* (Malibu, CA: Undena Publications, 2016), p. 186.

74. Ibid., p. 20.

75. Ibid., p. 3.

tered across the landscape from the Caspian Sea to the Persian Gulf, and from the Zagros Mountains in Iran to the Mediterranean Sea, it appears that the proto-Hurrian people, called the Kura-Araxes or Early Trans-caucasian culture, migrated during the second half of the fourth millennium BC from their original homeland on the Ararat Plain, on the border between modern Armenia and Turkey. They traveled northward across the Caucasus Mountains into Georgia and the Russian republics of Chechnya and Dagestan; east and south into Azerbaijan, northwest Iran, and the Kurdish regions of northern Iraq and Syria; westward into Anatolia; and southwest to the Mediterranean coast of Syria and Lebanon, reaching as far south as Bet Yerah on the southwest shore of the Sea of Galilee by about 2850 BC. Meanwhile, the Semites and Sumerians along the Tigris and Euphrates dominated the bulk of the Fertile Crescent from the Zagros to the Anti-Lebanon mountains, or what comprises western Iran and most of Iraq, Kuwait, Syria, and Jordan today.

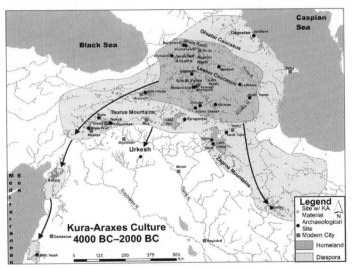

The Kura-Araxes (proto-Hurrian) culture and its migration from the Ararat Valley around 3500 BC, which reached as far as the Sea of Galilee and the Jordan River valley by 2850 BC.
Credit: Stephen Batiuk, CC BY-SA 4.0, https://www.asor.org/resources/photo-collection/maps/mid000011

Marilyn Kelly-Buccellati, who's devoted more than three decades of her life to excavating and interpreting the finds at Urkesh, describes the region controlled by the Kura-Araxes people, the proto-Hurrians, as the "Outer Fertile Crescent."[76] Urkesh is unusual not only because it either resisted or escaped being dominated by powerful southern kingdoms and maintained its Hurrian identity for more than two thousand years, but also because it is the largest and oldest city that can be positively identified as Hurrian.

And, finally, to get back on point: The temple atop the hill of Urkesh was dedicated to the city's patron god, Kumarbi.

The temple, sitting nearly ninety feet above the plain,[77] would have been visible for quite a distance. In majesty and splendor, it may have rivaled the Great Ziggurat of Ur, which wouldn't be built for about another fifteen hundred years, around 2100 BC.[78] The importance of Urkesh in Hurrian religion was preserved in Hittite-language copies of older Hurrian myths that name it as the city of Kumarbi—texts copied by Hittite scribes two thousand years after the temple was constructed on top of the elevated terrace above the plain.

What was it about Kumarbi or the temple that preserved and pro- tected Urkesh for more than two millennia? Perhaps it was the Hurrian belief that their chief deity was, like his father Alalu, a denizen of "the dark earth"—the underworld.

---

76. Marilyn Kelly-Buccellati, "Trade in Metals in the Third Millennium: Northeastern Syria and Eastern Anatolia." In P. Matthiae, M. Van Loon, and H. Weiss (eds.), *Resurrecting the Past: A Joint Tribute to Adnan Bounni* (Istanbul: Nederlands Historisch-Archaeologisch Instituut, 1990), p. 120.
77. Giorgia Buccellati and Marilyn Kelly-Buccellati, "Between Heaven and Hell in Ancient Urkesh," *Backdirt* 175 (2007), p. 67.
78. "The Ziggurat of Ur." *British Museum*, http://www.mesopotamia.co.uk/ziggurats/explore/zig.html, retrieved 5/18/21.

Chapter Six

THE ABI

The central feature of the temple at Urkesh was not a chapel or sanctuary, a place set apart for prayer and contemplation, or even a meeting hall for communal worship. It was a deep pit dug into the earth used to summon deities from the netherworld, including the chief god of the Hurrians, Kumarbi.[79]

Entities summoned from "the dark earth" were offered sacrifices in exchange for favors, often carrying some kind of evil back to the world below. It's known from later ritual texts found at Hattusa, the capital of the Hittite empire, that this pit was called an *abi*.[80] It's a distinctly Hurrian religious structure, unlike anything in southern Mesopotamia and not connected to the well-known Amorite *kispum* ritual.[81]

---

79. Marilyn Kelly-Buccellati, "Urkesh: The Morphology and Cultural Landscape of the Hurrian Sacred." In P. Matthiae and M. D'Andrea (eds.), *Ebla e la Siria dall'età del Bronzo all'età del Ferro* (Rome: Bardi Edizioni, 2016), pp, 99–100.

80. Giorgio Buccellati, "When Were the Hurrians Hurrian? The Persistence of Ethnicity at Urkesh." In J. Aruz, S. Graff and Y. Rakic (eds.), *Cultures in Contact* (New York: Metropolitan Museum of Art, 2013), p. 87.

81. The *kispum* is discussed in depth in our previous book, *Veneration* (see

To be clear, spirits of the dead do not freely roam the earth. Human spirits do not hang around waiting to appear when summoned through the correct rituals, communicate with mediums, or intercede for the living in the natural realm.

God may allow human spirits to return to the earth for His purposes. First Samuel 28 tells the story of the prophet Samuel, who delivered the disturbing news to Saul that he and his sons would fall in the coming battle with the Philistines. But nothing in Scripture even hints that this is a regular occurrence; indeed, the medium Saul consulted was shocked when the prophet appeared: "When the woman saw Samuel, she cried out with a loud voice."[82] The Hebrew word translated into English as "cried out," *zā'aq*, conveys the sense of shouting with alarm or calling for help.[83] In other words, the medium of En-dor expected to see a spirit, but not a *human* spirit.

Similarly, the Hurrian rituals preserved by the Hittites were used to summon spirit beings rather than humans. The *abi* at Urkesh was a monumental underground structure lined with stone, originally dug in a circle about thirteen feet in diameter. The pit has been excavated down to a depth of about twenty-six feet, revealing potsherds dated to about 2600 BC.[84] However, it's clear that the walls of the *abi* extend farther down, possibly another twenty feet, before reaching virgin soil.[85] This may push the date of the pit's creation back to the middle of the fourth millennium BC, around the time the city was first occupied and the niched building erected on the terrace above.[86]

---

pp. 41–61). For a scholarly treatment, see MacDougal, op. cit., pp. 117–287.

82. 1 Samuel 28:12a.

83. Strong's H2199, *BlueLetterBible*. https://www.blueletterbible.org/lang/lexicon/lexicon.cfm?Strongs=H2199&t=KJV, retrieved 2/15/21.

84. Kelly-Buccellati (2016), op.cit., p. 100.

85. Buccellati and Kelly-Buccellati (2007), op.cit., p. 68.

86. Kelly-Buccellati (2016), op.cit., p. 98.

At some point, one wall of the *abi* was removed and a square shaft excavated, creating a keyhole shape and giving the entire structure a total length, end-to-end, of about twenty-four and a half feet. A narrow staircase on the square end allowed access by a priest or the king and queen, who apparently conducted some of the rituals in the pit. The *abi* was not originally covered, although it appears there was a vaulted ceiling over the circular portion for a period of time, and it is almost certain that the square section of the "keyhole" was under a roof.[87]

The keyhole shape continued to have divine significance for thousands of years around the Mediterranean. It's well known as the symbol of Tanit, the consort of Baal Hammon (another aspect of Kumarbi, about whom more later). The keyhole is found on stelae at the tophets of Carthage and Motya (San Pantaleo Island, near Sicily), and at a number of sacred wells from the Bronze Age Nuragic culture on the island of Sardinia.[88]

Rituals in the *abi* were performed at sunset or at night inside a magic circle dug into the dirt of the pit with a hoe or shovel, or traced with a pin, knife, or dagger.[89] This is remarkably similar to modern occult rituals in which magicians use a magic circle, sometimes drawn with salt or chalk, to protect themselves from a spirit being summoned. Similar practices were known in Akkad, where a magic circle called a *zisurrû* was marked out with flour to protect one against demons or curses.[90]

---

87. Ibid.

88. The keyhole shape of the Nuragic holy wells is a mystery that needs further investigation. The wells are dated to the Bronze Age, prior to 1200 BC, but the first Phoenicians, who brought the worship of Tanit and Baal Hammon to the island, aren't supposed to have reached Sardinia until about five hundred years later, in the eighth century BC.

89. Marilyn Kelly-Buccellati, "Ein hurritischer Gang in die Unterwelt," *Mitteilungen der Deutschen Orient-Gesellschaft zu Berlin* 134 (2002), p. 138.

90. *The Assyrian Dictionary of the Oriental Institute of the University of Chicago*, Vol. 21: Z (Chicago: The Oriental Institute, 1961), pp. 137–138.

The purpose of a ritual pit was to allow the "primeval gods" or "former gods" to rise from the netherworld, drawn to the sacrifices, to hear the plea of the officiant:

> When at night on the second day a star leaps, the offerer comes to the temple and bows to the deity. Two daggers which were made along with the (statue of) the new deity they take (with them) dig a pit for the deity in front of the table. They offer one sheep to the deity [...] and slaughter it down in the pit.[91]

While a sheep is mentioned in the example above, and bones of goats and donkeys have also been found, the animals typically offered as sacrifices at the *abi* in Urkesh were most often piglets and puppies, which apparently served a purificatory purpose. Pigs may have been thought to have a connection to the underworld gods because of their habit of rooting in the dirt, but why young animals were preferred to adults is unknown.[92] The gods of the underworld apparently didn't mind offerings of animals considered unclean onto which additional impurities had been ritually transferred.

At the conclusion of a ritual, it was necessary to seal up the pit (or pits—some ritual texts required as many as nine, one for each of the underworld gods) that had been opened by covering it with loose dirt, loaves of bread, or a cloth.[93] These lids, fragile as they seem to us, were considered effective enough at sealing the exits to prevent sinister forces from escaping the underworld and wreaking havoc on the living.

---

91. From *Relocation of the Black Goddess*, KUB 29.4 rev iv 31–36, cited in Kelly-Buccellati (2016), op. cit., p. 101.

92. Billie Jean Collins, "A Channel to the Underworld in Syria." *Near Eastern Archaeology* 67:1 (2004), pp. 55–56.

93. Harry A. Hoffner, Jr., "Second Millenium Antecedents to the Hebrew ,Ôb." *Journal of Biblical Literature*, Vol. 86, No. 4 (Dec., 1967), p. 399.

The underworld deities were led by the sun-goddess of the earth, Allani, whose name means "the lady" (of the underworld).[94] The sun-deity's connection to the netherworld in the religions of the ancient Near East stems from the observable fact that the sun is below the horizon about half the time. Kumarbi, the father of the Hurrian pantheon, is not listed among the gods of the netherworld in these rituals, although he is mentioned in other texts as one of the "former gods" consigned to the underworld by the king of the pantheon, the storm-god Teshub.

Interestingly, these "primeval gods" were referred to in Akkadian translations as the Anunnaki, similar to Mesopotamian traditions that had developed by the time of Abraham, Isaac, and Jacob depicting the former chief deities of Sumer as gods of the underworld.[95]

Among the other infernal deities summoned in the Hurrian *abi* rituals was the personified Abi. This seems odd, contrary to our concept of the pagan gods of the ancient world as anthropomorphic, or at least semi-humanlike satyrs and centaurs. But a ritual pit as a god? Scholar Billie Jean Collins explains that the inclusion of "Abi" among the underworld deities "is not a testimony to its divine status in the proper sense as it is a recognition of its extra-human power to connect the realm of the gods with that of man."[96]

And remember that Hades was both a place and an underworld deity, so this isn't an unfamiliar concept.

Another aspect of the *abi* was the "divine watercourse," the rough

---

94. Alfonso Archi, "The West Hurrian Pantheon and its Background." In B. Collins and P. Michalowski (eds.), *Beyond Hatti* (Atlanta: Lockwood Press, 2013), p. 6.

95. Christopher B. Hays, *Death in the Iron Age II and in First Isaiah* (Tübingen: Mohr Siebeck, 2011), p. 52.

96. Billie Jean Collins, "Necromancy, Fertility, and the Dark Earth." In *Magic and Ritual in the Ancient World*, (Leiden, The Netherlands: Brill, 2014), p. 225.

translation into English of a site called the ^{d}KASKAL.KUR in ritual texts. This appears to be a sacred pool intended to resemble a river-bank where many of the sacred rituals of the Hurrians took place.[97] This term has only been found in nine Hittite texts, one of which is a treaty dated to about 1280 BC between the Hittite king Muwatalli II and Alaksandu of Wilusa.[98] Some scholars identify Alaksandu as Alexander of Troy,[99] better known as Paris, the guy who started the Trojan War by stealing the beautiful Helen away from her husband, King Menelaus of Sparta.[100]

We get a better sense of the term ^{d}KASKAL.KUR by breaking it down into its components, both of which are Sumerian words: KAS-KAL ("road," "journey," and/or "military campaign") and KUR, which means "mountain," but in this context surely points to its other mean-ing, "netherworld."[101] Interestingly, the sign ^{d}KASKAL.KUR was also used during the time of Abraham to refer to the Balikh River,[102] a tributary of the Euphrates that joins the big river near Raqqah, Syria, the city that was the de facto capital of the Islamic State between 2014 and 2017.

KASKAL was also the Sumerian equivalent for the Akkadian word *ḥarrānum* and the ideogram for Harran, the city from which Abraham began his journey to Canaan. Located on a key east-west trade route, Harran was appropriately named, because it was a crossroads connecting

---

97. Collins (2004), op. cit., p. 56.

98. Edmund I. Gordon, "The Meaning of the Ideogram ^{d}KASKAL.KUR = 'Underground Water-Course' and Its Significance for Bronze Age Historical Geography." *Journal of Cuneiform Studies*, Vol. 21 (1967), p. 73.

99. Wilusa is the name behind the title of Homer's epic poem about the Trojan War, *The Iliad.*

100. That's not certain, since the treaty is dated about fifty years earlier than the best guess for the date of the Trojan War.

101. Gordon, op. cit., p. 76.

102. Ibid., p. 77.

a number of key cultures in the biblical world, among them the Assyrians, Hittites, Amorites, and Hurrians. Harran also sits on the Balikh, which makes the river's ancient name, "Road to the Netherworld," doubly interesting—but I digress.

The point of this brief detour is that a stone drain installed in a platform alongside a palace at Urkesh may be an early form of the ^{d}KASKAL.KUR and connected to the rituals for contacting the underworld gods in the *abi*.[103]

In short, the *abi* was an underground portal to the netherworld. And the discoveries at Urkesh connect Hurrian religious rituals from western Syria and central Turkey as late as 1200 BC, with a monumental religious center constructed in northeastern Syria more than two thousand years earlier.

Now, why is this relevant to our understanding of the Bible, Christian theology, and the long supernatural war for the souls of humanity? Because Kumarbi and the "former gods" had been banished to the netherworld. This links those spirits to the sinful angels mentioned by Peter and Jude, an identification that, while admittedly speculative, is supported by the evidence. I intend to show that Kumarbi, known throughout history by a number of names, is the Watcher chief Shemihazah.

Forbidden rites to contact the spirit realm, documented at the Hurrian city of Urkesh more than five thousand years ago, have continued to this day. And the entity who inspired those rituals, the powerful Watcher called Shemihazah, still influences the world even from his pitch-black prison in the abyss.

---

103. Kelly-Buccellati (2002), op.cit., p. 143.

Chapter Seven

URKESH TO SINAI TO ZION

In Genesis 15, God made a remarkable and somewhat puzzling promise to Abraham:

> Then the LORD said to Abram, "Know for certain that your offspring will be sojourners in a land that is not theirs and will be servants there, and they will be afflicted for four hundred years. But I will bring judgment on the nation that they serve, and afterward they shall come out with great possessions. As for you, you shall go to your fathers in peace; you shall be buried in a good old age. And they shall come back here in the fourth generation, **for the iniquity of the Amorites is not yet complete.**" (Genesis 15:13–16, emphasis added)

If there is one thing we should be taught beginning in Sunday school, it's that no detail in the Bible is unimportant. What did God mean by "the iniquity of the Amorites"? Why did He single out a group of people that most of us have only heard of, if we've heard of them at all, in the list of nations that the Israelites had to push out of Canaan? There must have been something unique about the Amorites for God to call them out.

As it happens, scholars of the ancient Near East know a lot about the Amorites. Between the time of Abraham and the Israelites' sojourn in Egypt, roughly 2000 BC to 1500 BC, the Amorites dominated the lands of the Bible. It was the Age of the Amorites in what is now Iraq, Syria, Jordan, Kuwait, the northern parts of Arabia and Egypt, northwest Iran and southeastern Turkey. For about the last hundred years, it's been well known among academics that Amorite kings, chiefs, and tribal elders controlled most of what we call the Middle East. Their social structure was similar to what we know of the Israelites between the time of Abraham and Nebuchadnezzar's sack of Jerusalem, about 2000 BC to 586 BC. That isn't surprising, since Abraham, Isaac, and Jacob lived in a culture dominated by the Amorites. But there were other groups of people who also influenced the world of the patriarchs, and over the last forty years or so we've begun to appreciate the importance of the Hurrians.

As we noted earlier, the Hurrians emerged in Northern Mesopotamia, in the Kurdish region along the border between Syria, Iraq, and Turkey. The city of Urkesh was founded in the fourth millennium BC and appears to have been an important center of Hurrian religion for more than two thousand years, from about 3500 BC until the city was finally abandoned around 1200 BC. Even though Urkesh was settled several centuries before the earliest evidence of writing, the presence of the *abi* (ritual pit), a ritual structure "uniquely linked to the Hurrian tradition,"[104] the evidence is strong for Hurrian spiritual and political influence in Mesopotamia during the formative years of the Jewish—and, by extension, Christian—faith. And this Hurrian influence connects three very important mountains in the history of the Bible: Ararat, Sinai, and Zion.

We noted in a previous chapter that the proto-Hurrians, the Kura-Araxes (or Early Transcaucasian) people, migrated from their original homeland on the Ararat Plain. It's tempting, although we can't prove

---

104. Kelly-Buccellati (2002), op.cit., p. 132.

this, to connect the origin point of this culture and the survivors of the Flood of Noah, whose boat landed on a mountain somewhere near the Ararat Plain.

Entire books have been dedicated to making the case for or against the Flood. That topic is way outside the scope of what we're examining here. But for the sake of argument, let's speculate that a historic Flood did, in fact, deposit a boatload of survivors somewhere in the mountains of Ararat, possibly in the fifth millennium BC. As the descendants of Noah came down from the mountain and established themselves in new territories, a group of Japhethites, the Kura-Araxes people (named for the two rivers that drain the north and south sides of the Lesser Caucasus Mountains) established themselves by about 4000 BC in what is now Armenia, Georgia, Azerbaijan, and eastern Turkey. That part of the equation is guesswork, but archaeologists are confident that the Kura-Araxes culture spread from the Ararat Plain after 4000 BC to cover a broad area from northern Iran to eastern Turkey, north of the Caucasus Mountains, and south to the outer edge of the Fertile Crescent, eventually migrating south along the Mediterranean coast to reach the Sea of Galilee and the Jordan River valley by about 2850 BC.[105]

This is relevant to our study because the advent of writing in the early third millennium BC allows us to follow text evidence to track the influence of the Kura-Araxes (proto-Hurrian) people on ideas and beliefs through their words, and not just their architecture and pottery.

Scholars date the end of the Kura-Araxes culture at about 2000 BC,[106] just about the time the Amorites emerged as a cultural and political

---

105. Yael Rotem, Mark Iserlis, Felix Höflmayer, and Yorke M. Rowan, "Tel Yaqush—An Early Bronze Age Village in the Central Jordan Valley, Israel." *BASOR* 381 (2019), pp. 107–144.

106. Giulio Palumbi and Christine Chataigner, "The Kura-Araxes Culture from the Caucasus to Iran, Anatolia and the Levant: Between Unity and Diversity. A Synthesis." In: *Paléorient*, vol. 40, n°2 (2014), pp. 247–260.

force in the Near East.[107] However, the Hurrians, as descendants of the Kura-Araxes culture of the Ararat Plain and founders of Urkesh, connect the mountains of Ararat, the necromantic rituals of the *abi*, and people encountered by the patriarchs in Canaan.

The year 2000 BC is also roughly the time that Abraham began his migration from Ur to Harran (note: that is the correct spelling of the city's name) and finally to Canaan. And the Hurrians feature prominently in the stories of the biblical patriarchs.

First, we need to rethink the common assumption of Abraham's origins: Ur of the Chaldees (or Chaldeans) was not in Sumer, which is modern-day southern Iraq. In fact, for most of the last four thousand years, most people assumed that Abraham came from northern Mesopotamia. It was only when famed British archaeologist Sir Leonard Woolley found the fabulous "Royal Tombs of Ur" in 1922 that Jews, Christians, and Muslims decided that the fascinating and important Sumerian city was a fitting point of origin for Father Abraham. Until Woolley, Bible scholars generally believed the patriarch had come from southern Turkey. That's exactly where we find ancient Harran, on the Balikh River about ten miles north of the Syrian border.

In the early second millennium BC, Harran was an important trading center on the caravan route between the Mediterranean coast and Assyria in what was probably a key border zone between the Assyrians to the southeast, the Hurrians to the northeast, an emerging Amorite kingdom at Aleppo to the southwest, and the Hittites, who were arriving in Anatolia to the northwest around that time.

Close by Harran was Ura, a town known as a home base for traveling merchants,[108] as were cities bearing the names of Abraham's father,

---

107. Minna Silver, "The Earliest State Formation of the Amorites: Archaeological Perspectives from Jebel Bishri." *ARAM* 26:1&2 (2014), p. 244.

108. Cyrus H. Gordon, "Abraham and the Merchants of Ura." *Journal of Near Eastern Studies* Vol. 17, No. 1 (Jan. 1958), pp. 28–31.

grandfather, great-grandfather, and brother—namely Serug (Sarugi), Nahor (Nahur), Terah, and, of course, Haran, the father of Lot.[109] To be accurate, we should note that "Haran" and "Harran" are different words. As noted earlier, "Harran" derives from the Akkadian *ḫarrānum* ("road"), while "Haran" probably meant something like "mountaineer," from *har*, the Hebrew word for "mountain." Still, the names of his close family members suggest a much stronger connection between Abraham and northern Mesopotamia than with Ur in Sumer, about seven hundred miles to the southeast (and where there are no mountains).

Likewise, Abraham's lifestyle as a tent-dwelling nomad is more consistent with the Amorite culture of northern Mesopotamia than with Sumer. He was not a city-dweller, and neither were Isaac and Jacob. And this must be said: If Abraham's father, Terah, had meant to go from Ur in Sumer to Canaan, he would not have ended up in Harran, not even by mistake. A map of the caravan trails of the ancient Near East makes it obvious.

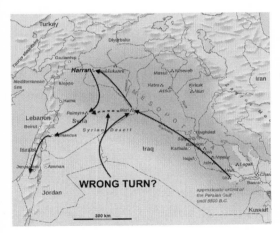

If Abraham traveled to Canaan from Ur in Iraq, he missed an important left turn at Mari. Credit: Goran tek-en, CC BY-SA 4.0, https://commons. wikimedia.org/w/index. php?curid=30851043

109. Mark Chavalas, "Genealogical History as 'Charter': A Study of Old Babylonian Period Historiography and the Old Testament." In *Faith, Tradition, and History: Old Testament Historiography in Its Near Eastern Context* (Winona Lake, IN.: Eisenbrauns, 1994), p. 122.

After following the Euphrates northward from Ur, Terah would have had to miss a left turn at Mari, near the modern border between Iraq and Syria. A well-known caravan trail there crossed the steppe to Tadmor (Palmyra) and Damascus before descending into Canaan by way of Bashan, the modern Golan Heights.

Harran isn't just a little out of the way; it's *ridiculously* out of the way. Going from Ur to Canaan by way of Harran is like driving from Atlanta to Dallas by way of Milwaukee.

Most important, the Bible supports a northern location for Abraham's Ur. When Joshua called on the tribes of Israel to remember their origins, he said:

> Thus says the LORD, the God of Israel, "Long ago, your fathers lived beyond the Euphrates, Terah, the father of Abraham and of Nahor; and they served other gods. Then I took your father Abraham from beyond the River and led him through all the land of Canaan, and made his offspring many." (Joshua 24:2–3)

The key phrase there is "beyond the Euphrates." Ur in Sumer is on the west bank of the Euphrates River. Abraham would not have crossed it to get to Canaan. Harran, and presumably Abraham's Ur, is on the far side of the river. As Cyrus H. Gordon argued in 1958, "It is now clear that Abraham was a merchant prince…from the Hittite realm."[110]

Perhaps, but it's possible that the realm was Hurrian rather than Hittite. There are scholars who believe that Ur-Kasdim ("Ur of the Chaldees/Chaldeans") points to Urkesh. The city-state was at the peak of its power near the end of the second millennium BC, especially after the fall of the Akkadian empire, but its influence began to wane after about 2000 BC. Urkesh is roughly 140 miles east of Harran on a well-traveled trade route coming south through the Mardin Pass and heading west toward markets like Ebla, Halab (Aleppo), and southward to Damascus,

110. Gordon, op. cit., p. 31.

Canaan, and Egypt. In a consonantal language like Hebrew, it is conceivable that a scribe in the post-Babylonian exile, writing fifteen hundred years later, might have come across the name of a long-forgotten city, *u-r-k-s*, and "corrected" it to one he was familiar with, *u-r-k-s-d-m*—Ur-Kasdim, the Sumerian Ur.[111]

We can only speculate, because it's not explicit in the Bible, but the Hurrians' worship of netherworld gods at Urkesh may be the reason Abraham insisted that Isaac not go back there:

> And Abraham said to his servant, the oldest of his household, who had charge of all that he had, "Put your hand under my thigh, that I may make you swear by the LORD, the God of heaven and God of the earth, that you will not take a wife for my son from the daughters of the Canaanites, among whom I dwell, but will go to my country and to my kindred, and take a wife for my son Isaac." The servant said to him, "Perhaps the woman may not be willing to follow me to this land. Must I then take your son back to the land from which you came?" Abraham said to him, "See to it that you do not take my son back there. The LORD, the God of heaven, who took me from my father's house and from the land of my kindred, and who spoke to me and swore to me, 'To your offspring I will give this land,' he will send his angel before you, and you shall take a wife for my son from there. But if the woman is not willing to follow you, then you will be free from this oath of mine; **only you must not take my son back there.**" (Genesis 24:2–8, emphasis added)

The route from Urkesh to Harran to Canaan was well-known to the Hurrians, so it's not surprising at all that would Abraham follow it. The Bible (and archaeology) reveals that Hurrians were scattered all over

---

111. Patricia Berlyn, "The Journey of Terah: To Ur-Kasdim or Urkesh?" *Jewish Bible Quarterly*, Vol. 33, No. 2 (2005), pp. 73–80.

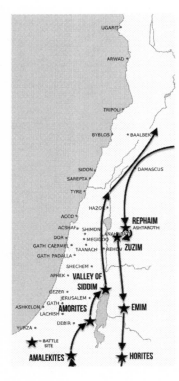

Probable route of the kings from the east in Genesis 14. Note the battle with the Horites (Hurrians) southeast of the Dead Sea.

the lands of the Bible. We first encounter them in Genesis 14:1–16, where we read of a military expedition led by Chedorlaomer, the king of Elam (western Iran), against enemies in the Transjordan and around the Dead Sea. The king and his Mesopotamian allies defeated a coalition led by the kings of Sodom and Gomorrah, who'd rebelled against Chedorlaomer's rule after serving him for twelve years. The battle was probably fought just north of the Dead Sea, possibly on the plain between Mount Nebo and Jericho.[112]

This appears to have been what modern politicians might call a "police action" by the kings of the east to assert their control over the profitable trade route from Egypt to Mesopotamia. The King's Highway crossed the Sinai Peninsula, turned northward at Aqaba, continued through the Arabah past Petra, then up the Transjordan to Damascus, and from there to the Euphrates by way of Tadmor (Palmyra). In the days of Abraham and Lot, Sodom, almost certainly the ruins called "Tall el-Hammam" about eight and a half miles northeast of the Dead Sea, dominated the south end of the Jordan valley. The city's massive walls enclosed about eighty-five acres, and the occupied zone outside

112. For the location of Sodom at Tall el-Hammam, Jordan, about 8.5 miles northeast of the Dead Sea, see Steven Collins and Latayne C. Scott, *Discovering the City of Sodom: The Fascinating, True Account of the Discovery of the Old Testament's Most Infamous City* (New York: Howard Books, 2013).

the walls included about 240 acres.[113] Sodom was the largest city in the southern Levant behind only Hazor and Ashkelon. For comparison, at that time, Jerusalem and Jericho covered only twelve and ten acres, respectively.[114]

We've covered the spiritual significance of Sodom elsewhere.[115] It's our belief that the city was the center of worship devoted to Baal Peor, the lord of the entrance to the underworld (about whom more later). The relevant point here is that the kings of the east fought a series of battles against tribal groups either identified as Rephaim or linked to the giants before confronting troops from the cities of the plain in the valley across the Jordan River from Jericho. This is the most logical place for the battle, given that Sodom holds a commanding defensive position on a spur overlooking the plain.

Chedorlaomer's army moved south along the King's Highway as far south as the Red Sea, and then marched north through the Arabah and along the west side of the Dead Sea. Its first battle was against the Rephaim at Ashteroth-karnaim, one of the cities named as the center of Bashan, the kingdom ruled by Og, last "of the remnant of the Rephaim."[116] The Mesopotamian force likewise had to deal with tribes of Emim and Zamzummim, whom we learn in Deuteronomy were as "tall as the Anakim," and like the Anakim, linked to the Rephaim. Other battles were fought with the Amalekites at En-mishpat, another name for Kadesh, where the Israelites spent many years during their wanderings in the wilderness, and against

113. Collins & Scott, op.cit., p. 157.

114. Leen Ritmeyer, "Chart Showing Relative Sizes of Major Cities in the Levant." Steven Collins, Carroll M. Kobs, and Michael C. Luddeni, *The Tall Al-Hammam Excavations: An Introduction to Tall al-Hammam with Seven Seasons (2005–2011) of Ceramics and Eight Seasons (2005–2012) of Artifacts, Vol. 1* (Winona Lake, IN: Eisenbrauns, 2015), pp. 173, 174.

115. Gilbert & Gilbert (2019), op.cit., pp. 51–72.

116. Deuteronomy 3:11.

the Amorites at Hazazon-tamar, identified as Ein Gedi on the west side of the Dead Sea.[117]

There was one other battle, and it's this one that attracts our interest: Before turning north to face the Amalekites and Amorites, the army from the east encountered "the Horites in their hill country of Seir as far as El-paran on the border of the wilderness."[118] This verse places the Horites in the vicinity of Mount Sinai in the time of Abraham. "Paran" was an alternate name for Sinai,[119] and "Seir" generally refers to the land of Edom, where the Shara mountains rise along the east side of the Arabah valley that connects the Dead Sea to the Red Sea.

Many believe that Mount Sinai is the mountain called Jebel al-Lawz in Saudi Arabia. We'll address that in a future book, but for now, the important detail is the link between Sinai, Seir, Paran, and the Horites. Why is this significant? Because the Horites, as you've probably guessed from the similarity of the names, were Hurrians.[120] And that establishes the presence of this people, their culture, and their religion in the Holy Land centuries before Moses and the Israelites escaped from Egypt. Indeed, the Bible tells us that the inhabitants of the land descended from Seir the Horite,[121] who apparently gave his name to the region south of the Dead Sea. To this day, Mount Hor, where Moses' brother Aaron died and was buried, is identified as Jabal Hārūn, one of the peaks overlooking Petra in Jordan.[122]

The Hurrians in the Transjordan during Abraham's day were pushed out by the descendants of Esau.[123] But they remained in control of two

---

117. 2 Chronicles 2:20.

118. Genesis 14:6.

119. Deuteronomy 33:2, Habakkuk 3.

120. Nicolas Wyatt, "A Ritual Response to a Natural Disaster: KTU 1.119.31 = RS 24.266.31 Revisited." *Ugarit-Forschungen* 50 (2019), p. 454.

121. Genesis 36:20.

122. Josephus, Antiquities of the Jews 4.4.7.

123. Deuteronomy 2:12, 22.

important cities in Israel down to the time of David: Shechem and Jerusalem.

Chapter 34 of the book of Genesis describes an unpleasant encounter between the family of Jacob and the citizens of Shechem, which was ruled by "Hamor the Hivite." However, the Septuagint translation of the verse uses the Greek word *Chorraios*, which means the Jewish translators probably worked with an older Hebrew text that described Hamor as *ḥōrî* rather than *ḥivî*—in other words, Hurrian and not Hivite.[124] Scholars have pointed out that the practice of a married couple living with or near the husband's father's group, while not typical Israelite practice, is attested in Hurrian texts found at Nuzi,[125] an ancient Mesopotamian city located near modern Kirkuk, Iraq.

Quick sidebar: Believe it or not, the Hivites of the Old Testament were actually Greeks. The Hebrew *ḥivî* probably derives from *Hiyawa*,[126] a Luwian (south Anatolian) form of Ahhiyawa, the Hittites' name for the Achaeans, who were the Mycenaean Greeks in Homer's epic poems *Iliad* and *Odyssey*. Short form equation: Hivite = Hiyawa = Ahhiyawa = Achaean = Greek.

This in turn helps to explain the presence of Anakim in Canaan in the days of Joshua, about two hundred years before the Trojan War: The name Anakim derives from *anax*, a Greek noun with four meanings: "the gods, Homeric heroes, the master of the house and ship masters)."[127] The Anakim, who were probably mentioned in Egyptian

---

124. Nicolas Wyatt, "The Story of Dinah and Shechem." In *The Archaeology of Myth* (London: Equinox, 2010), p. 20.

125. Ibid.

126. Billie Jean Collins, "The Bible, the Hittites, and the Construction of the 'Other'." In *Tabularia Hethaeorum: Hethitologische Beiträge Silvin Košak zum 65. Geburtstag.* Dresdner Beiträgezur Hethitologie 25 (Wiesbaden: Harrasowitz, 2007), p. 154.

127. E. C. B. MacLaurin, "Anak/ ̓αναξ." *Vetus Testamentum*, Vol. 15, Fasc. 4 (Oct., 1965), p. 472.

texts about five hundred years before Joshua and the Israelites chased them out of the hill country of Canaan,[128] were a hereditary ruling class, a proto-Greek aristocracy in Canaan.[129] Not surprisingly, pottery and DNA[130] evidence shows that the Philistines, a thorn in the side of the Israelites from the time of the judges through the reign of David, were originally Mycenaean Greeks from Crete and mainland Greece.[131]

But back to Shechem: Scholars note that Hamor's name, which means "donkey," probably wasn't included in the Genesis account by an Israelite scribe as an insult, as we might suspect, but as a reference to the Near Eastern practice of sacrificing a donkey to confirm a treaty.[132] The prospect of a deal with Jacob's family is what induced the men of Shechem to agree to be circumcised. "Will not their livestock, their property and all their beasts be ours? Only let us agree with them, and they will dwell with us."[133]

By the time of Jacob in the nineteenth century BC, an influx of proto-Indo-Aryans into the Near East brought new gods and a ruling elite class to the Hurrian homeland in the Khabur River region, and eventually to all of the lands of the Bible. The Hurrians emerged as a regional power with a kingdom based in northern Mesopotamia

128. "The Execration of Asiatic Princes." In J. B. Pritchard (Ed.), *Ancient Near Eastern Texts Relating to the Old Testament* (Princeton, NJ: Princeton University Press, 1969), p. 328.

129. MacLaurin, op. cit., pp. 469–470, 474.

130. Feldman et al, "Ancient DNA Sheds Light on the Genetic Origins of Early Iron Age Philistines." *Science Advances*, Vol. 5, no. 7 (2019). https://advances.sciencemag.org/content/5/7/eaax0061/tab-pdf, retrieved 2/20/21.

131. "The Philistines in Canaan and Palestine." Luwian Studies. https://luwianstudies.org/the-philistines-in-canaan-and-palestine/, retrieved 2/20/21.

132. Martin Noth, "Old Testament Covenant-making in the Light of a Text from Mari." In *The Laws of the Pentateuch and other Essays* (Edinburgh: Oliver & Boyd, 1966), pp. 108–17.

133. Genesis 34:23.

called Mitanni. Between the seventeenth and fourteenth centuries BC, Mitanni rivaled Egypt and the Hittite empire in size and power, struggling with both for control over what would become the Holy Land. The relevant point here is that the Hurrians introduced worship of the treaty-god Mitra to the Levant,[134] and it appears that Shechem was an important cult center for this god for centuries.

More than four hundred years later, the city of Shechem rebelled against the family of Gideon. Despite ridding the land of marauding Midianites with his valiant band of three hundred, the people of Shechem, who still identified as sons of Hamor,[135] backed a play by Abimelech, Gideon's son by his Shechemite concubine, to kill his half-brothers and prevent the establishment of a ruling dynasty—something that was hinted at by Abimelech's name, which means "My Father the King."

The book of Judges records that "as soon as Gideon died, the people of Israel turned again and whored after the Baals and made Baal-berith their god."[136] "Baal-berith" means "lord of the covenant," a descriptive term for the Hurrian treaty-god, Mitra. And money from the temple of Baal-berith paid the assassins of Gideon's sons:

> And they gave him seventy pieces of silver out of the house of Baal-berith with which Abimelech hired worthless and reckless fellows, who followed him. And he went to his father's house at Ophrah and killed his brothers the sons of Jerubbaal, seventy men, on one stone. (Judges 9:4–5a)

The spiritual significance of Shechem, attested in texts written a thousand years before the Exodus, is too big a story to tell in a few paragraphs, but we can highlight several important events that occurred at the city:

---

134. Wyatt (2010), op. cit., p. 21.
135. Judges 9:28.
136. Judges 8:33.

- God appeared to Abraham at the Oak of Moreh, on a hill over-looking Shechem (probably Mount Gerizim), to confirm that He would give the land to Abraham's descendants (Genesis 12:6–7).
- Jacob buried the teraphim stolen by Rachel from her father under that oak (Genesis 35:4).
- God told Moses and Joshua to designate Mount Gerizim and Mount Ebal, which overlook the city, the mountains of the blessing and the curse, respectively (Deuteronomy 11:29).
- Joshua renewed the covenant with God at Shechem (Joshua 24:1–28), presumably on Mount Ebal (v. 26: "The sanctuary of the LORD").
- The Samaritans live to this day on Mount Gerizim (which is not the same mountain as the mountain of the blessing in Joshua's day, but that's a topic for another time), and believe that the Jews are descendants of a faction that followed the high priest Eli to Shiloh in the eleventh century, thus usurping the priesthood from the sons of Aaron's grandson Phinehas.[137]

The idolatry of the Israelites just a couple of centuries later must have seemed like a victory to the rebellious small-g gods of the pagans. To this day, Shechem (modern Nablus) is a point of conflict between Israelis and Palestinians—and, of course, between rebellious principalities and powers and the God who created them.

Likewise, the struggle for the city where God has placed His Name, Jerusalem, is ancient. God signaled His intention to claim it almost four thousand years ago when He directed Abraham to take Isaac to Mount Moriah. Based on 2 Chronicles 3:1, we can identify this as the location of the threshing floor of Araunah the Jebusite, purchased by David on

---

137. Robert T. Anderson and Terry Giles, *The Keepers: An Introduction to the History and Culture of the Samaritans* (Peabody, MA: Hendrickson Publishing, 2002), pp. 10–12.

the orders of the angel of YHWH, delivered by the prophet Gad. This
piece of ground is where Solomon built the Temple.[138] As you know,
those thirty-seven acres of real estate are hotly contested by Jews, Muslims, and various denominations of Christians to this day.

Here's the bit that connects the story to this chapter: It's accepted
by scholars that the name "Araunah" in 2 Samuel 24 ("Ornan" in 1
Chronicles 21) is probably not a proper name, but a title based on the
Hurrian word *ewri-*, which means "lord" or "ruler."[139] In other words,
Araunah was probably the king of the Jebusites at Jerusalem. He may
even have been a priest-king because there is evidence from the ancient
world that threshing floors were considered portals—points of contact
between this world and the spirit realm.[140]

Interestingly, there is a cave underneath the Dome of the Rock,
directly below the Foundation Stone, that's believed to be where David
offered his sacrifice after buying Araunah's threshing floor. The cave is
attested as early as AD 333 by an anonymous pilgrim from near Bor-
deaux, France,[141] but since the Middle Ages it's been called the Well of
Souls, based on an Islamic legend that one can hear the spirits of the
dead awaiting Judgment Day—similar to the souls who'd been slain for
the word of God crying out from under the altar in heaven at the opening of the fifth seal in Revelation 6:9–11.

Can we connect this cave under the Temple Mount to the Hurrians
of three thousand years ago? No, not yet. We don't know anything about
the early use of the cave. As you can guess, archaeology underneath the

---

138. See 2 Samuel 24:18–25 and 1 Chronicles 21:18–30.

139. Michael T. Winger, *The "God of the Fathers" and Self-Identification in the
Hebrew Bible* (PhD dissertation: UCLA, 2017), p. 81.

140. We discuss threshing floors as portals in *Veneration*, especially pp.
109–126.

141. Jerome Murphy-O'Connor, *The Holy Land: An Oxford Archaeological
Guide from Earliest Times to 1700*, 5th edition (Oxford: Oxford University
Press, 2008), p. 97.

Dome of the Rock, especially work that might confirm an Israelite presence on the Temple Mount prior to 1967, would be met with violent
resistance. But that possibility does point our way to the next chapter,
where we'll see just why this Hurrian connection between the Caucasus
and the Holy Land is important.

Chapter Eight

RITUAL PITS, RESURRECTION, AND REPHAIM

Of all the names under which this old god has masqueraded through the centuries, "Kumarbi" may be the one least known. "Shemihazah" is likewise obscure, but at least he's mentioned in the Book of 1 Enoch, so those who've been exposed to the story of the Watchers on Mount Hermon are at least familiar with that name, if not the spelling. But the cult of Kumarbi died a long time ago, and the Hurrians, who considered him the father of their gods, had all but disappeared from history until modern archaeologists started digging up the Near East. The story of Kumarbi was lost until 1936, when Emil Forrer connected the Hittite texts about Kumarbi to Greek tales of the Titan king Kronos. And yet, in the supernatural history we're reconstructing, Kumarbi plays a key role.

We've established that the Hurrians are the link between the Chalcolithic (Copper Age) civilization of the Ararat Plain, the early urban center of Urkesh in northern Mesopotamia and its necromantic pit, the *abi*, and key sites in and around what became Israel—specifically, Shechem, the area around Mount Sinai, and Jerusalem. This is significant because the word for the sacred pit used by the Hurrians to summon the gods of the netherworld—the Infernal Council, if you will—is connected to several Hebrew words for spiritual practices expressly forbidden by God. In fact, the term was familiar to a number of cultures in the ancient Near East stretching from the Persian Gulf to the middle of Anatolia:

> A large degree of probability exists for deriving the Sumerian, Assyrian, Hittite, Ugaritic, and Hebrew terms from a common source. The chart below illustrates the similarity in sound shared by these various terms:
>
> | Sumerian | $ab(.l\grave{a}l)$ |
> |----------|-----------|
> | Hittite | a-a-bi |
> | Ugaritic | $'eb$ |
> | Assyrian | abu |
> | Hebrew | $'\bar{o}b$ [142] |

The Hebrew word $'\bar{o}b$ (pronounced "ove," with a long O) is usually translated into English as "medium,"[143] but some scholars believe a more accurate rendering is "spirit of the dead."[144] The word appears in the Old Testament sixteen times, often followed by $yidd\breve{e}'\bar{o}n\hat{\imath}$ ("necromancer"). The most famous use of $'\bar{o}b$ is in the story of Saul and the medium of En-dor, to whom Saul turned in desperation when he realized that he'd been abandoned by God. Note the description of Samuel's appearance:

> When the woman saw Samuel, she cried out with a loud voice. And the woman said to Saul, "Why have you deceived me? You are Saul." The king said to her, "Do not be afraid. What do you see?" And the woman said to Saul, "**I see a god coming up out**

---

142. Hoffner, op. cit., p. 385.

143. Strong's H178.

144. Josef Tropper, "Spirit of the Dead." In K. van der Toorn, B. Becking, & P. W. van der Horst (Eds.), *Dictionary of Deities and Demons in the Bible*, 2nd extensively rev. ed. (Leiden; Boston; Köln; Grand Rapids, MI; Cambridge: Brill; Eerdmans, 1999), p. 807.

of the earth." He said to her, "What is his appearance?" And she said, "An old man is coming up, and he is wrapped in a robe." And Saul knew that it was Samuel, and he bowed with his face to the ground and paid homage. (1 Samuel 28:12–14, emphasis added)

The spirit of Samuel, called "a god" (*elohim*) by the medium, "rose up out of the earth"—in other words, from the pit she used to contact netherworld spirits. This has led some scholars, because of the connection between the Hebrew term and the pagan divination pit of the Hurrians, prefer to translate 'ōb as "ritual pit." Compare the ESV and NET translations of 1 Samuel 28:8 (emphasis added):

ENGLISH STANDARD VERSION	NEW ENGLISH TRANSLATION
So Saul disguised himself and put on other garments and went, he and two men with him. And they came to the woman by night. And he said, "Divine for me by a spirit and bring up for me whomever I shall name to you."	So Saul disguised himself and put on other clothing and left, accompanied by two of his men. They came to the woman at night and said, "Use your ritual pit to conjure up for me the one I tell you."

In light of the evidence, the NET translators are correct. We can't fault the ESV translators; the NET Bible may be the only English translation to choose "ritual pit" as the translation for 'ōb in that verse. But it's only been since about 1980 that scholars have accepted the existence of a cult of the dead in and around ancient Israel. The idea that the pagan neighbors of the Hebrews summoned gods of the netherworld is not usually discussed by Bible scholars. And the *abi* of Urkesh was only discovered in 1999, so the influence of the Hurrians on these necromantic rituals is only now coming into focus.

So, kudos to the translators of the NET Bible. Citing the paper we excerpted above, the translators of the NET point out that the common understanding of 'ōb in the days of Saul and David was not "medium" but "owner of a ritual pit."[145] And it's clear that Saul and his servants knew exactly what the pit was used for.

As noted above, the concept of the *'ōb*, a pit used to summon spirits from the underworld, connects the Hebrews to older cultures in the ancient Near East going all the way back to Sumer. The Sumerian word, *ab*, means "sea," and it's related to *abzu*, the term for the cosmic underground freshwater domain of the god of wisdom, Enki, whom we mentioned in an earlier chapter. It was from the *abzu* that Enki sent forth the *abgal* (usually referred to by the Akkadian word *apkallu*), semi-divine sages who delivered the gifts of civilization to humanity. And, as we noted, *abzu* (Akkadian *apsû*) is where we get the English word "abyss."

Amar Annus demonstrated in a groundbreaking 2010 paper that the *apkallu* can be positively identified as the Hebrew Watchers.[146] There is a striking similarity between the activity of the *abgal/apkallu*, the rebellious Watchers (especially Asael), and the Titan Prometheus. We don't think this is a coincidence. Annus interprets the Hebrew stories of the Watchers and their progeny, the Nephilim, as "*deliberate inversions* of the Mesopotamian source material,"[147] polemics against the sorcery and bad behavior of their pagan neighbors who celebrated the *apkallu* as heroes. More than that, however, the Hebrew accounts of the Watchers and their monstrous offspring were a different spin on a shared spiritual history in which the *apkallu* were judged according to the moral standards set by God, rather than those of the fallen "sons of God" placed over the nations after the Tower of Babel.

The connection between the *abzu* of Sumer and the *'ōb* of the Hebrews is obvious (pardon the pun). The *apkallu* were called upon for

---

145. NET notes for 1 Samuel 28:3. https://netbible.org/bible/1+Samuel+28, retrieved 2/23/21.

146. Amar Annus, "On the Origin of Watchers: A Comparative Study of the Antediluvian Wisdom in Mesopotamian and Jewish Traditions." *Journal for the Study of the Pseudepigrapha* 19.4 (2010), pp. 277–320.

147. Ibid., p. 280.

favors, especially to protect the home or royal building projects,[148] and it was common for Mesopotamian kings to compare themselves to, or claim to be descendants of, the *apkallu*:

[Nebuchadnezzar], king of Babylon…distant scion of kingship, seed preserved from before the flood…[149]

To a Jew in the ancient world, a "seed preserved from before the flood" meant a descendant of the Watchers. (By the way, that inscription was carved for Nebuchadnezzar I, who ruled Babylon in the late twelfth century BC, about five hundred years before the Nebuchadnezzar most of us have heard of.) The Assyrian king Ashurbanipal compared his wisdom, including an ability to understand "antediluvian inscriptions," to the first of the *abgal/apkallu* to emerge from the *abzu*, Adapa, and claimed to be his descendant to boot.[150]

The point is that it was widely believed in the ancient Near East that supernatural beings from the netherworld had power and knowledge that was useful, even though they were sometimes considered evil beings with strong connections to Mesopotamian demonology, and were sometimes considered demonic themselves.[151] The linguistic link between the Sumerian *ab* and Hebrew *'ōb* connects the practice of trying to appease these underworld spirits and the necromantic activity of the woman consulted by Saul the night before his death.

Before we decide that we've firmly nailed this connection, new research deserves to be considered. As we saw above, Bible translators who've made a career of studying ancient Hebrew, Aramaic, Akkadian, and Greek haven't settled on a firm definition for *'ōb*. The context seems clear enough, but does the word mean "medium" or "ritual pit"? In 1 Samuel 28:7, the

---

148. Ibid., p. 289.

149. Ibid., p. 295.

150. Ibid., p. 294.

151. Ibid., p. 282.

woman Saul consults is called a *ba'alat 'ōb*. The translation "mistress of mediums" is odd (hence the NET note that the original Hebrew means "owner of a ritual pit").

Christopher B. Hays has suggested a new interpretation of *'ōb* based on an Egyptian etymology. He's argued elsewhere, convincingly, for Egyptian loanwords in the Bible, especially in the book of Isaiah.[152] In this case, Hays and his coauthor Joel M. LeMon suggest that the word may derive from an Egyptian cognate, *3b(w)t.*[153] Not surprisingly, they find the word in the book of Isaiah applied to Egyptian religious practices:

> ...and the spirit of the Egyptians within them will be emptied out,
> and I will confound their counsel;
> and they will inquire of the idols and the sorcerers,
> and the mediums [*'ōbot*] and the necromancers. (Isaiah 19:3)

The argument is fairly technical, but their conclusion is this: The Hebrew word *'ōbot* is related to Egyptian *3b(w)t* and means "dead ancestors who could be represented through images."[154] They go too far in crediting the Egyptians with inventing the word, given the evidence of similar terms going back to Sumer as early as 3000 BC, more than two thousand years before Isaiah.[155] Still, connecting this matrix of ideas to images or stat-

---

152. Referring specifically to the "loathed branch" of Isaiah 14:19. Christopher B. Hays, "An Egyptian Loanword in the Book of Isaiah and the Deir Alla Inscription: Hebrew *nṣr*, Aram. *nqr*, and Eg. *nṯr* as '[Divinized] Corpse'." *Journal of Ancient Egyptian Interconnections* Vol. 4:2 (2012), pp. 17–23.

153. Christopher B. Hays and Joel M. LeMon, "The Dead and Their Images: An Egyptian Etymology for Hebrew *ôb*." *Journal of Ancient Egyptian Interconnections* Vol. 1:4 (2009), pp. 1–4.

154. Ibid., p. 3.

155. "Abzu (water)." The Pennsylvania Sumerian Dictionary. http://psd. museum.upenn.edu/epsd/epsd/e114.html, retrieved 2/23/21.

ues that represented the venerated dead fits what we know of the culture that produced the patriarchs. Genesis 31 records the story of Jacob's flight from his father-in-law, Laban. Besides his anger at losing his moneymaking son-in-law, Laban was furious that his "household gods" (teraphim) had gone missing. While the idols are not called 'ōbôt in the Genesis account, the sense of the word is the same. The teraphim gave a physical location to ancestral spirits during the monthly *kispum* rite, and since those spirits were summoned for blessings and protection, losing access to them was a disaster. It was serious enough in the days of Abraham, Isaac, and Jacob that wills have been found cutting off disobedient children from the family gods.

Hebrew 'ōbôt is usually translated into English as "spirits of the dead," but a similar word, 'ābôt (based on the root 'āb), means "fathers," as in "deceased ancestors." The difference is subtle. It's even plausible that 'ābôt and 'ōbôt are essentially the same word,[156] and it's impossible to ignore the similarity to the Arabic word *abu*, which means "father of." These words and ideas are linked to a puzzling reference in Ezekiel 39:11 related to the prophesied war of Gog and Magog, who foresaw the battle's end in the *gê ha-ōberim* ("Valley of the Travelers"). "Travelers" was a term used by the pagan Amorites of Ugarit around the time of the judges to refer to the Rephaim,[157] spirit beings believed to be the deified dead kings of old, equivalent to the Nephilim of Genesis 6.

The Ugaritic Rephaim Texts, in which these Travelers are summoned to a feast in their honor, reveal information about the Rephaim that should be startling to Christians:

> In spite of the damaged text, we may read the opening lines of KTU 1.20 i 1–3 as follows:
>
> [*rp*] *um tdbḥn*   [The sav]iours will feast
> [*šb*] *'d ilnym*   [seve]n times the divinities
> [*tmnid*] *mtm*   [eight times] the dead...

---

156. Hays and LeMon, op. cit., p. 1.
157. The Ugaritic Rephaim Texts, designated by scholars KTU 1.20–22.

This amounts to a statement that the *rpum* [Rephaim] are indeed divine: they fall into the category of *ilnym* [*elohim*], that is, chthonian gods, who are in turn qualified as *mtm*, "dead." This gives them the aura of underworld associations, rather than merely denotes that they are defunct. These dead are powerful!...

The *rpum* texts contain other pieces of information. Apparently summoned to a cultic performance, usually interpreted as a *kispum* rite, **the Rapiuma [Rephaim] come in chariots on a three-day journey** to a location variously identified as a threshing-floor (*grn*), a plantation (*mtct*), a sanctuary (*atr*) and a house (*bt*, ‖ palace, *hkl*), which may denote a temple and its constituent sacral areas, and which is at the same time on a mountain summit in the Lebanon (KTU 1.22 i 24–5). **The three days of their journeying hints at a lunar symbolism tied to the theme of resurrection**, as perhaps evidenced in Hosea 6:2. This is circumstantial evidence supporting the view that they are dead. The apparent location of the sanctuary, and especially the allusion to the Lebanon, not as we might expect to somewhere directly associated with Ugarit (such as the city itself, or [Mount] Saphon [modern Jebel al-Aqra near Antakya, Turkey]) suggests that the narrative is keying directly into the tradition of the Hauran (biblical Bashan) as the territory associated with the Rapiuma.[158] (Emphasis added)

In the Ugaritic text designated KTU 1.22 i 13–15, the Rephaim are called ʿbrm, a Ugaritic cognate for ōberim, which is variously translated as "travelers," "vagabonds," or "those who came over," in the sense of the dead "crossing over" from the spirit realm to the land of the living. And note that these "travelers" were summoned through a necromancy ritual to the "threshing-floor" of the Canaanite creator-god El, which scholars generally agree was the summit of the mountain that was visible nearly

158. Wyatt (2010), op. cit., pp. 50–51.

everywhere in Bashan, Mount Hermon.[159] According to the text, after two days of riding, the Rephaim arrive at the threshing-floor "after sunrise on the third."[160] The purpose of the ritual was nothing less than the resurrection of the Rephaim:

> There, shoulder to shoulder were the brothers,
> whom El made to stand up in haste.
> There the name of El revivified the dead,
> the blessings of the name of El revivified the heroes.[161]

If you're a Christian, the concept of resurrection at dawn of the third day should be obvious. In fact, finding it in a pagan text written twelve centuries before the Resurrection of Christ should make the hair stand up on the back of your neck! To put it plainly, this is the most important concept in our faith. As Paul wrote, "If there is no resurrection of the dead, then not even Christ has been raised. And if Christ has not been raised, then our preaching is in vain and your faith is in vain."[162]

As we continue, we'll see that the timing and the location of the Resurrection take on new significance against the backdrop of the rebellion of the Watchers and their chief, Shemihazah.

---

159. Lipiński, op. cit., pp. 13–69.

160. KTU 1.22 ii 25. Nicolas Wyatt, *Religious Texts from Ugarit* (London; New York: Sheffield Academic Press, 2002) p. 320.

161. Spronk (1986), op. cit., p. 171.

162. 1 Corinthians 15:13–14.

Chapter Nine

THRESHING FLOORS AND PORTALS

It's no coincidence that David purchased the threshing floor of the Hurrian king Araunah as the future site of Solomon's Temple. In our book *Veneration*, Sharon devoted an entire chapter to explaining why threshing floors were considered portals to the spirit realm in the ancient world. She noted:

> These were communal spaces in the human sense, in that the floors were often clustered together, allowing locals to share news while working. But they were also communal in the spiritual sense, allowing contact with local deities. In fact, the Canaanite word for "grain" is *dagan*, which is very close to the name of their grain-god, Dagan (later called "Dagon" by the Philistines of Samson's day). Around the time of Abraham and Isaac, Dagan was called *bēl pagrē* at the Syrian city of Mari, an epithet that's been translated "lord of corpse offerings, lord of corpses (a netherworld god), lord of funerary offerings, and lord of human sacrifices." This has led some scholars to conclude that Dagan was at least a god with a strong connection to the underworld,

if not part of the royal ancestor cult—and perhaps the recipient of human sacrifice.[163]

Even the circular shape of the threshing floor is a callback to the magic circle dug into the dirt of the *abi*. And just as the threshing-floor/portal connects Mount Hermon to Mount Zion, so too does the transfiguration of Jesus on "a high mountain"[164] near Caesarea Philippi, which can only have been Hermon. Think about that! Jesus literally declared His divinity *on the threshing floor of El.* Then He proceeded on to Jerusalem to fulfill His mission—which, as you know, culminated with His resurrection on the third day.

The point here is that Ezekiel's prophesied Travelers are not vacationers at the Dead Sea, they are Rephaim—the spirits of the Nephilim—who will be foot soldiers in the army of the Antichrist at the final battle of the age, Armageddon.

To Christians, the three-day journey of the Rephaim to a sacred place connected to resurrection has obvious significance. Resurrection on the third day is at the heart of the gospel message:

> For I delivered to you as of first importance what I also received: that Christ died for our sins in accordance with the Scriptures, that he was buried, that he was raised on the third day in accordance with the Scriptures. (1 Corinthians 15:3–4)

Peter linked this event to baptism in a verse that suddenly makes sense when you connect it to the Watchers and their rebellion on Mount Hermon:

> For Christ also suffered once for sins, the righteous for the unrighteous, that he might bring us to God, being put to death

---

163. Gilbert and Gilbert (2019), op. cit., p. 110.
164. Matthew 17:1.

in the flesh but made alive in the spirit, in which he went and proclaimed to the spirits in prison, because they formerly did not obey, when God's patience waited in the days of Noah, while the ark was being prepared, in which a few, that is, eight persons, were brought safely through water. (1 Peter 3:18–20)

The "spirits" to whom Jesus "proclaimed" are not deceased humans. The word translated "spirits" (Greek *pneumasin*) is never used in the New Testament in an unqualified way to refer to human souls.[165] Peter is telling us that Jesus literally descended to Tartarus,[166] a level of the underworld separate and distinct from Hades/Sheol, to have a word with the rebellious spirits imprisoned there. By connecting it to baptism, Peter shows us that the rite is a declaration of victory over those disobedient entities; it is a reminder that another human soul is now set apart for resurrection into an incorruptible body at the sounding of the last trump.

The prophet Hosea revealed that the three-day period leading to resurrection did not originate in the first century with Jesus. It's an old concept that was *reversed* by Christ at His resurrection! And it's a template for what's in store for those who place their trust in Him:

After two days he will revive us; on the third day he will raise us up that we may live before him. (Hosea 6:2)

This concept is embedded in the Sumerian myth *Inanna's Descent to the Netherworld*, in which the headstrong goddess travels through seven gates to the Great Below, the domain of her sister Ereshkigal, queen of the underworld. Ereshkigal knew that Inanna, already called the Queen

---

165. Douglas Mangum, "Interpreting First Peter 3:18–22." In *Faithlife Study Bible* (Bellingham, WA: Lexham Press, 2016).

166. 2 Peter 2:4. The word translated "hell" is Greek tartarōsas; literally, "thrust down to Tartarus."

of Heaven, wanted to take her throne as well and so fixed Inanna with the "stare of death." With help from Enki, Inanna escaped the netherworld on the third day—at the cost of her husband, the shepherd-king Dumuzi (Tammuz in the Bible), who was dragged off to the underworld by demons in her place.

The concept of resurrection on the third day appears to have been incorporated into pagan rituals for the dead condemned by Isaiah:

> I spread out my hands all the day
> to a rebellious people,
> who walk in a way that is not good,
> following their own devices;
> a people who provoke me
> to my face continually,
> sacrificing in gardens
> and making offerings on bricks;
> who sit in tombs,
> and spend the night in secret places;
> who eat pig's flesh,
> and broth of tainted meat is in their vessels. (Isaiah 65:2–4)

Pork was taboo in a number of Near Eastern cultures, coming from "a 'cthonian' animal, which its nature intended to be offered to infernal divinities" and thus "reserved for more or less secret rites."[167] The "tainted meat" may not refer specifically to pork, but to eating a funeral feast on the third day after a death, a practice known in Greek and Roman times.[168] It may be that this activity is behind God's prohibition on eating sacrifices on the third day:

---

167. Roland de Vaux, "Les sacrifices de porcs en Palestine et dans l'Ancien Orient." *Von Ugarit nach Qumran: Festschrift O. Eissfeldt* (ed. J. Hempel and L. Rost) BZAW 77 (Berlin: Topelmann, 1958), p. 261.

168. George Heider, *The Cult of Molek: A Reassessment* (Sheffield: JSOT Press, 1985), pp. 390–391.

If any of the flesh of the sacrifice of his peace offering is eaten on the third day, he who offers it shall not be accepted, neither shall it be credited to him. It is tainted, and he who eats of it shall bear his iniquity. (Leviticus 7:18)

If it is eaten at all on the third day, it is tainted; it will not be accepted, and everyone who eats it shall bear his iniquity, because he has profaned what is holy to the LORD, and that person shall be cut off from his people. (Leviticus 19:7–8)

God is not opposed to remembering the dead. He is often referred to as "the God of Abraham, the God of Isaac, and the God of Jacob" in the Old and New Testaments. However, sacrificing to the dead and eating meat offered to the dead is another matter entirely. Psalm 106:28–31 makes clear that it was precisely that sin that provoked God to send the plague that killed twenty-four thousand Israelites on the plains of Moab.[169] It's not a coincidence that "the matter of Peor" occurred near the stations of the Exodus called Oboth ("spirits of the dead") and Iye-Abarim ("ruins of the Travelers") below Mount Nebo, which God called "this mountain of the Abarim [Travelers]."[170]

The link between the ʿōberim, abarim, ʾōbôt, ʾābôt, ʾōb, and the older words in Ugaritic, Hittite, Assyrian, and Sumerian may have a common ancestor. Until recently, scholars would have assumed that Sumerian must be the oldest, and thus original, form of the word. But as early as 1967, long before the discovery of ancient Urkesh and its monumental ritual pit, eminent Hittitologist Harry A. Hoffner argued that it was phonetically impossible for the Hittite word a-a-bi (from the Hurrian *ay(a)bi) to derive from Sumerian ab. Thus, Hoffner argued, it was better "to accept the Hurrian *ay(a)bi as the prototype."[171] In other words, on the basis of texts alone, Hoffner proposed that it was the Hur-

---

169. Numbers 25:1–18.
170. Deuteronomy 32:48–49.
171. Hoffner, op. cit., pp. 388–389.

rians, not the Sumerians, who brought to Mesopotamia the concept of a ritual pit to summons gods and spirits from the netherworld. Now, with the recent discovery of the Hurrian *abi* at Urkesh, a ritual complex that developed around the same time as the great cities of Sumer like Ur and Uruk (if not earlier), there is archaeological support for Hoffner's linguistic argument.

Here's the kicker: Archaeologist and historian Dr. Judd Burton recently published a paper tracing the origin of the various Eurasian words for "king" or "ruler" to an Akkadian word meaning "prince."[172] I reached a similar conclusion in my book *Last Clash of the Titans*, citing the work of University of Michigan professor Brian B. Schmidt:

> In the light of the repeated occurrence of *rp'um* [Rephaim] in military and heroic contexts and the inadequacy of alternative hypotheses, the significance of Ugaritic *r-p-'* might best be understood in the light of Akkadian *raba'um* "to be large, great", and its derivative *rabium* (< *rabûm*) "leader, chief". Thus, the *rp'um* would be "the Great Ones" or "the Mighty Ones."[173]

Burton argues that morphemes, the smallest word components, suggest that "'r-' indicates royalty and 'ap/ab' indicates a relationship with the Mesopotamian watery underworld: the '*apsu*,' or 'abyss.'"[174] While the *apsû/abzu* was located in Eridu (Sumer, southeast Iraq), the original homeland of the Sumerians was probably the region between the Black

---

172. Judd Burton, "The War of the Words, God-kings, and Their Titles: A Preliminary Report on the Linguistic Relationship Between the Rephaim and Royal Titles in Eurasian Languages." *Bulletin of the Institute of Biblical Anthropology* (2021), p. 7.

173. Brian B. Schmidt, *Israel's Beneficent Dead: The Origin and Character of Israelite Ancestor Cults and Necromancy* (Doctoral thesis: University of Oxford, 1991), pp. 158–159.

174. Burton, op. cit.

and Caspian seas,[175] a theory recently supported by research into similarities between the languages of the Sumerians and Hurrians.[176]

So, the origin of the term for "king" or "ruler" in languages from Western Europe to East Asia is a word used by our distant ancestors for the pre-Flood god-kings, the Rephaim. This word was preserved by the descendants of Noah who spread out from the lands around the resting place of the ark in the mountains of Ararat. And, thanks to recent discoveries by archaeologists, linguists, and geneticists, this movement of people, language, and religious beliefs is confirmed.

Summing up this tour through the realms of the ancient dead: Around 3500 BC, the Kura-Araxes people, ancestors of the Hurrians, began to migrate from the Ararat Plain to settle along the outer edge of the Fertile Crescent in a great arc from northwest Iran to eastern Anatolia and down through Lebanon to the Jordan valley. Their first urban center, Urkesh, commanded the Mardin Pass into the Taurus Mountains, an area rich with timber, copper, and silver that was traded with the areas to the south and west in Mesopotamia and the Levant.

The heart of Urkesh was its temple, built in a southern Mesopotamian style around 3500 BC. It sat above a necromantic pit called the *abi*. This pit was used to summon the "infernal deities," called "former gods" (or by the Akkadian name Anunnaki), who were offered sacrifices in exchange for their blessings and protection. These "former gods" had been sent to the underworld by the king of the pantheon, the storm-god Teshub, the Hurrian form of Baal, Zeus, and Jupiter. The father of the Hurrian gods was Kumarbi, and his home, according to several Hurrian ritual texts, was Urkesh.

By the time of Abraham, Isaac, and Jacob, Hurrians had lived in

---

175. Ibid.
176. Alexei Kassian, "Lexical Matches between Sumerian and Hurro-Urartian: Possible Historical Scenarios." Cuneiform Digital Library Journal (2014:004), https://cdli.ucla.edu/pubs/cdlj/2014/cdlj2014_004.html, retrieved 3/5/21.

Canaan for centuries, settling near the Sea of Galilee as early as 2850 BC. A Mesopotamian army battled Hurrians (Horites) near Mount Sinai, Jacob's sons Simeon and Levi slaughtered the Hurrian men of Shechem, and more than four hundred years later, Gideon's son Abimelech conspired with the Hurrian "sons of Hamor" to kill his half-brothers, only to die in a rebellion by his former comrades a short time later.

And, of course, there is the threshing floor that David bought from Araunah, the Hurrian king of Jebusite Jerusalem, a site of profound spiritual significance to this day. It is likely where Abraham was tested in the binding of Isaac; the place where David and Araunah saw the Angel of YHWH with a drawn sword "standing between earth and heaven,"[177] his hand stayed only by the mercy of God.

In short, the Hurrians have had a profound and, until now, unrecognized influence on history, world religions, and the Bible. The concepts of the *abi* (ritual pit), magic circles, contact with gods of the underworld, offerings to the ancestral dead, and veneration of long-dead kings—the "mighty men who were of old," the Nephilim/Rephaim—was spread throughout the ancient Near East and continue around the world to this day.

All of this was inspired by the spirit beings who descended to Mount Hermon in the distant past. Despite his present status as a prisoner in a deep, dark hole (which may have inspired the preferred means of contact—at night, underground, in a ritual pit), Shemihazah, chief of the rebel Watchers, perhaps working through the spirits of his children destroyed in the Flood, launched an alternate spirituality that reaches out not to our Father in heaven, but to the gods of the world below, the realm of the dead. This religion is still practiced in various forms all over the world today.

The Mount Hermon rebellion, and the spirit who led it, had a lasting impact on ancient Israel. It's also shaped the Western world through its influence on the religions of the Greeks and Romans. Kumarbi, the

---

177. 1 Chronicles 21:16.

god-father of the Hurrians, who we identify as the Watcher chief Shemi-hazah, has been called by many names over the centuries. And it appears his cult was spread by the dispersal of the descendants of Noah from the Ararat Plain.

Chapter Ten

EL

We're moving through the religions of the ancient world to trace the ancient god called "Shemihazah," "Kumarbi," and many other names in roughly chronological order. We began with the Watchers on Mount Hermon and followed, perhaps surprisingly, with the Hurrian god called "Kumarbi." You might think that we would move next to the religion of Sumer, which, until the recent discoveries at places like Urkesh, Tell Brak, and Hamoukar, was believed to be where urban civilization began.

Until recently, you would have been correct. But instead, we're looking west, at civilization along the Mediterranean coast where the father of the gods was called El.

El was the creator-god of the Canaanite pantheon and supreme among the gods, at least in name. While he played an active role in Canaanite religion, he appeared to be rather disinterested in running the show. He took no part in settling the matter of who'd take his place as king of the gods. (The question of *why* El was replaced at the head of the pantheon is not addressed in any of the Ugaritic texts found thus far.) The *Baal Cycle* describes the storm-god's violent struggle for kingship with the god of death, Mot, and the chaos-god of the sea, Yamm, both of whom were described in Ugaritic texts as "beloved of El."[178]

It's not a coincidence that the conflict between Baal, Yamm, and Mot is echoed by the tension between the Greek gods of storm, sea, and underworld, Zeus, Poseidon, and Hades. It's more evidence that the religions of Greece and Rome borrowed heavily from the Semitic people of the Near East.

El is mentioned more than five hundred times in the Ugaritic texts,[179] where he is portrayed as an old god, with the gray hair of his beard a sign of wisdom as well as age. Like Kumarbi, he's depicted as the father of the gods, but El was also credited with the creation of humanity.[180] A common epithet of the god, *Tôr 'Il*, "Bull El," is thought to refer to El's power and dignity—and possibly his generative powers, which are referred to fairly often.[181]

We can't miss the fact that the name of "El" was also a noun, the generic word meaning "god" in Ugaritic and Hebrew and the root behind *elohim*. For that reason, many scholars conclude that El and Yahweh were the same deity. And, to be fair, God did call Himself "El" for a long time:

> God spoke to Moses and said to him, "I am the LORD [YHWH]. I appeared to Abraham, to Isaac, and to Jacob, as God Almighty

---

178. Frank Moore Cross, *Canaanite Myth and Hebrew Epic: Essays in the History of the Religion of Israel* (London; Cambridge: Harvard University Press, 1973) pp. 40, 115.

179. Wolfgang Herrmann, "El." In K. van der Toorn, B. Becking, & P. W. van der Horst Eds., *Dictionary of Deities and Demons in the Bible,* 2nd extensively rev. ed. (Leiden; Boston; Köln; Grand Rapids, MI; Cambridge: Brill; Eerdmans, 1999) p. 275.

180. Cross (1973), op. cit., p. 15.

181. John Day, *Yahweh and the Gods and Goddesses of Canaan* (London; New York: Sheffield Academic Press, 2000) p. 34.

[El Shaddai], but by my name the LORD I did not make myself known to them. (Exodus 6:2–3, content in brackets added)

But there are too many differences between El and Yahweh to confuse the two. Yahweh, the God of the Bible, is an active warrior god, remembered for defeating Leviathan, riding on the clouds (a description of the storm-god repurposed from the *Baal Cycle*), and fighting for Israel against its enemies. El, on the other hand...

El summoned his drinking-companions;
El took his seat in his feasting house.
He drank wine to satiety,
new wine until intoxication.
El went off to his house;
he stumbled off towards his dwelling;
Thukamun and Shanim supported him.
A creeping monster approached him,
with horns and tail!
He floundered in his (own) faeces and urine:
El fell down as though dead;
El was like those who go down into the underworld.[182]

That is *not* the God of the Bible. Yet there were those in Israel who wanted to return to the worship of the old god, especially after the division of Israel and Judah during the reign of Solomon's son, Rehoboam. In the book of Hosea, the prophet recalled the idolatry of Jeroboam, the man who led the rebellion of the northern tribes:

I have spurned your calf, O Samaria.
My anger burns against them.
How long will they be incapable of innocence?

---

182. Wyatt (2002), op. cit., pp. 409–412.

For it is from Israel;
a craftsman made it;
it is not God.
The calf of Samaria
shall be broken to pieces. (Hosea 8:5–6, emphasis added)

This is Hosea's polemic against the golden calf idols set up by Jeroboam, who led the rebellion of the northern tribes against Rehoboam. The phrase, "For it is from Israel," comes from the Masoretic Hebrew text, *kî miyyiśrā'ēl*. The literal reading of the Hebrew is the clunky phrase, "For from Israel."[183] Frankly, that doesn't make sense.

But separating the characters differently yields *kî mî šōr 'ēl*, which changes verse 6 to this:

For who is Bull El?
a craftsman made it;
it is not God.
The calf of Samaria
shall be broken to pieces.[184] (Hosea 8:6, modified; emphasis added)

That's a huge difference! Jeroboam may have set up worship sites at Bethel and Dan to rival the Temple for political reasons. If the northern tribes continued to travel to Jerusalem for the feasts as required by the Law, they might switch their loyalty back to the House of David. Apparently, Jeroboam felt that reestablishing the worship of El, or adopting it from the pagan neighbors of the Israelites, was close enough to do the trick. Hence, the golden calves.

---

183. Nicolas Wyatt, "Calf." In K. van der Toorn, B. Becking, & P. W. van der Horst (Eds.), *Dictionary of Deities and Demons in the Bible: 2nd extensively rev. ed.* (Leiden; Boston; Köln; Grand Rapids, MI; Cambridge: Brill; Eerdmans, 1999), p. 181.
184. Ibid.

El occupied the same place in the Canaanite cosmic hierarchy as Kumarbi did for the Hurrians. So, by extension, we can likewise identify El as Shemihazah, leader of the rebellious Watchers on Mount Hermon. By erecting the golden calves, Jeroboam drew the northern tribes into the worship of a god whose rebellion introduced the pre-Flood world to the occult knowledge that Babylon was so proud of preserving. This crossed a big red line, and God made it immediately clear that it was unacceptable:

> You have done evil above all who were before you and have gone and made for yourself other gods and metal images, provoking me to anger, and have cast me behind your back, therefore behold, I will bring harm upon the house of Jeroboam and will cut off from Jeroboam every male, both bond and free in Israel, and will burn up the house of Jeroboam, as a man burns up dung until it is all gone. (1 Kings 14:9–10)

By reading "Bull El" in Hosea 8:6 instead of "Israel," the verse becomes a polemic directed not just at the idols of Jeroboam, but against the creator-god of the Canaanites. It fits the context of the passage better than the common English translation.

Not surprisingly, this isn't the only place in the Bible where that substitution may come closer to the Hebrew original. Here's the King James translation of Deuteronomy 32:8:

> When the most High divided to the nations their inheritance, when he separated the sons of Adam, **he set the bounds of the people according to the number of the children of Israel.** (Deuteronomy 32:8, KJV, emphasis added)

Now, consider this alternative for the second half of the verse:

> The epithet has also been identified recently in a perceptive study of Deuteronomy 32:8 by Joosten, in which he proposed a

similar consonantal regrouping in the expression *bny yśr'l (bĕnê yiśrā'ēl)* to read *(bĕnê šōr 'ēl)*. Since LXX [the Septuagint translation] (ἀγγέλων θεοῦ, some [manuscripts] υἱῶν θεοῦ), and one Qumran text, 4QDeut¹ *(lmspr bny 'lhym)*, already read a divine reference here, rather than the "Israel" of MT [the Masoretic Hebrew text], this proposal has much to commend it:

yaṣṣēb gĕbulōt 'ammîm (he set up the boundaries of the nations)

lĕmisparbĕnê šōr 'ēl (**in accordance with the number of the sons of Bull El.**)[185] (Emphasis added)

Most English translations agree with the King James Bible and render Deuteronomy 32:8, "the number of the sons of Israel." A few, such as the ESV, follow the Septuagint ("angels of God" or "divine sons") and the text of Deuteronomy found among the Dead Sea scrolls ("sons of Elohim"). What Simon and Nicolas Wyatt propose is reading the Hebrew as "sons of Bull El" instead at the end of the verse. And it fits.

That may sound borderline heretical, like we're playing fast and loose with the text. But note: In the Genesis 10 Table of Nations, there are seventy names, and in Canaanite religious texts, El had seventy sons.[186] That, dear reader, is not a coincidence. As mentioned in an earlier chapter, God placed lesser *elohim* over the nations after the Tower of Babel incident.

Were there exactly seventy tribes or nations at the time of Babel? Possibly not. The point is not the specific number seventy, it's what the number *represented*:

---

185. Simon Wyatt and Nicolas Wyatt, "The longue durée in the Beef Business." In O. Loretz, S. Ribichini, W. G. E. Watson, & J. Zamora (Eds.), *Ritual, Religion and Reason* (Münster: Ugarit-Verlag, 2013), p. 346.
186. Ugaritic text KTU 1.4, vi, 46.

The Aramaean inscription from Zinjirly of Bir-Rakib concerning of his father Panamuwa notes that Bir-Ṣur from Šam'al's seventy brothers were killed by an usurper. The Tel-Dan Inscription (line 6) notes that King Hazael slew seventy kings. In the biblical texts, Abimelech slaughtered Gideon's seventy sons (Judg 9:5–6) and Yehu Ahab's seventy sons (2 Kgs 10:6–7). **In all these instances, the number seventy is symbolic of complete destruction, not one person escaping.**[187] (Emphasis added)

In the ancient Near East, "seventy" was another way of saying "the complete set." Thus, the seventy sons of El on Hermon and the seventy *bene ha'elohim* of the Bible were the gods of the nations—all of the nations except Israel, which was "the LORD's portion," "His allotted heritage."[188]

El's home is described in the Ugaritic texts as a tent. This was similar to the tabernacle of the Israelites, Yahweh's home for more than four hundred years between the Exodus and the construction of Solomon's Temple. El's tent was located at "the source of the rivers, at the midst of the springs of the two deeps."[189] This is reflected in a psalm that takes on new meaning in this context:

> My soul is cast down within me;
> therefore I remember you
> **from the land of Jordan and of Hermon,**
> **from Mount Mizar,**
> **Deep calls to deep**
> **at the roar of your waterfalls;**
> all your breakers and your waves
> have gone over me. (Psalm 42:6–7, emphasis added)

---

187. Noga Ayali-Darshan, "The Seventy Bulls Sacrificed at Sukkot (Num 29:12–34) in Light of a Ritual Text from Emar (Emar 6, 373)." *Vetus Testamentum* 65:1 (2015), pp. 7–8.

188. Deuteronomy 32:8.

189. Ibid., p. 131.

Not to put too fine a point on it, but Psalm 42 points to the abode of El! Mount Hermon is the source of the Jordan River, and Mizar is probably the name of another peak in the Hermon range.[190] The word translated "deep" is *tehom*, which means the abyss, the deepest parts of the earth, and there was a belief in the Near East that the two deeps of the world—a subterranean ocean that emerged as a fountain from Banias (the Grotto of Pan at the base of Hermon), and the celestial ocean that produced the rain—came together at the great mountain.[191]

The rendering of Psalm 42 in the NET Bible offers a deeper insight into the reason for the psalmist's distress:

> I am depressed, so I will pray to you **while I am trapped here in the region of the upper Jordan.** (Psalm 42:6a, NET, emphasis added)

The psalmist is downhearted because he's stuck in enemy territory, the ancient land of Bashan. More specifically, the psalm points to the land seized by the tribe of Dan during the time of the judges. This included the area around Banias, the cave called the Grotto of Pan that was formerly the source of the Jordan River. Dan was remembered in the Bible as the first of the tribes of Israel to turn to idolatry. When the tribe moved north and took the city of Laish at the foot of Mount Hermon, it set up a carved image and established its own priesthood under Jonathan, the grandson of Moses.[192] When Jeroboam led the rebellion of the northern tribes, he set up one of his two golden calves at Dan, which Hosea condemned for serving the cult of "Bull El."

Periodic references to Bashan and Hermon in the Old Testament are clues that God takes this rebellion seriously. As you'll see, there are more references to El, in his many guises, than there are to Satan in the

---

190. Lipiński, op. cit., p. 40 (note 133).

191. Ibid., p. 41.

192. Judges 18:30–31.

Old Testament, sometimes shaped as polemics against the mountain of El's abode:

> O mountain of God, mountain of Bashan;
> O many-peaked mountain, mountain of Bashan!
> Why do you look with hatred, O many-peaked mountain,
> at the mount that God desired for his abode,
> yes, where the LORD will dwell forever?
> The chariots of God are twice ten thousand,
> thousands upon thousands;
> the Lord is among them; Sinai is now in the sanctuary.
> You ascended on high,
> leading a host of captives in your train
> and receiving gifts among men,
> even among the rebellious, that the LORD God may dwell there.
> (Psalm 68:15–18)

The "many-peaked mountain" of Bashan is Mount Hermon. Now, because you're sharp, you know that Hermon is not the mountain of God. That's the Temple Mount, in Jerusalem—the "mount that God desired for His abode." However, the Hebrew phrase *har elohim* can be singular or plural, depending on the context. In this passage, considering the supernatural history of Mount Hermon, reading the verse, "O mountain of *the gods*, mountain of Bashan," is more accurate.[193] Think about that for a moment: At some point in history, Yahweh led His heavenly army against Hermon and took prisoners!

Scholars aren't in agreement on the meaning of this psalm, but since Paul quoted it to describe Christ's victory over the dark domain (Ephesians 4:8), we can assume that the psalmist had some sort of battle in the spiritual war in mind. It's possible that the Psalm 82 courtroom scene

193. Michael S. Heiser, *The Unseen Realm: Recovering the Supernatural Worldview of the Bible* (Bellingham, WA: Lexham Press, 2015), p. 291.

was in view. Since 'el in Hebrew can be a generic word for "God" or a reference to the Canaanite creator-god, depending on the context, the phrase *ădat- 'el* ("divine council") in the first verse of that Psalm could be translated this way:

> God stands in **the assembly of El**;
> in the midst of the gods he renders judgment. (Psalm 82:1, NET, emphasis added.)

In the New English Translation, the Hebrew phrase 'adat 'el is taken as a reference to the Canaanite high god and his assembly, rather than the divine council of Yahweh. In other words:

> Israel's God invades El's assembly, denounces its gods as failing to uphold justice, and announces their coming demise.[194]

Think about that! Rather than a courtroom drama in God's heavenly throne room, Psalm 82 may depict Yahweh appearing in the middle of El's *infernal* council to pass sentence on the rebels! And Psalm 68 may record a battle that took place at Mount Hermon around that time—a supernatural military action that ended with God taking away "a host of captives."

But this battle isn't restricted to the Old Testament. The significance of Mount Hermon and its connection to the Canaanite creator-god is why Jesus made a special trip to the north of Israel:

> And after six days Jesus took with him Peter and James, and John his brother, and led them up a high mountain by themselves. And he was transfigured before them, and his face shone like the sun, and his clothes became white as light. And behold,

---

194. "Psalm 82:1." Biblical Studies Press, *The NET Bible First Edition* (Biblical Studies Press, 2005).

there appeared to them Moses and Elijah, talking with him. (Matthew 17:1–3)

While Mount Tabor, at the eastern end of Israel's Jezreel Valley, is the traditional site of the Transfiguration, clues in the text identify the mountain as Hermon. Matthew 16:13 places the event in "the district of Caesarea Philippi," which was the city outside Banias at the foot of Mount Hermon. Understand the significance of that: Jesus climbed the mountain to the threshing floor of El and sent a message to the old god and his demonic offspring. Christ's transfiguration into a being of light, and the miraculous appearance of Moses and Elijah, was a flare shot into the spirit realm. The Fallen were put on notice that Jesus of Nazareth was, in fact, Yahweh in the flesh.

Upon His descent from the mountain, He cast a demon out of a boy[195] (another message to the Fallen Realm) and then sent seventy-two disciples (or seventy, depending on the translation; from a numerological standpoint, the meaning was the same) into Galilee.[196] They returned, rejoicing, "Lord, even the demons are subject to us in your name!" This, too, was a message to the Fallen, essentially telling them that *His* seventy would ultimately replace the "seventy" that God allotted to the nations after Babel.

But a close reading of the Gospels hints that this wasn't the first time Jesus engaged the enemy on Mount Hermon. Matthew 4:8 notes that it was on "a very high mountain" that Satan showed Jesus "all the kingdoms of the world and their glory," offering them to Christ if He would fall down and worship the Adversary. While the text doesn't specify Hermon as the location of this encounter, it's easily the tallest mountain in or near Israel. At 9,232 feet above sea level, Mount Hermon is more than twice as high as any of the extinct volcanoes on the Golan Heights, more than three times higher than the Mount of Olives, and nearly four times the elevation of the Temple Mount.

---

195. Luke 9:37–43.
196. Luke 10:1–20.

Interestingly, the Ugaritic texts also suggest that the "two deeps" of the abode of El are "in the general vicinity of, if not actually in (or under) the Kinnereth [Sea of Galilee] itself."[197] This adds another dimension to Jesus calming the storm and walking on the water: Not only did He subdue the storm-god, Baal, and literally walk across the sea, which represents chaos (i.e., Leviathan), these may have been additional reminders to the fallen Watcher, Shemihazah, and his colleagues in their underground prison that God is still on His throne.

The biggest difference between El and Kumarbi is in the way power was transferred to the storm-god. Where Kumarbi was overthrown by Baal's Hurrian equivalent, Teshub, the *Baal Cycle* depicts El as semi-retired, declining to intervene in the wars of succession as his sons fought to become the next king of the Canaanite pantheon. Baal did not contend with El directly for the throne; instead, El instructed his son, the chaos-dragon Yamm ("Sea"), the "Beloved of El," to drive Baal from "from the throne of his kingship."[198]

After clubbing Yamm into submission (literally, with two maces named "Expeller" and "All-Driver" fashioned by the craftsman-god, Kothar-wa-Hasis), Baal was challenged by another "Beloved of El," the death-god Mot—and for a time, he succeeded. Baal's temporary death was reversed after much wailing and self-mutilation by El, which is odd given that he was okay with Yamm taking Baal's throne not long before. El's bloodletting is also reminiscent of the frenzied cutting by the prophets of Baal on Mount Carmel during the showdown with the prophet Elijah. In any case, Baal returned from the underworld for a rematch with Mot, an epic battle that finally ended when the sun-goddess Shapash intervened and convinced Mot to stand down.

The battles between Baal and his brothers, the sea-god and death-god, are echoed by the tension in Greek myths between their Hellenic

---

197. Baruch Margalit, *The Ugaritic Poem of AQHT.* (Berlin; New York: Walter de Gruyter, 1989), p. 412.

198. KTU 1.1 iv 23. Wyatt (2002), op. cit., p. 50.

counterparts, Zeus, Poseidon, and Hades. Over the last half-century or so, scholars have increasingly abandoned the old Eurocentric view that the Greek and Roman gods were inherited from a prehistoric Proto-Indo-European religion. The evidence points to the Levant and Mesopotamia, possibly by way of the Hittites and Hurrians who occupied the lands to the north and west of what is now Iran, Iraq, and Syria.

It's also possible that the cults of Semitic gods like El (Kronos/Saturn), Baal (Zeus/Jupiter), Astarte (Aphrodite/Venus), Yamm (Poseidon/Neptune), and Resheph (Apollo in Greece and Rome) were brought to the west by the proto-Greeks themselves. Philistine pottery was Mycenaean Greek. The Hivites encountered by Joshua and the Israelites were the people of Ahhiyawa (Mycenaean Greeks), and the Anakim were probably so named from the Greek *anax*, meaning "god," "king," or "ruler." In addition, modern research has revealed that the Girgashites, mentioned only seven times in the Old Testament, were probably the Teucrians who settled the city of Gergis on the west coast of Asia Minor between Troy and Miletus. The Teucrians have been identified as the Tjekker, one of the Sea Peoples who attacked Egypt during the reign of Ramesses III. An Egyptian text records that the Tjekker were inhabitants of Dor, a port city in Israel between Joppa and Mount Carmel.[199]

So, we shouldn't be surprised by the similarities between the gods and heroes of Greece and the deities of the Amorites. This is why the renowned scholar of the ancient Near East Edward Lipiński wrote:

> Mount Hermon is the cosmic mountain which joins the earth with the lowest heaven. The same conception lies behind the episode of the sons of God in the Book of Enoch. The celestial beings gather on the summit of Mount Hermon because this is the mountain of the gods, the Canaanite Olympus.[200]

199. Othniel Margalith, *The Sea Peoples in the Bible* (Wiesbaden: Harrassowitz, 1994), pp. 58–59.
200. Lipiński, op. cit., pp. 34–35.

However, it's more complex than that, which is not unexpected, given that we're dealing with multidimensional entities who have existed for thousands of years. In his landmark paper, "El's Abode," Lipiński concluded that there were *two* mountains that served as the Semitic Olympus.[201] Citing clues in the Ugaritic texts, the Gilgamesh epic, and other ancient sources, he places the other abode of El at the source of the Euphrates in the mountains of Armenia, which was known until the time of Daniel and Ezekiel in the sixth century BC as Urartu—Ararat, which some scholars believe is the location of Aratta, the rival kingdom to Nimrod's Uruk.

It may seem confusing for El to claim at least two separate locations as his mount of assembly (Hebrew: *har mô ʿēd*). I say "at least" because his identity among the Hurrians, Kumarbi, was described as being at home in the Taurus Mountains of southern Turkey. But remember, the memory of this rebellious Watcher was preserved by the human survivors of the Flood who came to ground in the mountains of Ararat. When the Kura-Araxes culture, the proto-Hurrians, migrated from the Ararat Plain in the fourth millennium BC, stories of the old god and the wonderful, magical things he and his colleagues had given to humankind went with them to Sumer, northern Mesopotamia (Urkesh), and the Levant (Mount Hermon).

The move to Mesopotamia resulted in one of the most spectacular interventions by God in human history and a throne-room vision by a Hebrew prophet that is still misinterpreted as a UFO encounter to this day.

---

201. Ibid., p. 69.

Chapter Eleven

ENLIL

The chief god of Mesopotamia before the political rise of Babylon was the deity called the "Great Mountain," Enlil. Scholars used to believe that the god's name was a combination of the Sumerian words *en* ("lord") and *líl* ("air/wind" or "storm").[202] As scholars have looked deeper into the nature of the deity, however, a growing number have concluded that "Lord Wind" or "Lord Aether" is too simple. The stories and descriptions of Enlil don't include any characteristics you'd expect from a wind or storm-god.[203] Based on his identification with El, Kumarbi, and others we'll discuss before we reach the end of this book, Enlil should be understood not as lord of the air, but as "a universal god who controls different spheres and domains, different areas without any defined specialization."[204]

In other words, Enlil was simply "the" god. That makes the etymology of Enlil's name easier to grasp: Rather than Sumerian *en* + *líl*, it's

---

202. Lluis Feliu, "Concerning the Etymology of Enlil: The An=Anum Approach." *Aula Orientalis-Supplementa* 22 (2006), p. 229.
203. Ibid., p. 246.
204. Ibid.

most likely derived from a doubling of the Semitic word *ilu* ("god"), *il* +
ilû, meaning "god of gods,"[205] or "god of all the gods."[206]

That fits the character of Enlil, El, and Kumarbi in their respective
pantheons. All of them were considered creators of the world, described
by epithets like "father of the gods," "ancient one," and so on. To people
in the ancient world, Enlil/El/Kumarbi bridged the gap between time
immemorial and the present day. In each case, "the" god had assumed
kingship over the pantheon by replacing a primordial deity who represented the sky or heaven. Enlil and Kumarbi supplanted Anu, while El
took the place of Šamêm ("Heaven").[207] In my view, this is the Fallen
Realm's twisted tale to diminish the true God of heaven (and earth, and
all creation), Yahweh, by slandering the sky-god as remote, disinterested,
and, in some accounts, literally neutered.

This recent reconsideration of the nature of Enlil is quite different
from the way the god has traditionally been understood by scholars.
Rather than emerging from Sumer in the south, as Mesopotamian civilization is assumed to have done, recent research shows that "the" god was
imported into Sumer by migrants from the north or northwest.

When Amorites first encountered the civilizations of Akkad and
Sumer in the twenty-fourth century BC, the two most popular deities
among the newcomers were the moon-god, Erah (also spelled "Yarikh";
called "Sîn" in Akkad and "Nanna" in Sumer) and "the" god, under the
Amorite name "El." This is documented by the Amorite personal names
logged in official Sumerian and Akkadian records:

---

205. Christopher B. Hays, "Enlil, Isaiah, and the Origins of the *ʾĕlîlîm*: A
Reassessment." *Zeitschrift für die alttestamentliche Wissenschaft*, 132(2) (2020),
p. 226.
206. Feliu (2003), op. cit., p. 230.
207. Frank Moore Cross, *Canaanite Myth and Hebrew Epic: Essays in the
History of the Religion of Israel* (Cambridge: Harvard University Press, 1973),
p. 41.

If we then take a look at the 43 most popular Amorite names (in this case: Amorite names occurring three times or more). **We can see immediately the moon-god Erah and El ('God') are the two most popular (and only) theophoric elements in these early Amorite personal names.** This is a striking parallel with the Akkadian personal names. This parallel pleads against the "Amorites" as newcomers, because such a phenomenon is typically the result of long-term contact and/or acculturation.[208] (Emphasis added)

This is new research, just published in 2014. During the time of Abraham and Isaac, in texts dated between 1900 BC and 1791 BC,[209] the only two gods attested among the Amorites of Mesopotamia were the moon-god and "the" god. Considering the number of gods in the Mesopotamian pantheon, it's significant that Amorites in Akkad and Sumer during the lifetime of Abraham only honored two of them.

Why these two? I discussed the moon-god in some detail in my book on the spiritual forces behind Islam, *Bad Moon Rising*. It appears that the moon-god was considered the "god of the Amurru-land"—in other words, the god of the Amorites:

We may reasonably conclude, therefore, that the god worshiped by the nomadic Amurru-peoples in the Balikh-Harran region by the epithets "Amurru" and "Bêl Šadê," at the time of the Mari and Old Babylonian texts, was a lunar deity. Sometimes he is specifically named (or at least identified with) Sîn.[210]

---

208. Rients de Boer, "Amorites in the Early Old Babylonian Period" (Dissertation: Leiden University, 2014), p. 69.

209. Ibid.

210. Lloyd R. Bailey, "Israelite 'Ēl Šadday and Amorite Bêl Šadê." *Journal of Biblical Literature*, Vol. 87, No. 4 (Dec., 1968), p. 435.

This research identifies the Mesopotamian deity Amurru, generally considered a separate entity by most scholars, as the moon-god, and places the center of his cult in the very region that produced the family of Abraham—the area along the Balikh River and around the city of Harran, which was home to a well-known temple to Sîn.

The similarity between Bêl Šadê ("lord of the mountain"), referring to Amurru/Sîn, and Yahweh's epithet El Shaddai ("God of the mountain") is obvious. The Fallen Realm doesn't hesitate to steal that which belongs to their Creator. The Balikh-Harran region is roughly a hundred miles west of Urkesh, where "the" god had been worshiped under the name "Kumarbi" for probably fifteen hundred years by the time of Abraham. And it's known that Urkesh and Harran were connected by an important trade route, linking the resource-rich mountains north of Urkesh to markets in northern Syria and the Mediterranean port near Antioch. It's not a stretch to theorize that the cult of "the" god, Kumarbi/El/Enlil, was carried to Harran by travelers along that route over the centuries.

This also establishes a link between the Hurrians and the Amorites, and suggests a path of transmission from the north to Sumer. While the Hurrians remained in the "Outer Fertile Crescent," the Amorites moved south along the Euphrates and Tigris during the second half of the third millennium BC. They developed a pretty rough reputation, especially the Tidanu tribe (about whom more later), that contributed to the collapse of the last Sumerian kingdom to rule Mesopotamia. By the time of Abraham, around 1900 BC, Amorites controlled nearly everything from western Iran to the Mediterranean.

A trilingual god list from Ugarit, composed during the time of the judges, confirms that the Amorites, Hurrians, Akkadians, and Sumerians all worshiped "the" god with this handy linguistic equation: Enlil = Kumarbi = El.[211] Like the Amorites, the name "Kumarbi" may come from northern Syria. It probably means "he of Kumar," a site identified with the modern village of Kīmār, about twenty-five miles northwest

---

211. Feliu (2003), op. cit., p. 299.

of Aleppo.[212] Today, it's home to about six hundred souls in war-torn Afrin province of northwestern Syria; in the second millennium BC, it belonged to a kingdom called Mukish, which is likely why Hurrian religious texts name Kumarbi's vizier as Mukishanu.[213]

Kīmār is roughly halfway between Aleppo and the Amuq Valley, right in the middle of an area that includes ancient Antioch, a city of some importance to the early Christian church; Mount Zaphon (modern Jebel al-Aqra), the mountain on which Baal's palace was believed to sit; and the Amanus Mountains, the significance of which we'll explain as we get deeper into this book. The point of this geography lesson is that it was from this general area, northwest of Sumer and Akkad, that the Amorites migrated into southern Mesopotamia, bringing with them the worship of "the" god, *il-ilû* (Enlil).

This may explain the best-known epithet of Enlil, "Great Mountain." The Akkadian term is ŚA.DÚ ì-li ra-bí-um, literally, "the great mountain of the gods."[214] This title is attested from the time of Sargon of Akkad, who reigned in the late twenty-fourth and early twenty-third centuries BC, about three or four hundred years before the time of Abraham.

The equivalent of ŚA.DÚ ì-li ra-bí-um in Sumerian is ᵈEn-líl(É) *kur-gal* (*kur-gal* = "great mountain").[215] However, the epithet *kur-gal* has not been found in any Sumerian text prior to the rise of Sargon in the late twenty-fourth century BC,[216] evidence that this particular title of "the" god was introduced to Sumer by the Akkadians, rather than a holdover from the dim Sumerian past. This is a plausible scenario, given that the Sumerian homeland in southern Iraq is noticeably devoid of mountains.

---

212. Michael C. Astour, "Semitic Elements in the Kumarbi Myth." *Journal of Near Eastern Studies*, Vol. 27, No. 3 (July, 1968), p. 172.

213. Ibid., p. 173.

214. Wang, op. cit, p. 199.

215. Ibid.

216. Ibid., p. 134.

The rise of the Akkadians occurred around the same time that Amorite migrants began to arrive in southern Mesopotamia. I'm not aware of any research into whether these events and the emergence of Enlil's new title, "Great Mountain," are connected, but it seems unlikely that they were a coincidence. It's true that correlation does not imply causation, but the arrival in Sumer of that epithet at about the same time as groups of Semitic-speaking Akkadians and Amorites is strong circumstantial evidence. Remember, the Amorites of that era worshiped only two gods, "the" god Ilu (El) and the moon-god called Bêl Šadê ("lord of the mountain"). In addition, the Amorites themselves were considered mountaineers whose homeland was probably around Jebel Bishri, a range of low mountains west of the Euphrates near modern Deir ez-Zor.[217]

We should also remember that the Akkadians sealed a political alliance with the Hurrians around this time by marrying off the daughter of Narām-Sîn to the *endan* (king) of Urkesh. And the Hurrians, too, were familiar with highland life, as Urkesh controlled trade between their cousins in the Taurus Mountains to the north and the cities of Mesopotamia to the south.

Not to follow rabbits too far off the main trail here, but that begs the question: Were the Amorites and Hurrians related? Although the Amorites spoke a Semitic language, they were usually portrayed in Egyptian art with fair skin.[218] The Hurrians (the Horites of the Bible) and Amorites were among the tribes Joshua and the Israelites had to push out of Canaan. And the deity the Hurrians and Amorites considered the father of their gods, Kumarbi/El, was at home in the mountains and connected to an underground abode—the Hurrian *abi* and "the springs of the two deeps" under or near Mount Hermon. This, by the way, follows the broad outlines of Enlil's career:

---

217. Silver, op. cit., p. 244.

218. M. G. Easton, "Amorites." *Illustrated Bible Dictionary* (New York: Thomas Nelson, 1897). https://www.biblestudytools.com/dictionary/amorites/, retrieved 3/11/21.

A text from Nineveh recounts a myth in which divine beings break the wings of Enlil and Anu and cast them down into the Abyss (*apsû*). In the same text, it is said that Marduk "cast a [sp]ell against Illil in the Abyss, and consi[gned him] to the Anunnaki," that is, the underworld gods.[219]

In any case, Enlil's emergence as the kingmaker of Mesopotamia doesn't extend as far back in Sumerian history as was thought. It was widely believed that a human king's right to rule derived from the favor of Enlil; in fact, "kingship," the attribute of royalty that conveyed the divine authority of a king, was literally called "enlilship."[220] But until about 2450 BC, Enlil did not bestow that power to kings across all of Sumer. Before that, the androgynous goddess of sex and war, Inanna (called Ishtar in Akkadian), the patron deity of Uruk, conveyed "rulership" to leaders in southern Sumer where Enlil was apparently considered a foreign god.[221] His name was rarely used as the theophoric element in personal names before the Akkadian conquest of Southern Mesopotamia around 2300 BC.[222]

It was about this time that Enlil appears to have been elevated from the status of patron god of Nippur, a city located near the Euphrates about one hundred miles southeast of modern Baghdad, to head of the Mesopotamian pantheon. His temple also seems to have acquired the title E-kur ("House of the Mountain") with the rise of the Akkadian Empire.[223] With the emergence of Enlil as the chief god of the land,

---

219. Hays (2011), op. cit., p. 219.

220. Andreas Johandi, "Some Remarks about the Beginnings of Marduk." In S. Fink and R. Rollinger, eds., *Proceedings of the Ninth Symposium of the Melammu Project Held in Helsinki / Tartu* (Münster: Ugarit-Verlag, 2018), p. 566.

221. Wang, op. cit., p. 26.

222. Ibid., p. 136.

223. Ibid., p. 201.

Nippur, also transliterated as "Nibru," became the center of Mesopota-mian religion. The E-kur was the home of the divine council, the place where the gods convened to decide and decree the fates of the people under their domain.

Why Nippur was chosen is anyone's guess. It began as a collection of reed huts in a marsh alongside the Euphrates. Over time, garbage, debris, and earth were piled up to lift the town above the surrounding marsh. You'd think the "king of heaven and earth" and "father of the gods" could find a better piece of real estate.

Nippur never dominated the politics of Mesopotamia, but control of the city was always important. Enlil was subject only to Anu, the sky-god, and he was often portrayed as the only deity who could con-tact Anu. So, possession of Nippur was crucial for an ambitious ruler in Sumer. Ownership of Nippur was proof that Enlil wanted him to be king.

However, Enlil's days at the top of the virtual mountain were num-bered when the Amorite dynasty of Hammurabi transformed Babylon from a third-rate village into a political force in the eighteenth century BC. Like an aging movie star who gradually finds leading roles harder to come by as younger actors arrive in Hollywood, Enlil was eventually replaced as the king of Mesopotamian deities by the city-god of Baby-lon, Marduk, a process that was complete by about the twelfth century BC.[224]

But Enlil's prestige continued for centuries afterward. Even though his name isn't mentioned even once in our English Bibles, the proof of Enlil's power is written in the Old Testament.

---

224. W. G. Lambert, "Studies in Marduk." *Bulletin of the School of Oriental and African Studies*, University of London, 1984, Vol. 47, No. 1 (1984), p. 1.

Chapter Twelve

ISAIAH'S "WORTHLESS IDOLS"

Isaiah's love of wordplay is well known. Among his many artistic uses of language, it appears the prophet adapted the name of "the" god into a Hebrew word, 'ĕlîl, that became a common term for false gods and idols.[225]

> As it happens, however, a better suggestion [for the etymology of 'ĕlîl] was advanced in 1907 by A. T. Clay, who noted in passing that "[t]he origin of אלילים, the word translated 'idols' in the Old Testament [...] is probably to be found in the name of the Nippurian deity Ellil."[226]

As noted above, the best explanation for the origin of Enlil's name is the Semitic *il-ilû*, "god of gods." This would have been written in syllabic cuneiform as Illil,[227] so its use by the prophet is not as much of a stretch as it looks at first. This is especially plausible since Assur, the chief

---

225. Hays (2020), op. cit., p. 224.
226. Ibid., p. 226.
227. Ibid.

god of the Assyrians, was "the Assyrian Enlil."[228] When Assyria came to power, the temple of the god in the capital city, also called Assur, was renamed from *bit aššur* ("House of Assur") to E-kur,[229] the name of Enlil's temple in Nippur.

The turbulent political events of the day are reflected in Isaiah's writing. Assyria destroyed the northern kingdom of Israel during his lifetime and would have done the same to Judah without God's divine intervention.[230] One of the most interesting uses of *'ĕlîlim* by Isaiah describes the shift of power from southern Mesopotamia to the land of Assur, whose homeland was what is now the Kurdish region of northern Iraq:

> (The king of Assyria is speaking): As my hand has reached to
>   the kingdoms of the idols [*'ĕlîl*],
> whose carved images were greater than those of Jerusalem and
>   Samaria,
> shall I not do to Jerusalem and her idols [*'ăṣabbê*]
> as I have done to Samaria and her images [*'ĕlîle*]?"
> (Isaiah 10:10–11)

The clue is the singular form of the word *'ĕlîl* in verse 10, which makes the verse "my hand has reached to the kingdoms of *'ĕlîl*." In other words, the Assyrian king was referring to Sumer and Akkad, the lands that recognized Enlil as their chief deity. Chapter 10 of Isaiah depicts God speaking for the Assyrian king to *mock* the mighty Sennacherib for

228. Alasdair Livingstone, "Assur." In K. van der Toorn, B. Becking, & P. W. van der Horst (Eds.), *Dictionary of Deities and Demons in the Bible* (2nd extensively rev. ed.) (Leiden; Boston; Köln; Grand Rapids, MI; Cambridge: Brill; Eerdmans, 1999), p. 108.
229. Ibid.
230. The story is told in 2 Kings 18:13–19:37, 2 Chronicles 32, and Isaiah chapters 36 and 37.

daring to boast that he would do to the people of Yahweh what he'd just done to the people of Enlil:

In light of Assyrian propaganda, the singular use of לִילָא in 10:10 is telling. Rather than referring back to the small, regional kingdoms listed in v. 9 (in which case one would expect the plural מִילִילָא), it more likely refers to Sennacherib's victories in Babylonia. In multiple inscriptions, beginning in 702, Sennacherib boasted of his conquest of southern Mesopotamia—including Illil's home city, Nippur, and various other southern Mesopotamian (and Aramean) cities—in lengthy lists of rebellious peoples; and he goes on to characterize all the peoples ruled by Assyria as "subjects of the god Illil" (*ba'ulāt Illil*). (The Assyrians had by that point taken over both the city of Illil and the religious rhetoric associated with Illil.) That is to say, in this reflection of Assyrian rhetoric, the king's boast in Isa 10:10 is that he has seized "the kingdoms of Illil."[231]

God does not take such hubris lightly. Isaiah 10:12–19 records His decree of Sennacherib's fate:

When the Lord has finished all his work on Mount Zion and on Jerusalem, he will punish the speech of the arrogant heart of the king of Assyria and the boastful look in his eyes. (Isaiah 10:12)

That was fulfilled when the angel of the LORD struck down 185,000 Assyrians outside the walls of Jerusalem,[232] preserving Jerusalem and the kingdom of Judah for another century.

Most uses of *'ĕlîlim* in the Bible refer to carved images representing

231. Hays (2020), op. cit., p. 229.
232. Isaiah 37:36.

the gods of the pagans. The word eventually became an adjective used as an insult ("worthless").[233] However, there are Scriptures where it appears to refer specifically to Enlil, and more broadly to the entities who followed his example and rebelled against their Creator:

> For great is the LORD, and greatly to be praised;
> he is to be feared above all gods [*elohim*].
> For all the gods [*elohê*] of the peoples are worthless idols ['ĕlîlim],
> but the LORD made the heavens. (Psalm 96:4–5)

> The heavens proclaim [God's] righteousness,
> and all the peoples see his glory.
> All worshipers of images are put to shame,
> who make their boast in worthless idols ['ĕlîlim];
> worship Him, all you gods [*elohim*]! (Psalm 97:6–7)

Both of the psalms above equate elohim ("gods") with the 'ĕlîlim ("worthless idols"). In these contexts, they are not the graven images forbidden by God, but rebellious spirits called 'ĕlîlim. ("Enlilites"?) The term may be similar to "revolutionary," which describes those who take up arms against a legitimate government.

The Jewish scholars who translated the Septuagint three centuries before the birth of Jesus apparently understood, at least in some passages, that the 'ĕlîlim were not simply graven images:

> For all the gods of the nations are **demons** ['ĕlîlim],
> but the Lord made the heavens. (Psalm 96:5 LXX, emphasis added)

Isaiah, as you'd expect from a prophet of God, foretells a day when these mutinous spirits are destroyed:

---

233. Hays (2020), op. cit., p. 234.

For the LORD of hosts has a day
against all that is proud and lofty,
against all that is lifted up—and it shall be brought low;
against all the cedars of Lebanon,
lofty and lifted up;
and against all the oaks of Bashan; [...]
And the haughtiness of man shall be humbled,
and the lofty pride of men shall be brought low,
and the LORD alone will be exalted in that day.
And the idols ['ĕlîlîm] shall utterly pass away.
(Isaiah 2:12–13, 17–18)

The phrase "in that day" refers to the Day of the Lord, the ultimate fulfillment of prophecy. It describes the end of history when God finally pours out His wrath on the unrepentant—which will include "the host of heaven,"[234] a group that apparently includes the 'ĕlîlîm. You're familiar enough by now with the supernatural significance of Mount Hermon to know that the reference to "the cedars of Lebanon" and "the oaks of Bashan" is not a polemic against imported lumber; it's a condemnation of a supernatural enemy—in this case, the one who was believed to rule over Bashan and Lebanon from his abode atop Hermon.

But Isaiah was not the only prophet to deal with Enlil. And there is evidence that the false god's presence in the Bible is recorded much earlier than Isaiah.

---

234. Isaiah 24:21.

Chapter Thirteen

BABEL AND EZEKIEL'S WHEEL

Enlil was the chief god of Mesopotamia for more than a thousand years. As noted above, his "reign" began with the rise of the Akkadian empire in the twenty-fourth century BC. But if we look farther back in history, to the end of the Uruk Period around 3100 BC, we may find another hint at this god's arrogance and a very clear message from God that he was not going to be allowed out of the abyss before the appointed time.

I described earlier the effort by Nimrod, who was the Sumerian king Enmerkar, to expand the temple of the god Enki, the E-abzu ("House of the Abyss"), to serve as "an abode of the gods."[235] This temple, commonly called the Tower of Babel, was not at Babylon, despite the similarity between the names. The temple was, in fact, located at an ancient city called Eridu.

This isn't as odd as it might seem. The name "Babylon" was used for other Mesopotamian cities, including Eridu.[236] The ziggurat at Eridu is the oldest and, had it been completed, would have been the largest in all

---

235. Gilbert and Gilbert (2019), op. cit., pp. 190–192.

236. Stephanie Dalley, "Babylon as a Name for Other Cities Including Nineveh." In R. Biggs, J. Meyers & M. Roth (Eds.), *Proceedings of the 51st Rencontre Assyriologique Internationale* (Chicago: The University of Chicago, 2008), pp. 25–26.

of Mesopotamia, a description that's consistent with the little we know about the career and ambition of Nimrod. It also fits with archaeology of the fourth millennium BC, which, as we noted in an earlier chapter, was when the city of Uruk (biblical Erech), was, with Babel, the "beginning of his kingdom."[237]

In the late 1940s, archaeologists working at the site of Eridu, Tell Abu Shahrain in southeast Iraq, made a fascinating discovery. As builders worked on the new and improved E-abzu, the construction project was suddenly and inexplicably interrupted:

> The Uruk Period...appears to have been brought to a conclusion by no less an event than the total abandonment of the site.... In what appears to have been an almost incredibly short time, drifting sand had filled the deserted buildings of the temple-complex and obliterated all traces of the once prosperous little community.[238]

If you're familiar with the story of the Tower of Babel, then you don't need me to tell you that the discovery of the archaeologists tracks with the account in the book of Genesis:

> "Come, let us go down and there confuse their language, so that they may not understand one another's speech." So the Lord dispersed them from there over the face of all the earth, **and they left off building the city.** (Genesis 11:7–8, emphasis added)

---

237. Genesis 10:10.
238. Fu'ād Safar, Seton Lloyd, Muhammad 'Alī Muṣṭafá & Mu'assasah al-'Āmmah lil-Āthār wa-al-Turāth, Eridu (Baghdad: Republic of Iraq, Ministry of Culture and Information, State Organization of Antiquites and Heritage, 1981), p. 46.

The Uruk period ended around 3100 BC, after which the influence of Nimrod's city faded and power was shared with other Sumerian cities such as Ur, Lagash, Kish, and Umma.

Here's the reason for circling back to the account of the temple to Enki, who's often depicted as a rival to Enlil in Mesopotamian myths: It's generally accepted that the name "Babel" derives from the Akkadian words *bab ilû*, typically translated "god-gate" or "gate of the gods." While this is speculative, let me suggest a new idea: It's possible that *bab ilû* meant "gate of 'the' god," Enlil. Perhaps Nimrod's expansion of the "House of the Abyss" was intended to serve as a portal to contact Enlil in the *abzu*, similar to the use of the *abi* to reach Kumarbi at Urkesh. Or, since the poem *Enmerkar and the Lord of Aratta* describes the rebuilt E-abzu as an "abode of the gods," maybe it was Nimrod's hope that the Tower of Babel would allow Enlil/Kumarbi to *return* from the abyss.

Again, this is speculation. There is no evidence from the historic period that Enlil was ever worshiped at Eridu. However, the Tower of Babel occurred during the Uruk period, before the invention of writing. Is it possible that part of the story was lost or forgotten before *Enmerkar and the Lord of Aratta* was written on clay? We'll never know, but it's worth considering—especially since we're fairly sure, thanks to the evidence from ancient Urkesh, that Enlil was worshiped by the Hurrians in northern Mesopotamia (as Kumarbi) when Nimrod broke ground at Eridu.

And it is certain that God took this entity seriously. Jesus specifically declared His divinity at Hermon, the mountain sacred to this entity. Six hundred years earlier, God revealed His glory to Ezekiel at another place that is just as significant:

In the thirtieth year, in the fourth month, on the fifth day of the month, as I was among the exiles by the Chebar canal, the heavens were opened, and I saw visions of God. On the fifth day of the month (it was the fifth year of the exile of King Jehoiachin), the word of the Lord came to Ezekiel the priest, the son of Buzi, in the land of the Chaldeans by the Chebar canal, and the hand of the LORD was upon him there. (Ezekiel 1:1–3)

This is Ezekiel's famous vision of the cherubim and the "wheel within a wheel" that has so deluded the UFO community into believing that God is a space traveler. This has been sufficiently addressed elsewhere; suffice it to say that Ezekiel's readers knew that what he saw was a royal throne and its supernatural guardians, not a spacecraft.

The important point for us here is a geographic detail that was so important Ezekiel included it twice: He was "by the Chebar canal." Scholars used to connect the Chebar to the Hubur, a river that in Mesopotamian cosmology was similar to the Styx—the river one crossed to reach the netherworld. That idea has been discarded and it's now accepted that the Chebar canal was the Naru Kabari, which is today a dry riverbed called the Shatt en-Nil. Here's the important bit: Back in the day, it flowed right through the center of Nippur.[239]

Please take a moment to get your head around that: God revealed Himself to Ezekiel in all of His glory above the temple of the chief god of Mesopotamia! This was no more a coincidence than Jesus climbing Mount Hermon for the Transfiguration. In fact, this was so important to Ezekiel that he reminded his readers four more times (in chapters 3, 10, and 43) of the vision of glory he'd seen "by the Chebar canal."

Before we leave this chapter, I must call your attention to one more reference in the Bible clearly directed at this ancient enemy of God:

Then he said to me, "This is the word of the LORD to Zerub-babel: Not by might, nor by power, but by my Spirit, says the LORD of hosts. **Who are you, O great mountain? Before Zerub-**

---

239. Leonard W. King, *A History of Sumer and Akkad* (London: Chatto and Windus, 1910), p. 9.

babel you shall become a plain. And he shall bring forward the top stone amid shouts of 'Grace, grace to it!'" (Zechariah 4:6–7, emphasis added)

Because you're paying attention, you spotted the reference to the "great mountain" right away. Bible commentators usually take this as a metaphor for a difficult task, like the one that faced Zerubbabel—rebuilding the Temple. That analysis is too naturalistic. It completely misses the reference to a pagan deity who was well known, especially to Jews who'd been oppressed by invaders from Mesopotamia—first the Assyrians, and then the Chaldeans from Babylon—for about two hundred years by the time of Zechariah and Zerubbabel.

Zechariah's ministry began around 520 BC,[240] no more than seventy-five years after Ezekiel's vision of God's throne room above the city of Nippur. No, Zechariah was privileged to hear God literally *mocking* Enlil in the abyss! The LORD's message to the fallen Watcher was blunt: "My people will rebuild My house on My mountain. You, 'O Great Mountain,' are no mountain at all."

The sarcasm comes through loud and clear twenty-five hundred years later.

It's also worth noting that the Sumerian word usually translated "mountain," *kur*, has a dual meaning. It means "mountain," yes, but the Sumerians had another word that meant "mountain" and *only* "mountain." *Kur* meant "mountain," and it also meant "netherworld," a cognate for the Akkadian word *erṣetu*,[241] which is a match for the Hebrew *eretz*.

In other words, Enlil, the "Great Mountain," was appropriately titled, since "Great Mountain," in Sumerian, can also mean "Great

240. "Zechariah 1:1." *Faithlife Study Bible* (Bellingham, WA: Lexham Press, 2016).

241. Scott B. Noegel, "God of Heaven and Sheol: The 'Unearthing' of Creation." *Hebrew Studies*, Vol. 58 (2017), p. 121.

Below" or "Great Netherworld." In fact, by the time of the Exodus, Enlil was listed among the "former deities" in Hittite religious texts that summoned deities from the underworld. By the time of Saul and David in Israel, Mesopotamians believed Enlil was a permanent resident of the Great Below (note: "Illil," from *il-ilû*, is an alternate form of Enlil):

> Illil's fall into the underworld is recorded in first millennium texts which explain the mythical background of some cultic rites. A text from Nineveh, SAA III 37 (pp. 92–95), concerns some rituals in Marduk's temple Esagil in Babylon. It alludes to some divine beings who "set up a clamor against Illil and Anu, poured out their sheen on them, [...] broke their [win]gs and [cast them down] into the Abyss."[242]

Like his other identities, El and Kumarbi, and others we'll discuss in upcoming chapters, Enlil had a firm connection to the land of the dead by the time of Isaiah, Ezekiel, and Zechariah.

Peter and Jude tell us that he and his colleagues, the angels who sinned, will remain in the *kur*—the netherworld—until the time of the end. Their release is described in chapter 9 of the book of Revelation, and we'll discuss that later in this book.

---

242. William R. Gallagher, "On the Identity of Hêlēl Ben Šaḥar of Is. 14:12–15." *UF* 26 (1994), pp. 140–141.

Chapter Fourteen

DAGAN

Now we move to the part of Mesopotamia that lies between the areas that were home to the entities we've already discussed: Kumarbi, in the northern territory of the Hurrians; El, whose home was in the west; and Enlil, venerated mainly in southern Mesopotamia. In the middle of these territories we find their equivalent, Dagan.

Dagan was the chief god of the middle Euphrates region, the area along the great river in what is now Syria. The entity is still a mystery after two hundred years of archaeologists digging in the Syrian sand. You've no doubt noticed the similarity between the name of this god and Dagon, chief god of the Philistines. You're right—it's the same god, the one whose idol fell on its face before the Ark of the Covenant, losing its head and hands in the process, a rather important bit of symbolism. Scholars believe the way his name was pronounced changed over the centuries, which is why the last *a* became an *o* in English.

Contrary to popular belief, Dagan was not a fish-god. An Internet search for pictures of Dagan/Dagon usually turns up images of a man in a fish costume identified as Dagon or a priest of the god. This is an error that was first made popular around 1860 by Alexander Hislop's book *The Two Babylons*. While Hislop meant well, he didn't have access to more recent archaeology—and, to be honest, his scholarship left something to be desired.

Ironically, the guy in the strange fish cloak costume was one type of the supernatural being called *apkallu* in Mesopotamia. As noted earlier, the *apkallu* were the Watchers, the "sons of God" from chapter 6 of Genesis and the rebellious Watchers from the Book of 1 Enoch. (The other two types of *apkallu* were a winged, bearded man and a winged humanoid with the head of an eagle.) Since we're building a case that Dagan was just another name for Shemihazah, chief of the Watchers, then in a sense he actually *was* one of the fish-cloaked entities summoned for protection and good luck by Mesopotamians even though Dagan himself was worshiped as a grain-god and, more important, king of the Amorite pantheon in Syria.

The notion that Dagan was a god of fish may have started with a bit of folk etymology. *Dāg* is the Hebrew word for "fish,"[243] and since the Philistines lived on the coastal plain between Israel and Egypt, the worship of a fish-god seems logical. But Dagan first appeared in the middle Euphrates more than a thousand years before Samson started cutting down Philistines with the jawbone of a donkey. Since the Amorite kingdoms along the Euphrates were never based on fishing, the notion of a fish-god at the top of their pantheon just doesn't fit. Dagan as a grain-god is more consistent with the evidence. In fact, the Semitic root for "grain" is *dgn*, which leads to a chicken-and-egg question: Was grain named for Dagan, or the other way around?

In either case, Dagan was equated with the Hurrian god Kumarbi, who in turn was identified with El, Enlil, and with the Greek god Kro-

---

243. John F. Healey, "Dagon." In K. van der Toorn, B. Becking, & P. W. van der Horst (Eds.), *Dictionary of Deities and Demons in the Bible* (2nd extensively rev. ed.). (Leiden; Boston; Köln; Grand Rapids, MI; Cambridge: Brill; Eerdmans, 1999), p. 216.

nos, king of the Titans.[244] According to Greek myth, Kronos used a sickle to castrate his father, Ouranos, which, since sickles were used during the harvest, is more evidence that Dagan was likewise a grain-god.

One thing we do know: Dagan was very important in the ancient Near East, even if we don't know much about his character. His cult may have been spread across the region in the twenty-fourth century BC by the great conquerer Sargon of Akkad, who led his troops from near modern Baghdad all the way to the Mediterranean. On the way, Sargon stopped to pay homage at the temple of Dagan in Tuttul, a city on the Euphrates about ninety miles northwest of Baghdad. Sargon's grandson, Narām-Sîn, likewise credited Dagan with his military triumphs. And, since we've identified Dagan with Kumarbi, this might explain why Narām-Sîn chose to make an alliance with Urkesh, home of the *abi*, instead of conquering it outright.

This would be an interesting coincidence if I was a coincidence theorist. But since I'm not, I'll point out that, in the previous chapter, we saw that the conquests of Sargon coincided with the elevation of Enlil, another identity of Dagan, Kumarbi and El, to supreme status among the gods of southern Mesopotamia. It appears that the ruling dynasty of Akkad credited "the" god with their military success.

We know that Dagan/Dagon was still worshiped by the Philistines more than a thousand years after Sargon, although how the god moved from the middle Euphrates to the Gaza Strip is still a mystery. In an earlier chapter, we described the recent discovery of a Neo-Hittite kingdom near ancient Antioch called Palistin. This nation seems to have flourished briefly at about the same time as the new Israelite kingdom ruled by Saul and David.[245] It appears that the branch of the Sea Peoples we

---

244. This equivalence was noted by the Phoenician historian Philo of Byblos in the second century AD.

245. Jeffrey P. Emanuel, "King Taita and His 'Palistin': Philistine State or Neo-Hittite Kingdom?" *Antiguo Oriente*, volume 13 (2015), pp. 11–40.

call the Philistines, or a subset thereof, migrated from somewhere in the Aegean and set up a kingdom in what is now the border between Syria and Turkey. It lasted a short while at the beginning of the Iron Age, leaving behind only a place name for its successor state, Patin or Patina.[246]

The best-known king of Palistin was Taita, who left impressive statues of himself and Tarhunz (the Hittite name for the storm-god Hadad, better known to us as Baal in the Bible) at the temple of the Storm-God in Aleppo. The inscription on the statue of the king describes him as "King Taita, the Hero, the King of Palistin." Given the cultural and religious cross-pollination between the Amorite lands of Lebanon and Syria to the south and southeast and the Hurrian and Hittite lands to the north, east, and northwest, it's possible that this short-lived kingdom, located at the gateway from Mesopotamia to Anatolia, is where the Philistines first encountered Dagan/Dagon.

Palistin probably emerged from the chaos of the Bronze Age collapse around 1200 BC. That's the term scholars use to describe a period of chaos in which the aforementioned Sea Peoples swarmed out of the Aegean, overran the Hittites, and destroyed most of the kingdoms in the eastern Mediterranean. One of those was Ugarit, which reached its peak around the time of the Exodus. Ugarit, just twenty miles south of Mount Zaphon, may have been part of the territory absorbed by the new state of Palistin. Oddly, though, while Dagan was named among the chief deities of Ugarit, he doesn't appear at all in their myths. Dagan is mentioned only as the father of the king of the gods, Baal.

The puzzle is that Baal is also the son of Dagan's counterpart in the Canaanite pantheon, the creator-god El. A number of theories have been floated to explain Baal's dual parentage: El and Dagan were brothers, or El and Dagan played the roles of Ouranos and Kronos in an earlier version of the Greek myths, with Baal, a storm-god like Zeus, emerging as king of the pantheon.

---

246. Ibid.

Or maybe there's a simpler answer: Dagan and El were one and the same.

> This view is supported by the fact that KTU 1.118 and 1.47 have both El and Dagan sharing the same epithet, "father god" (*'ilib*). Additionally, inscriptions at what most scholars consider the temple of Dagan at Ugarit make an identification very likely, the Mesopotamian pantheon identified both Dagan and El with the supreme god (Anu/Enlil), and at Ebla Dagan is the high god, also called "lord of Canaan." [...] [I]n the words of del Olmo Lete, "there can be no doubt that the equation of Ilu and Daganu expresses the process of cultural and cultic identification of two (Canaanite/Amorite) pantheons." This fusion explains the dual reference to Baal's parentage alongside the clear descriptions of his kinship with the other sons of El.[247]

So, we've connected Dagan, chief god of the Amorites who lived along the Euphrates, to Enlil, El, and Kumarbi. Our working theory is that this entity is one and the same with the chief of the rebel Watchers on Mount Hermon, Shemihazah. Under different names, this ambitious *elohim* occupied the top slot in the pantheons of people from the Persian Gulf to the Taurus Mountains, and from the Zagros Mountains of western Iran to the Mediterranean. And all of that territory factored into the early history of the Hebrews.

A key connection between Dagan and his other identities is the god's link to the netherworld. One of Dagan's epithets was *bēl pagrê*, which has been translated "lord of the dead,"[248] "lord of corpse offerings, lord of

---

247. Michael S. Heiser, *The Divine Council in Late Canonical and Non-canonical Second Temple Jewish Literature* (Doctoral dissertation: Univ. of Wisconsin-Madison, 2004), pp. 47–48.

248. Hays (2011), op. cit., p. 96.

corpses (a netherworld god), lord of funerary offerings, and lord of human sacrifices."[249] Shamshi-Adad, the powerful Amorite king of northern Mesopotamia in the days of Hammurabi, once journeyed to Terqa, another important center of the Dagan cult located on the Euphrates River about fifty miles north of the modern border between Syria and Iraq. Shamshi-Adad arrived at Terqa on the day of the *kispum* and dedicated a *bīt kispim* ("house of the *kispum*") to Dagan.[250]

But scholars can't seem to agree on Dagan's relationship to the netherworld or how he was honored. The Semitic root *pgr* behind the Akkadian *pagrê* is a cognate (same word, different language) for the Hebrew *peger*, which means "corpse" or "carcass." Did the Amorites of Abraham's day literally sacrifice humans to Dagan? It seems unlikely that something so outrageous would have slipped past the prophets without a mention. Still, there was a connection between Dagan and the dead,[251] and that's the point. The living were required to make offerings to the dead, and Dagan played a role in the process.

Later, among the Philistines, Dagon (same god, but pronunciation had shifted over the course of centuries) seems to have been important to fertility—both of crops and humans. The story begins with the Philistines capturing the Ark of the Covenant and bringing it home as a trophy for their god, installing it at the temple of Dagon in Ashdod:

> And when the people of Ashdod rose early the next day, behold, Dagon had fallen face downward on the ground before the ark of the LORD. So they took Dagon and put him back in his place. But when they rose early on the next morning, behold, Dagon had fallen face downward on the ground before the ark of the LORD, and the head of Dagon and both his hands were lying cut off on the threshold. Only the trunk of Dagon was left to him.

---

249. Schmidt, op. cit.
250. MacDougal, op. cit., p. 31.
251. Spronk, op. cit., p. 151.

This is why the priests of Dagon and all who enter the house of Dagon do not tread on the threshold of Dagon in Ashdod to this day.

The hand of the LORD was heavy against the people of Ashdod, and he terrified and afflicted them with tumors, both Ashdod and its territory. And when the men of Ashdod saw how things were, they said, "The ark of the God of Israel must not remain with us, for his hand is hard against us and against Dagon our god." So they sent and gathered together all the lords of the Philistines and said, "What shall we do with the ark of the God of Israel?" They answered, "Let the ark of the God of Israel be brought around to Gath." So they brought the ark of the God of Israel there. But after they had brought it around, the hand of the LORD was against the city, causing a very great panic, and he afflicted the men of the city, both young and old, so that tumors broke out on them. So they sent the ark of God to Ekron. But as soon as the ark of God came to Ekron, the people of Ekron cried out, "They have brought around to us the ark of the God of Israel to kill us and our people." They sent therefore and gathered together all the lords of the Philistines and said, "Send away the ark of the God of Israel, and let it return to its own place, that it may not kill us and our people." (1 Samuel 5:3–11)

The priests and diviners of the Philistines advised their leaders to send the ark back to the Israelites, but with a guilt offering to appease Yahweh:

They answered, "Five golden tumors and five golden mice, according to the number of the lords of the Philistines, for the same plague was on all of you and on your lords. So you must make images of your tumors and images of your mice that ravage the land, and give glory to the God of Israel. Perhaps he will lighten his hand from off you and your gods and your land." (1 Samuel 6:4–5)

There are a couple of takeaways from this story—one obvious, one not so much. First, the collapse of the statue of Dagon two days in a row shows that it was not a coincidence. Its position, face down on the ground in front of the ark, was a clear sign that Yahweh was the superior God. And the idol's decapitation and loss of its hands was an image that meant more back then than it does today; removing heads and hands of a defeated enemy was a common practice to simplify the body count after a battle.[252]

But the affliction of the Philistines and the guilt offering recommended by their diviners needs a little explaining. Some Bible commentators explain the Hebrew word 'opalim ("tumors") as a disease like bubonic plague. You may have heard "tumors" in 1 Samuel 5:6 rendered "emerods," the word chosen by the King James Bible translators, or its modern form, "hemorrhoids," as in the NAB. That's a bit closer, but not quite specific enough. New archaeological finds at the sites of the Philistine cities has shed some light on this. It appears God hit the Philistines where it hurt—literally.

At Ashkelon, one of the most important cities of the ancient Levant, a cache of seven vial-shaped vessels called *situlae* was found in the mid 1990s. The small bronze artifacts bore representations of Egyptian-style gods. Based on their similarity to Egyptian imagery and cult practices, archaeologist Lawrence Stager "suggested that these vessels had a phallic connotation and were most probably associated with a cult of symbolic revivification."[253]

Before we share a laugh at the expense of the Philistines, let's explain the logic here. The word 'opalim likely derives from the same root ('pl)

---

252. Piotr Bienkowski, "Warfare." In P. Bienkowski & A. Millard (Eds.), *Dictionary of the Ancient Near East* (Philadelphia: University of Pennsylvania Press, 2000), p. 317.

253. Aren M. Maeir, "A New Interpretation of the Term 'opalim (עֲפָלִים) in the Light of Recent Archaeological Finds from Philistia." *Journal for the Study of the Old Testament*, Vol 32.1 (2007), pp. 25–26.

that gives us the word Ophel, the name of a hill in southeast Jerusalem. The implied meaning—something high or raised up—could well be construed as a euphemism.[254] In addition, phallic-shaped vessels of this type are evidence of yet one more point of difference between the Philistines and the neighboring Israelites:

> Quite obviously, the male reproductive organ is of importance in all human cultures. While such depictions are relatively common in Egyptian religious iconography, they are very rare in ancient Semitic religious and symbolic iconography. On the other hand, phallic symbolism is well known in early Greek cultures and occurs in various forms.
>
> Taking into account that there are very few phallic representations in the ancient Near East, while, in contrast, they are common in Aegean/early Greek cultures, this would seem to have special significance regarding our understanding of Philistine culture. As is well known, it is highly likely that the Philistine culture (or at least, significant portions of it) originated in the Aegean cultural milieu.[255]

This connects the Philistines and their veneration of Dagon to our earlier discussion of the Anakim, the Hivites, and the other identities of this god, Enlil, El, and Kumarbi.

Like his other identities, Dagon/Dagan was believed to be the father of the gods.[256] Because many of the gods of the pagans were actually demons,[257] that links him to Shemihazah, chief of the "sons of God" who defiled themselves with human women and fathered the monstrous Nephilim and their demonic spirits. Those spirits, called 'ōberim ("Travelers"), were summoned

---

254. Ibid., p. 30.

255. Ibid., p. 29.

256. Feliu (2003), op. cit., p. 273.

257. 1 Corinthians 10:20–21; Revelation 9:20.

through a *kispum*-like necromancy ritual to the threshing-floor of El on the summit of Mount Hermon to be "revivified." This recalls the summoning of the Hurrians' netherworld gods at the *abi* in Urkesh, the home of Kumarbi. That ancient ritual pit was connected to the *'ōb* of the Old Testament and the *'oboth* ("spirits of the dead") who were summoned at those pits. If the Philistine idols were objects used by a cult of revivification, we have another point of contact between Dagon/Dagan and the matrix of ideas around the cult of the dead inspired by the spirits of the Watchers' demonic offspring.

We mentioned in an earlier chapter that the Anakim were an elite class of warriors who ruled the hill country of Israel and Judah at the time of the Israelite conquest of Canaan. The summary of the war for Canaan in Joshua 11:21–22 makes it clear that defeating the Anakim was Joshua's priority. The Anakim were of Greek origin, possibly ethnic Hivites or Philistines. It's not a coincidence that, while the Anakim had been driven out of the hill country, "in Gaza, in Gath, and in Ashdod did some remain."[258] Those cities, along with Ashkelon and Ekron, were the five urban centers of the Philistines who fought against Israel from the period of the Judges through the time of Saul and David.

The Old Testament describes the battles fought by David and his men against four giants from Gath, Goliath's hometown, all of whom are called "descendants of the giants." This translation is misleading. The Hebrew phrase translated "descendants (or sons) of the giant(s)" is *yelîdê ha-rāpâ*—literally "sons of the *rapha*," singular, indicated by the definite article *ha* ("the") and *rapha*, the singular form of Rephaim.

The important thing to note is that the standard definition of *yelîdê*, "descendants," is too narrow and literal. The Hebrew word *yelîdê* never referred to direct genetic lineage, a blood descendant, but instead designated "one who is born into the group by adoption, initiation or consecration," and that "the second element in the phrase might then be the name of the group, or its emblem, or the name of the group's patron,

---

258. Joshua 11:22.

whether human or divine."[259] In other words, the *yelîdê ha-rāpâ*—Sons of the Rephaim—were not oversized half-divine demigods but a warrior cult who worshiped the spirits of the Nephilim—and were very likely possessed by the demon spirits they worshiped.

As evidence, we submit the name of one of the giants slain by David and his men:

> There was war again between the Philistines and Israel, and David went down together with his servants, and they fought against the Philistines. And David grew weary. And Ishbi-benob, one of the descendants of the giants, whose spear weighed three hundred shekels of bronze, and who was armed with a new sword, thought to kill David. But Abishai the son of Zeruiah came to his aid and attacked the Philistine and killed him. Then David's men swore to him, "You shall no longer go out with us to battle, lest you quench the lamp of Israel." (2 Samuel 21:15–17).

Ishbi-benob had a strange name. The etymology offered by Bible commentators usually something like "his dwelling is in Nob," which was a village of the tribe of Benjamin near Jerusalem. But Ishbi-benob was from Gath, in Philistine territory near the Mediterranean coast. That's nowhere near Jerusalem.

Author Brian Godawa suggested in his novel *David Ascendant* that we've been misspelling Ishbi's name. Brian's fiction is highly researched and theologically accurate. He suggests that the name of this Philistine giant should be "Ishbi ben Ob," or "Ishbi, son of the *'ob*"—son of the owner of a ritual pit, like the woman visited by Saul the night before he died in battle against the Philistines. (For his novel, Brian used some artistic license and made Ishbi the son of that

---

259. Conrad E. L'Heureux, "The *yelîdê hārāpā'*: A Cultic Association of Warriors." *Bulletin of the American Schools of Oriental Research*, No. 221 (Feb. 1976), p. 84.

woman. There's no evidence in the Bible for that relationship, but it's a fascinating idea.)[260]

The point of this rabbit trail is this: The "descendants of the giants" faced by David and his men were a Dagon-worshiping, demonic warrior cult.[261] The demons who led (or possessed) the group into which they were admitted "by adoption, initiation, or consecration" were created by Dagan/Shemihazah and his cronies. The Bible's repeated references to the Rephaim, Hermon, and Bashan point to this entity and the pivotal role he's played in this long rebellion by the fallen *elohim*.

---

260. *David Ascendant* is book 7 of *The Nephilim Chronicles*, which we recommend. For information, visit www.godawa.com.

261. The closest equivalent in relatively modern history are the berserkers of the Viking era. They were believed to be impervious to pain, fatigue, fire, and edged weapons like swords and arrows, and they were so dangerous on the battlefield, even to their own side, that the Vikings were eventually compelled to outlaw berserker war bands.

Chapter Fifteen

THE MOUNT HERMON INSCRIPTION

The work of archaeologists continues to confirm the account in the Bible. A new, just-published translation of an inscription discovered about a hundred and fifty years ago inside a temple on the summit of Mount Hermon adds more support for the theory that this entity, under a variety of names, has had a profound influence on human history and will play a devastating role before the final battle of the ages, Armageddon.

In September of 1869, a British military engineer and explorer named Charles Warren climbed to the summit of Mount Hermon on behalf of the Palestine Exploration Fund (PEF). The PEF was founded in 1865 under the patronage of Queen Victoria. The society included some of the giants in the field of archaeology, such as Sir William Flinders Petrie, Claude Conder, T. E. Lawrence ("of Arabia"), Kathleen Kenyon, and Sir Leonard Woolley,[262] who excavated Ur in the 1920s. It's no coincidence that many of those sent into the field had military training; by the second half of the nineteenth century, the Ottoman

---

262. "The History of the PEF." https://www.pef.org.uk/history/, retrieved 10/14/18.

Sir Charles Warren

Empire was crumbling and the great powers of Europe had their knives out, ready to carve up its carcass. We've learned a lot about the ancient world from the work of men like Warren, Petrie, and Lawrence, but the British government collected useful intelligence at the same time.

On top of Hermon, more than nine thousand feet above sea level, Warren visited an ancient temple called Qasr Antar, the highest man-made place of worship on the planet. It was probably built during the Greek or Roman period, placing its construction in the third century BC at the earliest. Inside the temple, Warren found an artifact that had been overlooked by visitors for two thousand years—a stela, a limestone slab about four feet high, eighteen inches wide, and twelve inches thick, with an inscription in archaic Greek:

> A later attestation of the sacred character of Mount Hermon appears in an enigmatic Greek inscription, perhaps from the third century C.E., which was found on its peak: Κατὰ κέλευσιν θεοῦ μεγίστου κ[αὶ] ἁγίου οἱ ὀμνύοντες ἐντεῦθεν ("According to the command of the greatest a[nd] holy God, those who take an oath [proceed] from here").[263]

Because the inscription is Greek rather than in a Semitic language like Aramaic, Hebrew, Canaanite, or Akkadian, the stela can't be dated earlier than Alexander the Great's invasion of the Levant in the late fourth century BC. Scholar George W. E. Nickelsburg, who's produced

---

263. George W. E. Nickelsburg, *1 Enoch 1: A Commentary on the Book of 1 Enoch, Chapters 1–36* (Minneapolis: Fortress, 2001), p. 247.

a modern translation of the Book of 1 Enoch and a detailed commentary on the book, connects the inscription to the Watchers of Genesis 6, whose mutual pact on the summit is described in 1 Enoch:

> Shemihazah, their chief, said to them, "I fear that you will not want to do this deed, and I alone shall be guilty of a great sin." And they all answered him and said, "Let us all swear an oath, and let us all bind one another with a curse, that none of us turn back from this counsel until we fulfill it and do this deed." Then they all swore together and bound one another with a curse. And they were, all of them, two hundred, who descended in the days of Jared onto the peak of Mount Hermon.[264]

The stela is currently in the possession of the British Museum, which it received from Warren in 1870, after some difficulty in wrestling the two-ton slab of limestone down the mountain. The stone broke into two pieces when Warren cut it down from twelve inches thick to four to reduce its original six-ton weight. For some reason, the stone wasn't unboxed until 1884, and then, because of questions over its origin, it wasn't translated until 1903. Renowned French orientalist Charles Simon Clermont-Ganneau, who worked with Warren to obtain the Moabite Stone, interpreted the Greek inscription this way:

> By the order of the god most great and holy, those who take the oath—hence![265]

---

264. George W. E. Nickelsburg, *1 Enoch: The Hermeneia Translation* (Kindle edition) (Minneapolis: Fortress Press, 2012), pp. 23–24.
265. Charles Simon Clermont-Ganneau, "Archaeological and Epigraphic Notes on Palestine." *Palestine Exploration Fund Quarterly Statement for 1903* (London: Palestine Exploration Fund, 1903), p. 138.

Stela discovered by Sir Charles Warren inside the temple on the summit of Mount Hermon

Like Nickelsburg, Clermont-Ganneau linked the stone to the Watchers' rebellion on Mount Hermon. In fact, he devoted some pages to Enoch's account of the Watchers in the same edition of the *Palestine Exploration Fund's Quarterly Report for 1903*, and came to some eye-opening conclusions:

> We are far from the remote times when the god in his high place received the homage of the primitive population in that part of Syria. But neither the place nor the god have changed, and no less the ceremonies that constituted his cult. It is to be supposed that it is to some one or the other of these rites that our inscription refers. It has the character of an imperative liturgical order. It is a command issued in the name of the god himself, and it seems to me that ἐντεῦθεν should be taken in its natural sense of starting from a place—"from here, hence"—a verb being understood. [...]
>
> Now, whether justified or not, this popular tradition existed in ancient times: **Mount Hermon was the "mountain of oath."**[266] (Emphasis added)

---

266. Ibid., pp. 231, 233.

In an earlier chapter, we discussed the Hurrians of Shechem who worshiped Baal-berith, "lord of the covenant." Our conclusion that the people of Shechem were Hurrian is based on the Septuagint translation, which used older Hebrew texts no longer available to us. Modern English translations, based on the Masoretic Hebrew text, identify the king of Shechem in Jacob's day as Hamor the Hivite. Joshua 11:3 puts the Hivites "under Hermon, in the land of Mizpah," and Judges 3:3 places the Hivites around "Mount Lebanon, from Mount Baal-Hermon as far as Lebo-Hamath," a site on the Orontes River valley about 120 miles north of Damascus.

The Hivites were the Ahhiyawa, Mycenaean Greeks, people with a long history of contact with the Hurrians, the Horites of the Bible. As we've seen, the Hivites and Hurrians were all over Canaan at least from the time of Abraham through the time of David. It's possible that Baal-berith, the "lord of the covenant" worshiped at the Hurrian city of Shechem, was not the Indo-Aryan deity Mitra, but the "lord of Hermon," Baal-Hermon—that is, El/Dagan, etc.

Clermont-Ganneau noted another unique feature of Mount Hermon: The summit has been scooped out like a giant bowl, probably to receive a drink offering, which scholars call "the rite of hydrophory."[267] This ritual was called *yarid* in Hebrew, based on a root that means "to come down," which it shares with the names "Jared" and "Jordan" (since the river "comes down" into the Galilee from Mount Hermon). This ritual was practiced at Heliopolis (Baalbek); Hierapolis, site of a famous temple to the goddess Atargatis (another name for Astarte, or Ishtar/Inanna); Tyre; and possibly even Jerusalem. The ritual "consisted chiefly in drawing water, which was borne in procession and thrown into a sacred tank."[268]

---

267. Lipiński, op. cit., p. 29.
268. Clermont-Ganneau, op. cit., p. 241.

I should not be surprised if the sanctuary of Hermon was formerly the scene of such a ceremony of this nature. Perhaps it was into the deep and remarkable cavity noticed by the explorers in the central cone that the consecrated water was thrown. Under these circumstances, if the sanctuary of Hermon really had its *yerid*, or *katabasis*, it would not be too rash, perhaps, to suppose that it was from this that the author of the *Book of Enoch* may have drawn his idea of the "descent of the angels in the days of Jared."[269]

In other words, the Watchers did not descend to Mount Hermon "in the days of Jared," but rather in the days when the *yarid* was performed on the summit of Hermon.

Why would this ritual have been performed on the mountain? Remember, it was the threshing-floor or tabernacle of El, whose abode was "the source of the rivers, at the midst of the springs of the two deeps." This is reminiscent of the ^{d}KASKAL.KUR, the "divine watercourse" of the Hurrians, the water that flowed to the netherworld to allow contact with Kumarbi and the gods of the great below.

And this is where things get really interesting. Thanks to new research by our friend, Dr. Douglas Hamp, we can connect the dots between Mount Hermon and the rebellion of the Watchers led by Shemihazah, El, Dagan, and Enlil.

Doug noticed that accepted translations of the "Watchers Stone" appear to gloss over a couple of words. For example, the text on the base of the stone, when it was displayed at the British Museum, reads:

GREEK INSCRIPTION
[4th–5th Cent. A.D.]
Warning: "Hence by order of the god those who do not take the oath"; probably an oath before celebrating the mysteries of the

---

269. Ibid.

temple on the summit of Mount Hermon, where this pillar was found. The god of Mount Hermon was Baal-Hermon—*Judges III, 3*

Presented by the Palestine Exploration Fund, 1903

So, we've seen three translations of the inscription:

- Nickelsburg: "According to the command of the greatest a[nd] holy God, those who take an oath [proceed] from here."
- Clermont-Ganneau: "By the order of the god most great and holy, those who take the oath—hence!"
- British Museum: "Hence by order of the god those who do not take the oath."

That's not exactly a consensus, but the bigger issue, Hamp contends, is that the Greek transcription on which those translations are based is flawed.

Words five and six βο *bo* and βατιου *batiou* are mysterious which could be why they were completely ignored by the British Museum, and amended by Nickelsburg; βο *bo* "a(nd)" and βατιου *batiou* as άγιου [*b*]*hagiou.*[270]

So, to compare, here is Nickelsburg's translation (my emphasis): *Katá kélefsin theoú megístou k[aí] agíou oi omnýontes entefthen.*

Hamp reads it this way: *Kata keleusin theou megistou* **bo batiou** *ou omnuontes enteuthen.*

Rejecting the reading by Clermont-Ganneau and Nickelsburg, Hamp proposes to read *bo* as a Greek prefix meaning "bull, ox, male

270. Douglas M. Hamp, *Corrupting the Image 2: Hybrids, Hades, and the Mount Hermon Connection* (Lakewood, CO: Eskaton Media Group, 2021), p. 174.

cattle."[271] He suggests that this fits with the bull imagery associated with Baal (Hadad), the West Semitic storm-god, whose equivalent in the Greek pantheon is Zeus.[272]

I agree with Doug to a point. The "bull" prefix fits perfectly the context of Mount Hermon as a pagan holy site. However, the connection is not with Baal/Zeus, but with the entity that we're investigating, El. His chief epithet, "Bull El," was so well known to the Hebrew prophets that we should read it in at least one, and possibly two, passages in the Bible—Hosea 8:6, certainly ("For who is Bull El?"), with Deuteronomy 32:8 ("the number of the sons of Bull El") a reasonable possibility.

So, what do we make of *batiou*? According to Hamp, the word is missing from lexicons, dictionaries, encyclopedias, scholarly sites, and journals. He concludes, "*batiou* simply is not Greek."[273]

He does, however, propose an elegant solution. It's too long to reproduce here, which would not do Doug justice. I refer you to his book *Corrupting the Image 2: Hybrids, Hades, and the Mount Hermon Connection* for details. In my opinion, Doug's detective work on the Mount Hermon inscription has drawn the first new information out of this artifact in more than a hundred years.

The summary is this: The Sumerian logogram BAD (or BAT), depicted as two inward-pointing horizontal wedges, designated both Dagan and Enlil. The *-iou* suffix, Hamp argues, makes the transliterated logogram "standard Greek."[274] Thus, Hamp's new translation reads: "According to the command of **the great bull-god** *Batios* [Dagan/Enlil], those swearing an oath in this place go forth."[275]

---

271. "Β β beeta (βῆτα) basis," *Greek Alphabet: Unlock the Secrets.* http://www. greekalphabeta.com/learn-about-beta-b-2.html, retrieved 3/18/21.

272. Hamp, op. cit., p. 175.

273. Ibid., p. 176.

274. Ibid., p. 180.

275. Ibid., pp. 181–182.

I agree, but with a small emendation: "According to the command of the great Bull El, those swearing an oath in this place go forth."

Since we've established that the names Dagan, Enlil, and El all refer to the same entity, my suggested change really does not constitute a disagreement with Doug's research.

It must be noted that not everyone will agree with his interpretation. Julien Aliquot, Research Fellow at Université Lyon in France, rejects the reading on which Doug bases his translation:

> On the stone, the eight lines of rough letters (4.5–10 cm) have been painted in red according to F. H. Marshall's erroneous facsimile, which distorts the reading of the inscription, if one confines to the current photograph [PLATE X-XI]. I reproduce here the transcription of Ch. Clermont-Ganneau, who was the first and last editor to publish the text correctly:
>
> Κατὰ κέ/λευσιν / θεοῦ με/γίστου κὲ / ἁγίου ὺ ὀμνύον/τες ἐντεῦ/θεν.
>
> L.4-5: κ(αὶ) / ἁγίου or κ[αὶ] / ἁγίου (Clermont-Ganneau) ; B[ο/β]ατίου (Marshall).
>
> L.6: Y for οἱ (Clermont-Ganneau); [ο]ὺ (Marshall).[276]

Hamp's translation generally agrees with those of Nickelsburg and Clermont-Ganneau. The important new connection Doug makes that's previously escaped scholars is identifying the Sumerian logogram BAD/BAT, which connects Dagan and Enlil to Mount Hermon, and thus to the Canaanite creator-god El and the Watcher chief Shemihazah. Recognizing the *bo-* prefix ("bull") strengthens the identification of Dagan/Enlil as "Bull El." (It's also more evidence confirming this god's identity

---

276. Julien Aliquot, "Sanctuaries and Villages on Mt. Hermon during the Roman Period." In T. Kaizer (Ed.), *The Variety of Local Religious Life in the Near East in the Hellenistic and Roman Periods* (Leiden; Boston: Brill, 2008), p. 82.

as Kronos, king of the Titans, but we'll deal with that in an upcoming chapter.) All in all, this is profound.

Amar Annus, whose work is referenced throughout this book, was consulted by Hamp on this new translation of the stela. Annus, in his book on the Akkadian god Ninurta, confirms the link between Dagan, Enlil, and mountains:

> The name of Dagan is written logographically ^{d}KUR in Emar [an ancient city near the bend in the Euphrates in northern Syria] as an alternative to the syllabic ^{d}Da-gan. ^{d}KUR is a shortened form of Enlil's epithet KUR.GAL "great mountain," which was borrowed by Dagan, and he is already described as the great mountain in a Mari letter. That in Emar there existed a cult for Dagan as ^{d}KUR.GAL points to the awareness of Sumerian traditions concerning Enlil, it "shows that some connection with the ancient title was preserved behind the common writing of the divine name as ^{d}KUR," and leaves no doubt that Enlil is the model behind Dagan in Emar.[277]

Given that the evidence shows that Enlil was imported to Sumer from the north or northwest, and that Mount Hermon was recognized as a sacred mountain in Babylonia as early as the time of the patriarch Jacob,[278] it's possible that the "Great Mountain" epithet, applied to Enlil and Dagan, may be attributed to the god's connection to Mount Hermon. And the double meaning of the Sumerian word *kur* ("mountain"/"netherworld") is likewise appropriate in the context of Hermon and its "double deeps."

---

277. Amar Annus, *The God Ninurta in the Mythology and Royal Ideology of Ancient Mesopotamia* (Helsinki: Neo-Assyrian Text Corpus Project, 2002), p. 178.

278. Lipiński, op. cit., p. 18.

This is reinforced by a text dated to the time of Israel's sojourn in Egypt, probably the seventeenth century BC, that mentions a king of Terqa offering "the sacrifice of Dagan ša ḪAR-*ri*."[279] Scholar Lluis Feliu compares this with a later text from Emar that mentions a "ᵈKUR EN *ha-ar-ri* that we may translate as 'Dagan, lord of the hole/pit'."[280] Then Feliu untangles the meaning of *ha-ar-ri* and reaches an interesting conclusion:

> A different question is the interpretation…of the term *ha-ar-ri*. The vocalisation in *a* suggests identifying this word with Akkadian *harrum* "water channel, irrigation ditch." However, the semantic and morphological similarity with *hurrum* "hole" makes it possible to understand the epithet, tentatively, as "The Dagan of the pit." This interpretation could find confirmation in the following line in the text Emar 6/3 384, where, after [ᵈKU]R EN *ha-[ar-ri]*, there occurs ᵈINANNA *a-bi*. [Note: Inanna is the Sumerian name and logogram for the goddess of sex and war, also known as Ishtar and Astarte during the biblical period.]
>
> As yet, the term *a-bi* has not been given a satisfactory translation and its meaning is much discussed. **One of the interpretations that has been proposed is "pit," based on Hurrian *a-bi*.**[281] (Emphasis added)

You probably recognize the link to the *abi*, the ritual pit of Kumarbi at ancient Urkesh and the pagan worship of the underworld spirits and gods it inspired. The ancient Amorite texts cited by Feliu connect Dagan to these necromantic practices and strengthen our theory that Dagan, Kumarbi, Enlil, El, and Assur are one and the same.

---

279. Feliu (2003), op. cit., p. 105.
280. Ibid., p. 106.
281. Ibid.

We've covered a lot of ground in this section, but another important piece of evidence links this entity in his guise as Dagan to the Bible. It also comes from Emar, the city that's provided us with solid evidence to identify Dagan as Enlil, and it's reflected in the most important annual feast given by God to the Hebrews.

The pagan religious calendar in the ancient Near East featured a festival called the *akitu* that dates back at least to the middle of the third millennium BC.[282] It was thought to be a new year festival held in the spring to honor the chief god of Babylon, Marduk, but more recent discoveries have shown that there were two *akitu* festivals, one in the spring, the harvesting season, and the other in the fall, the planting season, and some of them were performed to honor other gods. For example, the oldest known *akitu* is documented at ancient Ur in Sumer, which was the home city of the moon-god, Sîn.[283]

The *akitu* festivals began on the 1st of Nisan and 1st of Tishrei, close to the spring and fall equinoxes. Although the length of the festivals changed over the years, it appears they generally lasted eleven[284] or twelve days.[285] So, the Jewish festivals began a few days after their pagan neighbors finished their harvesting and planting rituals.

Sukkot is a seven-day festival. It's particularly interesting because of the sheer number of sacrificial animals required, especially because they were bulls. Numbers 29:12–34 spells out the requirements for the Feast of Booths.

282. Mark E. Cohen, *The Cultic Calendars of the Ancient Near East* (Bethesda, MD: CDL Press, 1993), p. 401.

283. Ibid.

284. Ibid., p. 403.

285. Jeremy Black & Anthony Green, *Gods, Demons and Symbols of Ancient Mesopotamia: An Illustrated Dictionary* (London: The British Museum Press, 1992), p. 136.

DAY 1	DAY 2	DAY 3	DAY 4	DAY 5	DAY 6	DAY 7
13 bulls	12 bulls	11 bulls	10 bulls	9 bulls	8 bulls	7 bulls
2 rams	2 rams	2 rams	2 rams	2 rams	2 rams	2 rams
14 lambs	14 lambs	14 lambs	14 lambs	14 lambs	14 lambs	14 lambs
1 goat	1 goat	1 goat	1 goat	1 goat	1 goat	1 goat

The Feast of Unleavened Bread, which was likewise a seven-day festival, required only one ram and seven lambs each day. But the biggest difference between the two feasts is that only two bulls were sacrificed each day during the Feast of Unleavened Bread.[286] In fact, none of the other festivals ordained by God for Israel required the sacrifice of more than two bulls per day.

This suggests that Sukkot was unique in the annual calendar. In fact, in several places in the Old Testament it's simply called "the festival" or "the feast."[287] But why so many bulls at this particular feast? And why the decreasing number of bulls slaughtered each day?

We may never know specifically, but it's fascinating (and not coincidental, in my view) that Sukkot bears an interesting resemblance to a festival called the *zukru* attested during the time of the judges at Emar:

On the month of SAG.MU (meaning: the head of the year), on the fourteenth day, they offer seventy pure lambs provided by the king...for all the seventy gods [of the city of] Emar.[288]

---

286. Numbers 28:16–25.
287. 1 Kings 8:65, Ezekiel 45:25.
288. Ayali-Darshan, op. cit., p. 6.

Seventy lambs for the seventy gods of Emar, headed up by Dagan, sacrificed over seven days during a festival that began in the first month "when the moon is full," just like at Sukkot.

Pop quiz: How many bulls were sacrificed at Sukkot?

$$13 + 12 + 11 + 10 + 9 + 8 + 7 = \mathbf{70}.$$

Dagan's underworld connection as the *bēl pagrê*, "lord of the corpse" or "lord of the dead," links this identity to El—Baal-Hermon, lord of the mountain that towers over Bashan, land of the entrance to the netherworld. Dagan was believed to be the father of "seventy gods"—i.e., "the complete set," or "all of them," in the same way that El held court on Mount Hermon with his consort, Asherah, and their seventy sons.[289]

Was this a coincidence? Dr. Noga Ayali-Darshan of Israel's Bar Ilan University thinks not:

> In light of the Emarite custom, I would like to propose that the law in Numbers 29 prescribing the offering of seventy bulls during Sukkot—which has no parallel in any other Israelite festival—reflects the old Syrian custom of offering seventy sacrifices to the seventy gods (i.e., the whole pantheon) at the grand festival celebrated in the month of the New Year.[290]

I would go further: In light of the seventy "sons of God" allotted to the nations after the Tower of Babel incident, which not coincidentally matches the number of names in Genesis 10's Table of Nations, God's requirement of seventy sacrificial bulls during Sukkot was a deliberate message to the Israelites, a reminder that He'd delivered them from the gods of the nations.

It was also a clear message to rebellious *elohim*, both the Watchers who'd descended to Mount Hermon and the group placed over the nations after Babel: This is what's in store for you.

---

289. KTU 1.4 vi 46. Wyatt (2002), op. cit., p. 107.
290. Ibid., p. 9.

Chapter Sixteen

ASSUR

The Assyrian kingdom emerged as the dominant political and military power in the ancient Near East toward the end of the tenth century BC, shortly after the division of Israel into the northern kingdom, which retained the name of Israel, and the southern kingdom, Judah. For the next three centuries, Assyria extended its borders to include all of the Middle East, including Egypt and the eastern half of Anatolia. It was during this period that the great king Sennacherib boasted of his conquests in Babylonia, mocking the "kingdoms of Enlil."

We also noted that Enlil, the Great Mountain, was singled out for scorn by Yahweh, specifically in Zechariah 4:7 and in Ezekiel's mentions of his vision of the throne room of God over Enlil's home city, Nippur. Then there are the condemnations of "worthless idols" in Isaiah 2, Psalm 96, and Psalm 97 that may in fact be references to the minions of Enlil (Shemihazah), the ʾĕlîlim who made a pact to rebel with their chief at Mount Hermon.

The Assyrians tried to conquer the Levant for more than a century before the northern kingdom fell in 722 BC. The subsequent resettling of the bulk of the Israelite population outside of the kingdom of Judah left a profound scar on the Jewish psyche. Contrary to their almost exclusively negative depiction in the Old Testament, the Assyrians clearly thought quite highly of themselves and their patron god:

> "Assur is king, Assur is king!" and, further on in the text, "May your (the king's) foot in Ekur and your hands (stretched) toward Assur, your god, be at ease! May your priesthood (šangūtu) and the priesthood of your sons be at ease in the service of Assur, your god! With your straight sceptre enlarge your land! May Assur grant you a commanding voice, obedience, agreement, justice and peace!"... "Assur is king—indeed Assur is king! Assurbanipal is the [...] of Assur, the creation of his hands. May the great gods establish his reign, may they protect the life [of Assurba] nipal, king of Assyria! May they give him a just sceptre to extend the land and his peoples! May his reign be renewed and may they consolidate his royal throne for ever!"[291]

"Assur is king, Assur is king!" We've heard that title before, and it's not coincidence. By now, it's been established that Assur was Enlil by a different name, and Enlil's identity has been linked to El, Dagan, and Kumarbi, all of which were considered the creator, father of the gods, and/or king of the pantheon. No surprise, then, that this entity convinced his Assyrian worshipers to likewise call him "king."

And since God directed His wrath at this entity under the names "El" and "Enlil," even though it's been hidden from us non-Hebrew speakers, it should likewise come as no surprise that God had choice words for Assur as well—although they, too, have been hidden by modern translations and our unfamiliarity with the world of the Hebrew prophets.

---

291. A. Livingstone, "Assur." In K. van der Toorn, B. Becking, & P. W. van der Horst (Eds.), *Dictionary of Deities and Demons in the Bible* (2nd extensively rev. ed.) (Leiden; Boston; Köln; Grand Rapids, MI; Cambridge: Brill; Eerdmans, 1999), p. 108.

Of course, it doesn't help that *'aššūr* in Hebrew can refer to the kingdom of Assyria or the small-*g* god Assur, depending on the context. This is admittedly somewhat speculative, but in the contexts of the verses we'll cite below, given the evidence we've already presented about the significance of this supernatural rebel who would be king, I think what you're about to read are prophecies of the ultimate destruction of this ancient enemy of God.

Isaiah 14 is one of the most remarkable chapters in the Bible. It's the source of the well-known verse, "How art thou fallen from heaven, O Lucifer, son of the morning! how art thou cut down to the ground, which didst weaken the nations!"[292] On the surface, the first part of the chapter is a polemic against the king of Babylon and a prophecy of that nation's destruction. Bear in mind, however, that at the time Isaiah was inspired to write this verse, Babylon was a vassal state of Assyria. Shalmaneser V had destroyed Samaria and carried off the northern tribes of Israel only twenty or thirty years earlier, and it would be almost a century before the Chaldeans established the Neo-Babylonian Empire.

There is more going on in Isaiah 14 than a prophecy of the destruction of Babylon or mocking Satan, who'd been reduced from his status in Eden to becoming the lord of the dead. (The "shades" who greet him upon his arrival in Sheol are *rephaim*,[293] the spirits of the Nephilim destroyed in the Flood.)

Consider the odd description of the rebel from Eden in verse 19:

All the kings of the nations lie in glory,
each in his own tomb;
but you are cast out, away from your grave,
like a loathed branch,
clothed with the slain, those pierced by the sword,
who go down to the stones of the pit,

---

292. Isaiah 14:12 (King James Bible).
293. Isaiah 14:9.

like a dead body trampled underfoot.
(Isaiah 14:19, emphasis added)

What did the prophet mean by calling the rebel from Eden "a loathed branch"? Most English translations agree that the Hebrew word *netser* means "branch," although a couple opt for "shoot." The range of adjectives chosen by translators includes "loathed," "repulsive," "rejected," "worthless," and "abominable," but they convey the same sense—someone or something utterly detestable. But even allowing for differences in culture and language over the last 2,700 years, the phrase "loathed/worthless/abominable branch" is odd.

The key is understanding that Isaiah didn't use the Hebrew word *netser*; he employed a similar-sounding word from another language that was common enough to his readers to be understood:

> [The] term is best explained as a loanword from the common Egyptian noun *nt̠r*. *Nt̠r* **is generally translated "god," but is commonly used of the divinized dead and their physical remains.** It originally came into Hebrew as a noun referring to the putatively divinized corpse of a dead king, which is closely related to the Egyptian usage.[294] (Emphasis added)

The Egyptians regularly used the word *nt̠r*, a homonym (a word that sounds the same as a completely different word) for *netser*, to describe Osiris, the Egyptian god of the dead. Given that Isaiah had just described the "Welcome to Sheol" party thrown by the Rephaim (the "shades" in Isaiah 14:9), calling him a "loathsome dead god" makes more sense than "loathed branch."

Why a loanword from Egypt? The influence of Judah's southwestern neighbor is evident in the book of Isaiah. The prophet warned Hezekiah not to trust in an Egyptian alliance to protect his kingdom (Isaiah

---

294. Hays (2012), op. cit., p. 17.

30:1–2, 31:1–3), which Isaiah called "a covenant with death" (Isaiah 28:15). However, recently discovered seals from King Hezekiah feature the image of a scarab (dung beetle), a sacred symbol in Egypt.[295] So, borrowing an Egyptian word would not have been unusual for Isaiah, especially given the poor opinion he had of Judah's neighbor.

The adjective translated "abhorred" or "abominable," Hebrew *ta ab*, is significant. It modifies the noun *netser*, which would normally have a positive connotation. In this context, *ta'ab* may suggest "ritually impure."[296] Isaiah made a profound declaration here about the rebel from Eden: The "loathed branch" was actually an "unclean god," the status of the divine rebel after he was kicked out of Eden.

What makes Isaiah 14 even more fascinating is another loanword, this time from Aramaic, a few verses further on:

> May the offspring of evildoers
> nevermore be named!
> Prepare slaughter for his sons
> because of the guilt of their fathers,
> lest they rise and possess the earth,
> and fill the face of the world with cities. (Isaiah 14:20b–21)

Now, God is not opposed to cities as such. He inspired Nehemiah, Ezra, Zerubbabel, and others to rebuild Jerusalem and its walls. So, how do we understand this?

Here's the key: The Hebrew word for "city" is *'iyr*. In Aramaic, the very same word means "Watcher." The plural forms are *'iyrim* and *'iyrin*, respectively. Thanks to Dr. Michael S. Heiser, we have a good example of an Aramaic word that was imported into the Bible and then corrected

---

295. Claude Mariottini, "The Seal of Hezekiah." *Dr. Claude Mariottini—Professor of Old Testament*, Aug. 5, 2014. https://claudemariottini. com/2014/08/05/the-seal-of-hezekiah/, retrieved 5/21/21.
296. Ibid., p. 18.

with the -*im* plural suffix, transforming *naphil(a)* ("giant") into *nephi-lim*, according to Hebrew rules of word formation.[297]

You can see right off how that would change the passage above in an important way:

> Prepare slaughter for his sons
> because of the guilt of their fathers,
> lest they rise and possess the earth,
> **and fill the face of the world with [Watchers]**. (Isaiah 14:21, emphasis added)

That puts a new spin on the whole chapter. Isaiah may have intended to record God's judgment against the offspring of the rebel angels on Hermon, the Watchers, and their progeny, the Nephilim. A similar prophecy was uttered by the prophet-for-prophet, Balaam:

> [A] star shall come out of Jacob,
> and a scepter shall rise out of Israel; [...]
> And one from Jacob shall exercise dominion
> and destroy the survivors of cities [Watchers]!
> (Numbers 24:17b, 19)

I stumbled onto this new reading of Isaiah 14 while researching my 2018 book, *Last Clash of the Titans*. At the time, I understood the passages cited above as the prophesied destruction of Lucifer/Satan and the Rephaim (i.e., the Nephilim). The cities/Watchers swap opens another dimension of understanding for Isaiah 14 and Numbers 24, too.

Obviously, we can't substitute "Watchers" for every occurrence of "cities" in the Old Testament. Most of the time, *'iyrim* means "cities."

---

297. Michael S. Heiser, "The Nephilim." *SitchinIsWrong.com*, http://www.sitchiniswrong.com/nephilim/nephilim.htm, retrieved 5/21/21.

But in the passages above, translating the word as "Watchers" fits the context better.

And in Isaiah 14, the fit is better yet if we consider that the chapter, contrary to the long-held consensus, doesn't refer to Lucifer/Satan at all, but was directed instead at another supernatural rebel: Assur.

Chapter Seventeen

HELEL BEN SHACHAR

On the surface, the last section of Isaiah 14 appears to refer to nation-states, specifically Babylon and Assyria. What I'm about to propose is something new, to the best of my knowledge—I suggest that the entire chapter is directed at those nations and the entity worshiped as the father of their gods:

> "I will rise up against them," declares the LORD of hosts, "and **will cut off from Babylon [*bābel*] name and remnant, descendants and posterity**," declares the LORD. "And I will make it a possession of the hedgehog, and pools of water, and I will sweep it with the broom of destruction," declares the LORD of hosts.
> The LORD of hosts has sworn:
> "As I have planned,
> so shall it be,
> and as I have purposed,
> so shall it stand,
> that **I will break the Assyrian [*'aššūr*] in my land,
> and on my mountains trample him underfoot;**
> and his yoke shall depart from them,

and his burden from their shoulder."
This is the purpose that is purposed
concerning the whole earth,
and this is the hand that is stretched out
over all the nations.
For the LORD of hosts has purposed,
and who will annul it?
His hand is stretched out,
and who will turn it back?
(Isaiah 14:22–27, emphasis added)

In the context of what precedes this section of Isaiah 14, I suggest that it refers to Babylon and Assyria as well as the spirit-beings connected to Babel and the "king-god," Assur.

First, remember that "Babylon" was a name applied to more than one city in Mesopotamia, including the ancient city of Eridu, the site of Babel. In fact, the Hebrew *bābel* translated "Babylon" in Isaiah 14:22 is the same word rendered "Babel" in Genesis 10 and 11. It doesn't mean that Babylon and Babel are the same place; it means we have to discern the meaning from the context.

God has promised that He will destroy "the offspring of evildoers" to prevent them from "fill[ing] the face of the earth with Watchers." In this interpretation of Isaiah 14, those "evildoers" are the sons of God from Genesis 6, and the "sons" and "fathers" of Isaiah 14:21 are the Nephilim/ Rephaim and the Watchers.

The prophecy against Babylon continues that thought. God's promise to "cut off from [*bābel*, "gate of 'the' god"] name and remnant, descendants and posterity" is more than a threat to destroy the Chaldeans, the rulers of Babylon in the time of Isaiah. The "name" in Old Testament theology is more complex and nuanced than a personal pronoun or a reputation. Without going too far down a rabbit trail, because this topic could fill a book, the "name" was another aspect of a supernatural being. For example, God told Moses and the Israelites to obey the angel He sent ahead of them "for my Name is in Him."[298] In short, "the Name in the OT is both Yahweh and a representation of Him, depending on the context. It's not merely a phrase, but a being."[299]

The pagans had a similar concept. As we noted earlier, the Rephaim were summoned through a necromancy ritual to Mount Hermon where "the name of El revivified the dead, the blessings of the name of El revivified the heroes."[300]

So, in Isaiah 14:22 God prophesied the absolute obliteration of the entities connected to Babel, as well as the destruction of Babylon. The latter was fulfilled in 536 BC when Cyrus took the city; the former should be viewed in the context of Psalm 82, the heavenly courtroom scene where God decreed the death of the gods.

But it's the reference to "the Assyrian" that's so fascinating. Yes, it can be read as a near-term prophecy of the collapse of the Assyrian kingdom. That was fulfilled in 609 BC when the father of Nebuchadnezzar II, Nabopolassar, destroyed what was left of the Assyrian army at the Battle of Harran. However, that was fought in northern Mesopotamia, near modern Sanliurfa, Turkey. When God refers to His land and His mountains, He means Israel.

The other relevant question is this: Why does God refer to "the Assyrian," singular? This type of description isn't used of any of the other traditional enemies of Israel. In other words, there are no prophecies or polemics directed at "the Edomite," "the Moabite," "the Philistine," or "the Egyptian"; it's always the plural form of the name—Edomites (adômîm), Egyptians (misrayim), etc. We haven't dug deeply enough into this passage or this character—because "the Assyrian" shows up elsewhere in the Bible.

---

298. Exodus 23:20–21.

299. Michael S. Heiser, "The Name Theology of the Old Testament." In *Faithlife Study Bible* (Bellingham, WA: Lexham Press, 2012, 2016).

300. Spronk (1986), op. cit., p. 171.

But first, I'm going to offer another paradigm-shifting suggestion: The "king of Babylon" to whom the prophecy of Isaiah 14:3–22 is addressed was not the Chaldean ruler of the region around the city of Babylon, nor was it Satan. Let me explain.

The Hebrew *melek bābel* also means "king of Babel." Given that Hebrew *bābel* derives from Akkadian *bab ilû* ("gate of the gods," or "gate of 'the' god"), and Isaiah 14's focus on the netherworld and its inhabitants (the Rephaim), I suggest that *melek bābel* means "king of the god-gate." Remember that Babel/Babylon was also a name for the ancient city of Eridu, home of the god Enki and his temple, the E-abzu ("House of the Abyss").

Here's what I'm getting at: I believe "the Assyrian," *'aššūr* in Hebrew, is Assur, otherwise known as Enlil, El, Dagan, Kumarbi, and Shemihazah, called by his followers "the king"—an idea we will develop further with additional evidence in an upcoming chapter. Here in Isaiah 14, we see this entity called *melek bābel*, "king of the god-gate," which, given Babel's location at Eridu, implies that this entity is king of the *abzu*—the abyss.

In short, the "king of Babylon" and "the Assyrian" were terms used by Isaiah for Assur, the principal object of the LORD's wrath in this chapter.

However, we can take this even further. Christian commentators generally agree that Isaiah 14 and Ezekiel 28 are parallel Scriptures that describe the fall of the same entity:

How you are fallen from heaven,
O Day Star, son of Dawn!
How you are cut down to the ground,
you who laid the nations low!
You said in your heart,
"I will ascend to heaven;
above the stars of God
I will set my throne on high;
I will sit on the mount of assembly

in the far reaches of the north;
I will ascend above the heights of the clouds;
I will make myself like the Most High."
But you are brought down to Sheol,
to the far reaches of the pit. (Isaiah 14:12–15)

The phrase "far reaches of the north," also translated ""sides of the north" or "uttermost parts of the north," is from the Hebrew *yarketê tsaphon*. That's a reference to Mount Zaphon, the mountain sacred to Baal:

A seat was prepared and he was seated at the right hand of Valiant Baal, until the gods had eaten and drunk. Then Valiant Baal said, "Depart, Kothar-and-Hasis! Hasten! Build a house indeed; hasten! Construct a palace! Hasten! Let them build a house; Hasten! Let them construct a palace, in the midst of **the uttermost parts of Zaphon**. A thousand square yards let the house take up, ten thousand acres the palace!"[301] (Emphasis added)

Since Baal was identified as Satan by Jesus Himself,[302] identifying "Day Star" or "Lucifer" (Hebrew *Helel Ben Shachar*, literally "Lightbringer, son of Dawn") as Satan seems like a slam dunk.

Maybe not. William R. Gallagher published a paper in 1994 that offers a compelling argument for identifying another candidate as Helel:

One could reasonably expect *hll* [Helel] to be the West Semitic form of Illil [that is, Enlil]. As the Ebla tablets suggest, Illil came into West Semitic directly from Sumerian. Thus this example is comparable to the development of E_2.GAL:

---

301. Ugaritic text KTU 1.4 v 49–57. In Wyatt (2002), op. cit., p. 104.
302. Matthew 12:22–26, Revelation 2:13.

| Sum. é-gal | Eblaite (?) | Ug. hkl | Heb. hêkāl |
| Sum. ᵈen-lil | Eblaite ᵈi-li-lu | Ug. hll | Heb. hêlēl[303] |

Yes, this is technical language geek stuff, but I need to show that I'm not pulling this theory out of thin air. While Gallagher had the route of transmission reversed, since the evidence shows that Enlil derives from the Semitic *il-ilû* ("god of gods") and not the other way around, he was correct in linking Helel to Enlil in Isaiah 14. And further, the etymology equating Helel with Enlil also identifies him as El, creator-god of the Canaanites.

This confuses things a bit. El's mount of assembly was Hermon, not Zaphon. So, how can we identify Helel (i.e., Lucifer) with El, the "lord of Hermon," if his five "I wills" in Isaiah 14 were all about establishing his mount of assembly at Zaphon?

It's possible that setting up shop on Mount Zaphon was his ambition, but that his plan was thwarted when God cast the rebellious "sons of God" into the abyss during the Flood of Noah. As Edward Lipiński wrote, "the modern Ğebel el-Aqra‘ [Mount Zaphon] seems to have been dedicated to El before it became the mountain of Baʿal. But there are no positive elements which should allow to characterize it as the Mountain of the divine Assembly."[304]

In short, what I suggest is that Helel Ben Shachar is not Lucifer/ Satan, but one and the same as the "king of Babel" and "the Assyrian." Isaiah 14:1–27, then, is a condemnation of this rebel and a prophecy of his future destruction.

In support of this theory, let's turn over a couple of additional pieces of evidence.

---

303. William R. Gallagher, "On the Identity of Hêlēl Ben Šaḥar of Is. 14:12–15." *Ugarit-Forschungen: Internationales Jahrbuch für die Altertumskunde Syrien-Palästinas*, 26 (1994), p. 137. Thanks to Dr. Douglas Hamp for calling my attention to this.
304. Lipiński, op. cit., p. 64.

In Isaiah 14:19, the "loathed branch" passage, Helel/Enlil is described as being "like a dead body trampled underfoot." The Hebrew word translated "dead body" is *peger*, a cognate for the Eblaite word *pagrê*, which we encountered earlier as one of the epithets of Dagan, *bēl pagrê* ("lord of the corpse"). Dagan is another identity of this creature. In Isaiah 14, the prophet masterfully incorporated several clues to the identity of the divine rebel—Helel = Enlil = El, while *peger* points to Dagan—and then mocked this entity and the cult of the dead that arose after the destruction of the Nephilim, the evildoers' offspring whose spirits were venerated as Rephaim by the pagan neighbors of Israel.

Upon arrival in Sheol, Helel is consigned to "the far reaches of the pit."[305] Besides being a humiliating reversal of his goal to establish his throne "in the far reaches of [Zaphon]," it identifies his new abode as a place of dishonor in the underworld. In fact, "far reaches of the pit" is a good description for the unbroken darkness of the abyss.

In Ezekiel 32, the chapter that refers to the chiefs of the *gibborim* "in the midst of Sheol," we find Assur (*'aššūr*) in Sheol with his host, "whose graves are set in the uttermost parts of the pit."[306] In other words, Assur and his company have the same underworld address as Helel Ben Shachar in Isaiah 14, the *yarketê bôr* ("far reaches/uttermost parts of the pit"). This may seem like hyperbole, a detail tossed in by the prophets to emphasize the evil of Helel/Assur, but it suggests that there's something unique about this entity:

> The notion that those killed in heroic battle have a special place in the afterlife is a shared feature of Ezekiel 32 and Greek heroic literature, even as Ezekiel 32 may be the only text in the Hebrew Bible to give such a detailed description of this geography. [...] Assur is relegated to the "uttermost edge of the Pit" (בור ירכתי) in

---

305. Isaiah 14:15.
306. Ezekiel 32:22.

v. 23—presumably in the sense of distance and ignobility—and
could thus be in a class of its own.[307]

Assur is the Watcher chief Shemihazah, and he is indeed in a class
of his own—the leader of a rebellion that affects the world, through his
demonic offspring, to this day.

In fact, if we turn back to Ezekiel chapter 31, we see a long diatribe
against the Pharaoh of Egypt. Like Isaiah 14 and Ezekiel 28, which con-
demn the king of Babylon and the prince of Tyre by comparing those
mortal rulers to divine rebels against the authority of God, Ezekiel 31
compares Pharaoh to Assyria, and there are reasons to read Assyria as
Assur, the small-*g* god who's the subject of this book.

> Son of man, say to Pharaoh king of Egypt and to his multitude:
> "Whom are you like in your greatness?
> Behold, [Assur] was a cedar in Lebanon,
> with beautiful branches and forest shade,
> and of towering height,
> its top among the clouds. (Ezekiel 31:2–3)

The reference to Lebanon is a clue. It's frequently used in the Old
Testament to evoke images of Bashan and its connection to Mount Hermon, the Watchers, the Nephilim, and the netherworld.

> The cedars in the garden of God could not rival it,
> nor the fir trees equal its boughs;
> neither were the plane trees
> like its branches;
> no tree in the garden of God

---

307. Brian R. Doak, "Ezekiel's Topography of the (Un-)Heroic Dead in
Ezekiel 32:17–32." *Journal of Biblical Literature*, Vol. 132, No. 3 (2013), pp.
619–620.

was its equal in beauty.
I made it beautiful
in the mass of its branches,
and all the trees of Eden envied it,
that were in the garden of God. (Ezekiel 31:8–9)

Here is where the identification becomes apparent. The trees in Eden represent other spirit beings, and Assur (Shemihazah, chief of the Watchers) was beyond compare. This is similar to the description of the rebel in Ezekiel 28:12–15—perfect, wise, beautiful, blameless in his ways. Since Ezekiel 28 and Isaiah 14 are parallel passages dealing with the same divine rebel, Ezekiel 31 appears to corroborate our theory that this entity, under his variety of names and identities, played a far more important role in this supernatural war than we've realized. And the punishment he received is appropriate for his crime:

"Thus says the Lord GOD: On the day the cedar went down to Sheol I caused mourning; **I closed the deep over it**, and restrained its rivers, and many waters were stopped. I clothed Lebanon in gloom for it, and all the trees of the field fainted because of it. I made the nations quake at the sound of its fall, when I cast it down to Sheol with those who go down to the pit. And all the trees of Eden, the choice and best of Lebanon, all that drink water, were comforted in the world below. They also went down to Sheol with it, to those who are slain by the sword; yes, those who were its arm, who lived under its shadow among the nations.

Whom are you thus like in glory and in greatness among the trees of Eden? You shall be brought down with the trees of Eden to the world below. You shall lie among the uncircumcised, with those who are slain by the sword.

This is Pharaoh and all his multitude," declares the Lord GOD. (Ezekiel 31:15–18, emphasis added)

The Hebrew word translated "the deep," *tehôm*, refers to the abyss.[308] What Ezekiel described was not a tree cast into Sheol; it was the punishment of Shemihazah and the Watchers, the "sons of God" who "left their proper dwelling" and are "in eternal chains under gloomy darkness until the judgment of the great day."[309] Such would be the fate, Ezekiel prophesied, of Pharaoh.

The difference between Pharaoh and Assur/Enlil/El, etc., is that the once-perfect chief of the Watchers gets out of the underworld for a brief time in the last days. Believe me, you don't want to be here when he returns from the abyss. The good news is you don't have to be.

———

This section has indulged in more speculation than other parts of the book, so it's worth recapping what we've covered. The chief god of Assyria, Assur, was Enlil by a different name—so much so that the name of Assur's temple was changed from the House of Assur to the House of the Mountain, the name of Enlil's temple in Nippur.

The identification of Assur with Enlil means the entity behind those names was also worshiped as Dagan, El, and Kumarbi. Our working theory is that this supernatural being was the chief of the Watchers who rebelled on Mount Hermon in the days of Jared (or in the days when the *yarid*, a libation ritual, was performed on the mountain).

Polemics directed at this entity have been hiding in plain sight, concealed in our Bibles by the translations, a lack of information about what the pagans around ancient Israel believed about their gods, and a consensus among modern Christians that pagan gods are imaginary—a belief that would have astonished the prophets, apostles, and early church. The

---

308. B. Alster, "Tiamat." In Karel van der Toorn, Bob Becking, and Pieter W. van der Horst (Eds.), *Dictionary of Deities and Demons in the Bible* (Leiden; Boston; Köln; Grand Rapids, MI; Cambridge: Brill; Eerdmans, 1999), p. 867.

309. Jude 6.

mockery of Dagan, spelled "Dagon" in the Bible, is obvious in the story of Samson. Condemnation of El requires a little digging into the original language, but it's there in Hosea 8:6 ("For who is Bull El?") and probably Psalm 82:1 ("God has taken His place in the assembly of El"), the references to Hermon[310] and Bashan[311] scattered through the Bible, and most clearly in Jesus' decision to climb Mount Hermon for the Transfiguration.

Enlil is not mentioned by name in our English Bible, but it's probable that Isaiah created the Hebrew word that came to mean "worthless idol," 'ĕlîl, from "Enlil." Likewise, Kumarbi does not appear by that name, but since we've traced the origin of the necromantic ritual pit, the 'ōb, to the *abi* of the Hurrians at ancient Urkesh, the influence of their chief god Kumarbi is felt throughout the Bible in references to mediums and necromancers.[312]

Assur is a different case. His name is found 130 times in the Bible, but in most cases it's unquestionably a reference to Assyria. However, it's probable that Ezekiel 31 and 32 contain references to Assur, and Isaiah 14:22–27 is most likely a polemic against Assur.

The biggest claim in this chapter is the suggestion that the divine rebel of Isaiah 14 and Ezekiel 28 is not Satan, but Shemihazah. Nothing in either chapter specifically names Satan, but it's been the consensus for so long that it's practically taken as a given. The case for identifying the rebel as the chief of the Watchers can be summarized thus:

- Etymology: Helel ("Lucifer") = Ellil = Enlil. And the story of the rebel's fall from heaven to the netherworld parallels the history of Enlil, the former chief deity of Mesopotamia who'd been relegated to the netherworld.

---

310. Psalm 42:6, 68:15–16, 89:2.

311. Psalm 22:12, Psalm 68:15–22; Jeremiah 22:20; Ezekiel 27:6, 39:18; Amos 4:1; Nahum 1:4; Zechariah 11:2.

312. Leviticus 19:1, 20:6, 20:27; Deuteronomy 18:11; 1 Samuel 28:3–25; 2 Kings 23:24; 2 Chronicles 33:6; Isaiah 8:19, 19:3. See also Acts 16:16–24.

- There is a stronger connection between Shemihazah and the Rephaim, the "shades" of Isaiah 14:9, than between the Rephaim and Satan, who played no role in the events of Genesis 6.

- The sons of God from Genesis 6 were thrust down to Tartarus, according to Peter, where they remain in chains until the judgment. There is nothing in the Bible that explicitly connects Satan to the underworld. Every time Satan appears as a character, he's either on the earth or in heaven (Job 1 and 2).

- This resolves the apparent contradiction over the type of entity Satan is. In Genesis 3, he's a *nachash* ("serpent"), a word used interchangeably with *saraph* in Numbers 21 ("fiery serpents" = *seraphim ha-nachashim*). But in Ezekiel 28:14 and 16, the divine rebel is called a "guardian cherub." So, is he of the seraphim or the cherubim? Who knows? But if the rebel in Ezekiel is Shemihazah and not Satan, the conflict disappears.[313]

- This also makes sense of Isaiah 14:21. If the chapter refers to Satan, who are his sons—and who are their guilty fathers? And why would their rise "fill the face of the world with [Watchers]"? However, the links between the Watcher chief Shemihazah, his colleagues, and their sons who threatened to "possess the earth" are clearly described in the Book of 1 Enoch.

Admittedly, this new identification of the rebel in Isaiah 24 and Ezekiel 28 is speculative, based on circumstantial evidence. It seems to be a tighter fit with the references to the spirits of the Rephaim and the

---

313. To be fair, the Septuagint renders Ezekiel 28:14, "I placed you with the cherub in the holy mountain of God" (emphasis added). The NET Bible follows this translation. This reading makes the rebel separate and distinct from guardian cherub, who ejects the rebel from Eden in verse 16. This also resolves the saraph/cherub conflict, and does so without replacing Satan in the story.

netherworld, but it's not a doctrinal hill to die on. I present it because it's helpful for understanding the nature of the war we're in and the enemy who opposes us.

But there are more layers of deception to roll back in our examination of this divine outcast. The Watcher wore yet another face to ensnare the people of the ancient world, including the Hebrews. You know his name, but you probably didn't expect to see him in this book.

Chapter Eighteen

MOLECH

Here is where Shemihazah's desire to be the king becomes most evi-dent. In this section of the book, we analyze the character and worship of yet another of his identities—Milcom, chief god of the Ammonites, who's better known to history as Molech.

If anything, Molech, which is sometimes spelled "Molek" or "Moloch," is even more mysterious than Dagan. Since ancient Semitic languages such as Akkadian, Ugaritic, and Hebrew had no vowels, it's difficult to tell when *mlk* means "king" (*melech*), "messenger" or "angel" (*malak*), and when it's the name of the dark god Molech. This condem-nation of idolatry from the book of Isaiah is a case in point:

> You journeyed to **the king** [*mlk*] with oil
> and multiplied your perfumes;
> you sent your envoys far off,
> and sent down even to Sheol. (Isaiah 57:9, emphasis added)

In that context, given the reference to Sheol, the Hebrew under-world, "the king" could just as easily read "Molech," a god linked almost exclusively to the netherworld. Obviously, that would change the entire sense of the verse.

Molech's first appearance in the Bible is in Leviticus 18, where God told the Israelites that they were forbidden to give their children as an offering to the dark god. Molech's cult, however, extends back at least a thousand years before Moses.

A god called "Malik" is known from texts found at Ebla, a powerful kingdom in northern Syria between about 3000 and 2400 BC, more than three hundred years before Abraham arrived in Canaan. Of the approximately five hundred deities identified from texts found at Ebla, one of most common theophoric elements in personal names—like -el in Daniel (" God is my judge") or -yahu in Hezekiah ("YHWH strengthens")—was ma-lik.[314]

Getting a handle on the character of Malik is difficult. It appears that by the time of Abraham, Isaac, and Jacob, he was still worshiped at Mari, a powerful city on the Euphrates River near the modern border between Syria and Iraq. Further, it appears that Malik was served by a group of underworld deities called maliku. And five hundred years later, during the time of the judges, Malik and the maliku (called mlkm by then) were still venerated at Ugarit.[315]

What's more, the Ugaritic texts link Malik with a god called "Rapiu," the "King of Eternity." This entity is interesting for a couple of reasons: First, Rapiu is a singular form of "Rephaim," similar to ha-rapha ("the rapha" or "the giant") in 2 Samuel 21 and 1 Chronicles 20. In other words, just as Malik had his band of netherworld followers, the maliku or mlkm, it's possible that Rapiu was "lord of the Rephaim."

Second, the Ugaritic texts connect both Malik and Rapiu to Ashtaroth, a city in Bashan near Mount Hermon.[316]

---

314. Heiser, op. cit., p. 96.

315. Ibid., p. 129.

316. Ibid., p. 115.

Mother Šapšu, take a message to Milku in 'Aṭṭartu [Ashtaroth]: "My incantation for serpent bite, For the scaly serpent's poison."[317]

Mother Šapšu was the sun-goddess in Ugarit. In this ritual, she was asked to carry a message to a god ruling in Ashtaroth, Milku, which is another form of the name "Molech." This isn't surprising; at the time of the judges in Israel, Bashan, the modern Golan Heights, was on the border of the relatively new nation of Ammon. The national god of the Ammonites was Milcom, who was one and the same with Molech.[318]

In fact, Rapiu had two cities connected to his kingdom: He is described as "the god enthroned at Ashtaroth, the god who rules in Edrei."[319] Those two cities are the same two from which Og, last of the living Rephaim, ruled over Bashan.[320] To the pagan Amorites, the kingdom of Og was literally the entrance to the underworld.

To be clear, despite the evil reputation of Molech/Malik, archaeologists have yet to find physical evidence of child sacrifice at Ugarit, Mari, or Ebla. Nor has any turned up near Jerusalem, despite references in the Bible to the ritual practice outside the walls of the city in the Valley of Hinnom. If children were being slaughtered for Molech in the Levant before the Israelites arrived, scholars haven't confirmed it yet.

Still, the Bible mentions it in Moses' day, around 1400 BC; Solomon built a high place for Molech around 950 BC;[321] and about 325

---

317. RS 24:244:40–41. Translation by Dennis Pardee & Theodore J. Lewis, *Ritual and Cult at Ugarit* (Vol. 10). (Atlanta, GA: Society of Biblical Literature, 2002), p. 177. Ugaritic text RS 24:251:42 also places the god Milku in Ashtaroth.

318. 1 Kings 11:5 calls Milcom "the abomination of the Ammonites," and 1 Kings 11:7 uses the same description for Molech.

319. Wyatt (2002), op. cit., p. 395.

320. Deuteronomy 3:1; Joshua 12:4, 13:12.

321. 1 Kings 11:7.

years later, King Josiah defiled the Topheth in the Valley of the Son of Hinnom, which was used to burn children as offerings to Molech.[322]

Now, here's where things get interesting: Molech was equated with the Mesopotamian plague-god and gatekeeper of the underworld, Nergal. Not only are both connected to death and the afterlife, Akkadian deity lists record the equation "Malik = Nergal." Further, Semitic *mlk* and Sumerian NERGAL can both be understood as "king," confirming the identification.[323]

There's a similar link between NERGAL and Kumarbi. An inscription, probably from a foundation deposit at the temple at Urkesh dated to about 2250 BC, reads, "Tish-atal, king of Urkesh, built the temple of NERGAL."[324] Without getting lost in the details, the conclusion of the archaeologists was this: The Sumerian logogram [d]KIŠ.GAL (NERGAL) represents a Hurrian divine name, not the proper name of the plague-god Nergal. Since the only god known to "live" at Urkesh is Kumarbi, "we may therefore identify the great Temple complex as being that of Kumarbi."[325] So, since "Malik = Nergal," we can infer that the "NERGAL" ("king") of Urkesh, Kumarbi, is also Malik/Molech.

The other aspect of the cult of Molech that's relevant to our investigation is the clear connection in the Bible between the dark god and the practice of consulting the *'ōbôt*, the spirits of the dead. We turn first to Leviticus:

---

322. 2 Kings 23:10.

323. Rebecca Doyle, *Faces of the Gods: Baal, Asherah and Molek and Studies of the Hebrew Scriptures* (Doctoral thesis: University of Sheffield, 1996), p. 129.

324. Giorgio Buccellati and Marilyn Kelly-Buccellati, "The Great Temple Terrace at Urkesh and the Lions of Tish-atal." *Studies on the Civilization and Culture of Nuzi and the Hurrians* - 18 (2009), p. 59.

325. Ibid., p. 63.

The LORD spoke to Moses, saying, "Say to the people of Israel,
Any one of the people of Israel or of the strangers who sojourn
in Israel who gives any of his children to Molech shall surely
be put to death. The people of the land shall stone him with
stones. I myself will set my face against that man and will cut
him off from among his people, because he has given one of
his children to Molech, to make my sanctuary unclean and to
profane my holy name. And if the people of the land do at all
close their eyes to that man when he gives one of his children
to Molech, and do not put him to death, then I will set my face
against that man and against his clan and will cut them off from
among their people, him and all who follow him in whoring
after Molech.

    If a person turns to mediums ['ōbôt] and necromancers
[yiddĕ'ōnîm], whoring after them, I will set my face against that
person and will cut him off from among his people. (Leviticus
20:1–6)

The significance here is that God Himself directly linked the cult of
Molech to the gods and spirits of the netherworld.

The unifying principle of vv. 1–6 is not merely "illegitimate cultic practices," but the practice of the cult of the dead. This realiza-
tion makes sense, also, of the condemnation of the guilty party's
entire clan (mispahto) in v. 5: as we saw at Mari and Ugarit, the
cult of the dead is a family affair, to secure the blessings (and
avert the wrath) of past family for the sake of the family present
and yet to be.[326]

A passage similar to Leviticus 20 is found in Deuteronomy 18:

---

326. Heiser, op. cit., p. 251.

There shall not be found among you anyone who burns his son
or his daughter as an offering [to Molech], anyone who practices
divination or tells fortunes or interprets omens, or a sorcerer or a
charmer or a medium or a necromancer or one who inquires of
the dead, or whoever does these things is an abomination to the
LORD. (Deuteronomy 18:10–12)

After the prohibition on burning children as offerings, there are seven
specific activities described as "abomination to the LORD." All seven were
intended to "gain information from or influence over a divine being or
beings."[327] The connection of the Molech cult to these activities and
underworld entities suggests that Molech is indeed the deity we met earlier in this study—Kumarbi, the god summoned from the *abi*, which, as
we've seen, is the Hurrian original behind the Hebrew words for "ritual
pit" (*'ôb*) and the spirits of the underworld (*'ōbôt*).

It's generally accepted that the various forms of the name
"Molech"/"Malik"/"Milcom" (and the chief god of Phoenician Tyre,
Melqart) derive from the Semitic root *mlk* ("king"). The identification
of this deity with Nergal, the gatekeeper of the underworld in Akkad
and Babylon, suggests that the true meaning of the name was "King
of the Underworld." This is consistent with our theory that this entity
was the god worshiped by the Moabites, and perhaps by the people of
Sodom in the days of Abraham and Lot, as Baal-Peor ("lord of the opening to the netherworld").

What I'm suggesting is that "Molech," like "Baal," was not a proper
name, but a title: "King/Lord (of the Underworld)." And it refers to the
entity at the heart of our study under his many names: Shemihazah,
Kumarbi, El, Enlil, Dagan, Assur, and a few others still to be explored.

Further evidence for this hypothesis comes from the small and
mostly forgotten kingdom of Ammon:

---

327. Ibid., p. 259.

The dominance of the theophoric element 'l in Ammonite personal names suggests the importance of the deity El in the context of family religion. [...]

The occurrence of the Ammonite name element 'l [El] with approximately the same percentage as Kemosh [national god of Moab], Qos [national god of Edom], and onomastic forms of Yahweh in theophoric names in Moabite, Edomite, and Hebrew, respectively, suggests that **among the Ammonites, too, the most popular family deity likewise corresponds to the chief national deity, in this case El.** [...]

In contrast with the more traditional and widespread form of family piety expressed in personal names, the differentiation of Ammonite El in more nationalistic contexts like the Amman Citadel Inscription and in biblical texts, was expressed through the title Milkom—a title distinct to the Ammonite form of El in his capacity as royal god, a role reflected in the Ammonite statuary. [...]

In sum, given the present state of the evidence, **Milkom is best understood as a distinctly Ammonite form of El.**[328] (Emphasis added.)

In short, there was no Milcom/Molech. The name is simply a title—"king"—that the Ammonites used to refer to their chief god, El. "Molech" was the form of the title used by the Hebrew prophets in which they switched out the vowels to make the name an insult, the same way they transformed "Baal" into "Bosheth" ("shameful thing") and "Astarte" into "Ashtoreth."[329]

---

328. Joel S. Burnett, "Iron Age Deities in Word, Image, and Name: Correlating Epigraphic, Iconographic, and Onomastic Evidence for the Ammonite God," *Studies in the History and Archaeology of Jordan* 10 (2009), p. 161.

329. Morris Jastrow, Jr. & George A. Barton, "Ashtoreth." *Jewish*

Here's another idea to consider. This was suggested by my wife, Sharon, who is obviously more observant than me: Since the name "Anakim" probably derives from Greek *anax* ("king" or "god"), a title given to Agamemnon, high king of the Greeks during the Trojan War, and an epithet of Zeus ("Zeus Anax"), because of his status in the Greek pantheon as overlord of creation,[330] it's possible that the Anakim were called by that name because they served the original fallen Watcher who was called *anax* ("king"), "Milcom"/ "El. "

In other words, "Anakim" would roughly mean "men of the 'high king'" and the "descendants of Anak" (*yelîdê ha-anaq*) in Numbers 13:22, like the "descendants of the giant" (*yelîdê ha-rapha*) defeated by David and his men, were not literal blood descendants of a giant man named Anak, but were servants of the supernatural *anax*—Milcom/El, the so-called king.

This is speculative, but not out of the realm of possibility. The Assyrians and their capital city shared the name of the chief god, Assur. The Amorites were associated with a god named Amurru, and an Amorite kingdom in northern Syria called Amurru is attested in Egyptian texts from the time of the Judges. And the Egyptian Execration Texts appear to place the Anakim in the Transjordan,[331] where we've established the existence of cults for this entity under the names El, "Milcom," "Malik," and probably "Baal-Peor."

Given that this god led the rebellion that created the Nephilim, who became the Rephaim spirits upon their deaths in the Flood, this could explain the link between the Anakim and Rephaim, and why Joshua

---

Encyclopedia, https://jewishencyclopedia.com/articles/2005-ashtoreth, retrieved 3/30/21.

330. "The Linear B Word wa-na-ka." Paleolexicon, http://www. palaeolexicon.com/Word/Show/16631, retrieved 4/12/21.

331. The leaders of the Iy'anaq are listed next to rulers of the Shutu, which probably refers to Moab (cf. the "sons of Sheth" in Numbers 24:17).

fixed on the destruction of the Anakim as Israel's first objective in the conquest of Canaan.

The connection between this entity, necromancy, and the cult of the dead—not to mention the sacrifice of children—adds a new dimension to the prophet Hosea's condemnation of Bull El. Isaiah, writing a few years after Hosea, wove a condemnation of the cult of the dead into prophecies of the coming Assyrian invasion and the birth of the Messiah:

> Behold, I and the children whom the LORD has given me are signs and portents in Israel from the LORD of hosts, who dwells on Mount Zion. And when they say to you, "Inquire of the mediums [ōbôt] and the necromancers [yiddĕ'ōnîm] who chirp and mutter," should not a people inquire of their God? **Should they inquire of the dead on behalf of the living?** To the teaching and to the testimony! If they will not speak according to this word, it is because they have no dawn. **They will pass through** ['ābar] **the land**, greatly distressed and hungry. And when they are hungry, **they will be enraged and will speak contemptuously against their king** [melek] **and their God** [elohay], and turn their faces upward. And they will look to the earth, but behold, distress and darkness, the gloom of anguish. And they will be thrust into thick darkness. (Isaiah 8:19–22, emphasis added)

There are several important points to note in this passage. First, the word rendered "inquire" (Hebrew *dirshu*) is translated "seek" or "search" about twice as often as "inquire." Compare Isaiah's words to the question asked by the angels of the women who'd come to prepare the body of Jesus after dawn of the third day: "Why do you seek the living among the dead?"[332] In other words, Isaiah condemned the people of Judah for

---

332. Luke 24:5b.

seeking the dead among the living, where the true "signs and portents" from God were to be found.

The prophet described those who looked to the spirit realm for oracles as people who were already dead: They live in darkness, and they're "greatly distressed and hungry," like the pagan dead of Mesopotamia who are not properly cared for by their descendants. In verse 21, Isaiah makes the connection to the dead explicit, writing that these unhappy souls will "pass through" the land. The Hebrew verb 'ābar is based on the same root, 'br, from which we get 'ōberim—"Travelers," as in the spirits of the dead who "travel" or "cross over" from the land of the dead to the world of the living; it's the same word used by the pagan Canaanites to describe the Rephaim summoned from the underworld through rituals to the threshing-floor of El on Mount Hermon.

What Isaiah described is the punishment for those who defied God by using ritual pits to summon the spirits of the dead—they become like the unhappy dead themselves. When they realize their fate, "they will be enraged." But in the context of the passage, with an understanding of the cult of the dead and the role of the "king" god in it, a better translation of the following sentence is this: "And they shall curse by Molek and by their ghosts."[333] (*Elohim*, the word translated "ghosts," isn't always a reference to God. The basic meaning is "one who lives in the spirit realm." Context is king, and here "ghosts" or "spirits" is a more accurate reading than "God.")

It's difficult for us in the twenty-first century to understand how an underworld god whose cult involved necromancy and child sacrifice survived in Israel and Judah for eight hundred years, but it did. The Israelites fell into the worship of Baal-Peor, another title or identity worn by this god, in the time of Moses and Joshua in the late fifteenth century BC, and it continued at least until the reforms of Josiah in the late seventh century BC.

But perhaps the most audacious example of this god's hubris is found on top of a hill just outside the walls of Jerusalem. And it was put there by the son of Israel's best and most beloved king.

---

333. Heiser, op. cit., p. 331.

Chapter Nineteen

MOUNT OF THE DESTROYER

Even though he's been imprisoned in the abyss since the Flood of Noah, Milcom/Molech has continued to exercise his considerable supernatural power on the earth. Through the foreign wives Solomon collected during his reign, the dark god influenced Solomon to build a high place for him that overlooked the Temple Mount:

> For when Solomon was old his wives turned away his heart after other gods, and his heart was not wholly true to the LORD his God, as was the heart of David his father. For Solomon went after Ashtoreth [Astarte] the goddess of the Sidonians, and after Milcom the abomination of the Ammonites. So Solomon did what was evil in the sight of the LORD and did not wholly follow the LORD, as David his father had done. Then Solomon built a high place for Chemosh the abomination of Moab, and for Molech [Milcom] the abomination of the Ammonites, on the mountain east of Jerusalem. (1 Kings 11:4–7)

The mountain east of Jerusalem can only be the Mount of Olives, which rises nearly three hundred feet above the Temple Mount. Solomon probably built those high places after 950 BC, and they stood for about three centuries until the time of King Josiah, who reigned from about 640 BC until his death in 609 BC:

> And the king defiled the high places that were east of Jerusalem, to the south of **the Mount of Corruption**, which Solomon the king of Israel had built for Ashtoreth the abomination of the Sidonians, and for Chemosh the abomination of Moab, and for Milcom the abomination of the Ammonites. (2 Kings 23:13, emphasis added)

Note the name given to the Mount of Olives by the author of 2 Kings: The Mount of Corruption. The Hebrew word rendered "corruption," *mašḥît* (pronounced *mash-kheeth*), means "destruction." But the Hebrew text reads *har ha-mašḥît*, which more precisely means "Mountain of the Destroyer."[334] That's a very different sense of the mountain's name and the god who was worshiped there.

Mašḥît is used twice in the Old Testament to identify a supernatural entity charged with exterminating large groups of people. In Exodus 12:23, "the destroyer" (*ha-mašḥît*) passes through the land of Egypt to take the lives of the firstborn. Second Samuel 24:16 and the parallel passage in 1 Chronicles 21:15 describe the Angel of Yahweh as the *mal'ak ha-mašḥît*, the "destroying angel." He must have been a terrifying sight; David and the elders of Israel, on seeing the Angel of Yahweh "standing between earth and heaven, and in his hand a drawn sword stretched out over Jerusalem," threw themselves to the ground, face down.[335]

However, it's unlikely that the faithful priests and chroniclers who condemned Solomon's pagan high places would use describe them with

---

334. Julian Morganstern, "The King-God among the Western Semites and the Meaning of Epiphanes." *Vetus Testamentum*, Apr., 1960, Vol. 10, Fasc. 2 (April, 1960), pp. 179–180.
335. 1 Chronicles 21:16.

a term that specified the Angel of Yahweh, who was "the second power in heaven," the pre-incarnate Christ.[336]

Now, here is where things get weird: While it appears that three gods were honored by Solomon on the Mount of Olives, it may only have been two. Sir Charles Warren, the British archaeologist mentioned in an earlier chapter, was instrumental in finding the pieces of what we call the Moabite Stone, or the Mesha Stela. It describes the political situation between Moab and the divided kingdoms of Israel and Judah in the time of King Jehoshaphat and the prophet Elisha, sometime around 850 BC.

> And Chemosh said to me, "Go, take Nebo from Israel!" So I went by night and fought against it from the break of dawn until noon, taking it and slaying all, seven thousand men, boys, women, girls and maid-servants, for I had devoted them to destruction for (the god) Ashtar-Chemosh. And I took from there the [...] of Yahweh, dragging them before Chemosh.[337]

This account of the slaughter of Nebo, which was probably at or near where Moses got his only look at the Promised Land, is similar to the treatment given by Joshua and the Israelites to the Amorite cities declared *khērem* ("under the ban"), a phrase usually translated into English as "devoted to destruction" or "annihilated." The sense of the word is hard for us in the modern West to grasp because we aren't taught that things can be so sacred or set apart that just touching them is punishable by death. For example, the first use of the word *khērem* in the Bible is in Exodus 22:

> Whoever sacrifices to any god, other than the LORD alone, shall be **devoted to destruction.** (Exodus 22:20, emphasis added)

---

336. Heiser (2004), op. cit.

337. "The Moabite Stone." Pritchard, op. cit., p. 320.

It's not a coincidence that *khērem* is the root word behind the name "Hermon," the mountain where Shemihazah and his fellow Watchers began their rebellion, and where the pagan Amorites believed their creator-god El held court with his consort and their seventy sons.

The Mesha Stele confirms that Chemosh and his followers understood the concept of *khērem*. And that's not all. Before the slaughter of the Israelites of Nebo, this happened:

> When the king of Moab saw that the battle was going against him, he took with him 700 swordsmen to break through, opposite the king of Edom, but they could not. Then he took his oldest son who was to reign in his place and offered him for a burnt offering on the wall. And there came great wrath against Israel. And they withdrew from him and returned to their own land. (2 Kings 3:26–27)

Verse 27 can be a difficult verse for Jews and Christians to understand. Why, after the prophet Elisha told the kings of Judah, Israel, and Edom that God would grant them victory, was there "great wrath against Israel"? And did the wrath come from Yahweh or Chemosh? The most likely explanation is this: God's anger was directed at the armies of Judah and Israel for losing faith in His ability to deliver on His promise.

The shocking detail in that passage, of course, is that Moab's King Mesha believed that his god, Chemosh, accepted child sacrifice. Does this identify Chemosh as Molech, and thus another name or epithet of El? Not necessarily, but it demonstrates the nature of the gods who have rebelled against their Creator. Human blood is definitely on their menu.

The other point we need to emphasize from the Mesha Stele is the connection the identification of Chemosh and Ashtar, an alternate spelling of Attar (the male war-god aspect of Astarte), as a single entity.

How can that be? Well, trying to pin down precise correlations between the gods and goddesses of the ancient world is a good way to drive yourself crazy. They change names and genders over the centuries—and besides, they lie. It's possible that the names of these deities are, at least in some cases, more like job titles than proper names. For example, in the Hebrew Old Testament, Satan is actually "*the* satan" (i.e., "the adversary" or "the accuser").

So, did Chemosh take on the mantle of "the *attar*" (the war-god) at some point after Israel established itself in Canaan? About that time, the violent, male side of Astarte, the war-god Attar/Ashtar, was deemphasized if not entirely split from her character. By the time she became "Aphrodite" of the Greeks and Venus of the Romans, the warlike aspect of her personality was nearly gone, maybe set aside in favor of emphasizing her identity in the Western world as the Queen of Heaven.[338]

The point of this rabbit trail is to suggest that perhaps Astarte and Chemosh ("Aphrodite" and "Ares" to the Greeks, "Venus" and "Mars" to the Romans) are just alternate aspects of the same supernatural entity. We're dealing with entities who operate in more dimensions than we can perceive. The sex-goddess/war-god personalities may be finger puppets manipulated by a single entity who finds the alternate identities useful for her/his/its devious schemes.

This is speculative, but I bring it up because of the influence of both entities since the dawn of human history. Inanna/Ishtar (also known to us as "Astarte," "Aphrodite," and "Venus," among others) was one of the most prominent and powerful entities of ancient Mesopotamia. As the Queen of Heaven, this entity has deceived millions for at least five thousand years—down to the present day, in fact, in the form of the cult of the Virgin Mary.[339]

Meanwhile, the war-god Attar has shed blood around the world through his followers in what will become the world's largest religion

---

338. C. Houtman, "Queen of Heaven." In K. van der Toorn, B. Becking, & P. W. van der Horst (Eds.), *Dictionary of Deities and Demons in the Bible (2nd extensively rev. ed.)*. (Leiden; Boston; Köln; Grand Rapids, MI; Cambridge: Brill; Eerdmans, 1999), p. 678.

339. Ibid., p. 679.

within the next fifty years, Islam.[340] During Muhammad's rise to power in the early seventh century, there were only three gods in Arabia who'd survived from ancient Mesopotamia—the astral triad of sun, moon, and Venus. That included the male war-god, Attar, who was the only one of the more than one hundred deities attested in southern Arabia (modern Yemen and Oman) worshiped by every tribe in the region.[341]

I argued in my book *Bad Moon Rising* that Allah of the Muslims is not a single entity but a collective or corporation made up of the old Mesopotamian gods who'd been caught offguard by the resurrection of Jesus—namely, El or Enlil (from Arabic *al-ilah*, "'the' god"); Hadad, the storm-god (Baal in the Bible, but better known as Satan);[342] Inanna/Ishtar; Chemosh/Attar, the war-god; Sîn, the moon-god; Shamash, the sun-god; and Resheph, the plague-god called Nergal in Babylon and Apollo by the Greeks and Romans.

Of that group, only El (Milcom/Molech) is in the abyss right now. The others were among the later group of "seventy" *bene ha'elohim* placed over the nations after Babel. That suggests that the old god still has influence with the second wave of rebellious *elohim*. It's my belief that the god called El, Enlil, Dagan, Kumarbi, or simply "king" (Molech/Milcom) is tremendously powerful, maybe even more powerful than Satan—that is, when he's not chained up in the abyss.

---

340. "The Changing Global Religious Landscape." Pew Research Center, April 5, 2017. https://www.pewforum.org/2017/04/05/the-changing-global-religious-landscape/, retrieved 3/25/21.

341. D. T. Potts, "The Arabian Peninsula, 600 BCE to 600 CE." *Coinage of the Caravan Kingdoms* (New York: American Numismatic Society, 2010), p. 42.

342. Jesus specifically identifies Baal (Beelzebul = "Baal the prince") as Satan in Matthew 12:22–26, and names Pergamum as the place "where Satan dwells" in Revelation 2:13. That's a reference to the Great Altar of Zeus, who was the Greek form of Baal.

Chapter Twenty

GOLIATH'S SKULL

We know that Solomon set up places of worship to Milcom (El/ Enlil, etc.), Astarte (Ishtar/Inanna), and Chemosh (Attar/Ares/ Mars) on the Mount of Olives. But it appears that pagan cult sites existed on that mountain before Solomon, and maybe even before David:

> But David went up the ascent of the Mount of Olives, weeping as he went, barefoot and with his head covered. And all the people who were with him covered their heads, and they went up, weeping as they went. [...]
>
> While David was coming to the summit, **where God was worshiped**, behold, Hushai the Archite came to meet him with his coat torn and dirt on his head. (2 Samuel 15:30, 32; emphasis added)

The phrase "where God was worshiped" (Hebrew *asher-yishtakhaveh sham l'elohim*) can also mean "where **the gods** were worshiped." Translators assume that *elohim* in 2 Samuel 15:32 refers to Yahweh, but neither the text nor the context excludes the possibility of pagan worship on the summit of the Mount of Olives. Nothing in 1 Kings 11, the story of Solomon building the high places, suggests that places of worship formerly dedicated to Yahweh were defiled or destroyed to make room for Astarte, Chemosh, and Milcom. With Solomon's new Temple just across the Kidron Valley on Mount Moriah, why would there be?

The Ark of the Covenant had been in the City of David since early in David's reign (see 2 Samuel 6), and the tabernacle was in the city of Gibeon, five miles northwest of Jerusalem, where it remained until Solomon built the Temple. It seems more likely that Yahweh worship would have been centered in the City of David or on Mount Moriah, the site of Araunah's threshing-floor, than on the Mount of Olives.

This leads to some intriguing observations about the life of Jesus. He met Mary, Martha, and their brother Lazarus at the village of Bethany on the southeast slope of the Mount of Olives. It was there that he raised Lazarus from the dead,[343] which certainly got the attention of the spirit realm. As we noted in an earlier chapter, the Rephaim Texts from Ugarit appear to be a necromancy ritual that summoned the demonic spirits of the Nephilim to the summit of Mount Hermon, the threshing-floor of El (Milcom), to be "revivified" after dawn of the third day. Greek and Roman funeral rites in the time of Jesus, which may date back to older practices from the eastern Mediterranean (cf. Isaiah 65:4), included a ritual meal on the third day after death.

John notes that when Jesus learned of Lazarus' illness, He deliberately "stayed two days longer in the place where he was" so that He arrived at Bethany when "Lazarus had already been in the tomb four days."[344] This was not a coincidence. Jesus deliberately waited so He could glorify God by raising his friend from the dead on the *fourth* day!

When Jesus returned to Jerusalem for the Passover from Caesarea Philippi and the Transfiguration on Mount Hermon, He approached Jerusalem from the east. The Jews of Jesus' day avoided Samaria, so in coming from the north He would have crossed over the Jordan to Perea, the part of Herod's kingdom east of the Jordan River between the Sea of

---

343. John 11:1–44.
344. John 11:6, 17.

Galilee and the Dead Sea, and then crossed back over the river at Jericho. As they neared Jerusalem, Jesus sent two disciples into Bethphage, a village on the eastern slope of the Mount of Olives, to obtain a donkey and her colt:

> "If anyone says anything to you, you shall say, 'The Lord needs them,' and he will send them at once." This took place to fulfill what was spoken by the prophet, saying,
>   "Say to the daughter of Zion,
>   'Behold, your king is coming to you,
>   humble, and mounted on a donkey,
>   on a colt, the foal of a beast of burden.'" (Matthew 21:3–5)

The other Gospels mention only the colt, but the meaning of his gesture was clear in that time and place: Jesus signaled to all who watched, human and divine, that He was the true and rightful king.

From our perspective, horses are the appropriate ride for kings, noble steeds worthy of their riders' royal image. But that's us reading our modern worldview backwards into the Bible. Jesus' entry into Jerusalem on the back of a donkey was a clear message to the principalities and powers behind the people who'd dominated the culture of the Near East since the time of the patriarchs, the Amorites.

Amorite kings never rode horses. In their world, as odd as it seems to us, donkeys were the symbol of royalty. Horses were for soldiers, who were usually commoners. Around the time of Isaac and Jacob, an Amorite official in the kingdom of Mari, which was based on the Euphrates River near the modern border between Syria and Iraq, offered some political advice to his king, Zimri-Lim:

> "May my lord honor his kingship. Since you are the king of Hanean (tribesmen), and also are the king of the Amorites, may my lord not ride horses; instead, he ought to ride a chariot or mules, so that he could honor his kingship." Therefore, when

Christ entered Jerusalem on a donkey, the population, as well
as the authorities, knew how to read the symbolism at stake
(Matthew 21).[345]

The Bible tells us that Jesus will ride a white horse when He returns,
but that's because He comes back as a soldier, and He'll be leading the
greatest army in the history of the universe.

From His triumphal entry, Jesus proceeded to the Temple Mount
and chased the moneychangers from the Temple, which, despite being
rebuilt by the wicked King Herod, was still His Father's house. After the
events of that day, which no doubt had all of Jerusalem talking, Jesus
returned to the Mount of Olives and lodged at the village of Bethany.

It was during the week between the Triumphal Entry and His arrest
that Jesus shared key information with His disciples about the last days.
The Olivet Discourse, recorded in Matthew 24 and 25, Mark 13, and
Luke 21, contains Jesus' most detailed descriptions of the signs of the
end times and His return. Matthew and Mark specify that these prophecies were delivered on the Mount of Olives.

The Gospel accounts agree that after the Last Supper, Jesus crossed
the Kidron from Jerusalem to Gethsemane, a garden at the foot of the
Mount of Olives within sight of the Temple Mount. It was there that He
was betrayed by Judas to the authorities. And, contrary to tradition, it
was also there that our Lord was crucified. The Church of the Holy Sepulchre in Jerusalem is historic, to be sure, but it's in the wrong place. The
church was established on the site endorsed by Helena, the mother of
Constantine, who'd legalized the Christian faith in the Roman Empire
about fifteen years before her pilgrimage to the Holy Land between AD
326 and 328. Before Helena's visit, there'd been no connection between
the Crucifixion and the site, which is in the Christian Quarter of the
Old City of Jerusalem.

---

345. Jack M. Sasson, "Thoughts of Zimri-Lim," *Biblical Archaeologist*, June
1984, pp. 118–119.

However, John 19:20 tells us that the site was "near the city"—in other words, outside the walls—and that's confirmed by Hebrews 13:12, which says that Jesus was executed "outside the gate." Further, the sign placed by Pilate on the cross, "Jesus of Nazareth, the King of the Jews,"[346] was meant to be seen by the thousands of pilgrims coming to Jerusalem for the Passover. The Church of the Holy Sepulchre is on the site of a temple to Venus built in the second century AD in an unused quarry—which, since it was below ground level (as you'd expect for a quarry), was not very visible. Nor was it on a hill, which is at least implied by the name of the Crucifixion site, Golgotha, Aramaic for "Place of a Skull."

The English rendering doesn't quite capture the sense of the name. The Greek word *kraniou* more accurately describes the top of the head, the brain pan, rather than the entire skull.[347] Those who've searched for a creepy-looking hill with features resembling empty eye sockets and nasal cavity followed a dead-end trail.

Not only does the Mount of Olives better fit the description of Golgotha, a little-known first-century Roman law confirms it as the site of the Crucifixion: Enemies of the state sentenced to be crucified were to be executed at the scene of their crime, and if that wasn't possible, at the place of their capture.[348] Although the exact location of the Garden of Gethsemane is unknown, eyewitnesses agree that it was on the Mount of Olives, and Jesus fit the legal definition of an enemy of the state, at least for the purposes of the Sanhedrin.

The case for identifying the Mount of Olives as the Crucifixion site was perhaps made first by Dr. N. F. Hutchinson for the *Palestine Exploration Fund Quarterly* in 1870 and 1873. Hutchinson presented

---

346. John 19:19.

347. "κρανίον." Wiktionary, https://en.wiktionary.org/wiki/κρανίον#Ancient_Greek, retrieved 3/30/21.

348. Ernest L. Martin, *Secrets of Golgotha: The Lost History of Jesus' Crucifixion* (Portland, OR: Associates for Scriptural Knowledge, 1996), pp. 73–74.

compelling arguments in his 1873 article that the Crucifixion was visible from only one of the approaches to Jerusalem in the first century, the road from Jericho through Bethany that wound around the Mount of Olives and entered the city from the east by the Fish Gate.[349]

There is one more bit of evidence: As the Gospels note, Golgotha was the "Place of a Skull." Our friend, messianic Rabbi Zev Porat, coauthor of *The Rabbi, the Secret Message, and the Identity of Messiah*, believes that the name refers to a specific skull—the head of Goliath, which David brought to Jerusalem,[350] and is perhaps buried on the Mount of Olives. Golgotha, then, would be the place of Goliath's skull.

But there's another possible explanation for the name: The Scripture from 2 Samuel 15 we quoted above describes David's flight from Jerusalem to escape the rebel army led by his son Absalom. Verse 32 notes that David paused at the summit of the Mount of Olives. The Hebrew word translated "summit" is *rosh*, which means "head." So, 2 Samuel 15:32 literally reads, "When David was coming to '**the head**,' where God was [or, "the gods were"] worshiped…" In other words, Golgotha (and Calvary, which derives from the Latin word for "bald") may simply refer to the summit of the Mount of Olives, the most visible piece of ground for people arriving at the city from the east or those looking out across the Kidron Valley from the Temple Mount.

The Apostle John then adds this detail as to the temporary resting place of Christ:

> Now in the place where he was crucified there was a garden, and in the garden a new tomb in which no one had yet been laid. So because of the Jewish day of Preparation, since the tomb was close at hand, they laid Jesus there. (John 19:41–42)

---

349. N. F. Hutchinson, "Further Notes on Our Lord's Tomb." *Palestine Exploration Fund Quarterly Statement* 5.3 (July 1873), pp. 113–115.
350. 1 Samuel 17:54.

Understand what that means: Jesus spent the final week of His life living and teaching in two places—in the Temple and on the Mount of Olives, where almost a thousand years earlier Solomon had erected a high place for the "king-god," Milcom/Molech. Jesus' final night as a mortal on this earth was spent in prayer in a garden on that mountain, where He was arrested, and the following day crucified, died, and was buried.

From there, Christ descended into the abyss and "proclaimed to the spirits in prison."[351] Now, the meaning of this verse has been debated for two thousand years. On the surface, it appears that Jesus, as a spirit, "preached" (Greek *kēryssō*) to human spirits in hell. That is not what Peter meant. "Proclaimed" or "declared" is a better English translation for *kēryssō*. Jesus didn't preach; He straight up told the spirits, "This is how it's going to be." The context and grammar of the sentence make clear that the spirits He addressed weren't human:

> The NT never uses the word for "spirit" in an unqualified fashion to refer to the human soul. Therefore, the reference in 1 Peter 3:19 may point to nonhuman supernatural beings. This interpretation is strengthened when the passage is read in the context of Genesis 6–9 because of the reference to Noah and the flood in 1 Pet. 3:20. The flood reference also draws in the traditions of 1 Enoch, so the "spirits in prison" may have been understood to be the fallen angels or "sons of God" of Genesis 6:1–4.[352]

Jesus descended to the abyss to declare victory over the rebellious "sons of God," the Watchers, whose chief Shemihazah—under the names "Milcom," "Molech," and "El"—had been worshiped at the top

---

351. 1 Peter 3:19.
352. D. Mangum, "Interpreting First Peter 3:18–22." In *Faithlife Study Bible* (Bellingham, WA: Lexham Press, 2016).

of the Mount of Olives, and in the Valley of Hinnom at the foot of the mountain.

Then, to pour salt in their wounds, Christ rose from the dead at dawn of the third day on that mountain, reversing the centuries-old pagan ritual that summoned the Rephaim to El's mount of assembly, Hermon—from which no one in history has ever risen from the dead.

And if that wasn't enough, note the place of Christ's ascension:

And he led them out as far as Bethany, and lifting up his hands he blessed them. While he blessed them, he parted from them and was carried up into heaven. (Luke 24:50–51)

Bethany. Yes, Jesus Christ departed this world from the Mount of Olives.

We've covered a lot of material over the last six thousand or so words. To sum up:

- "Molech" is a deliberate twisting of the Semitic word for "king," *melek*, substituting vowels in the same way that Baal became *bosheth* ("shameful thing") and Astarte became *ashtoreth*.
- Molech was known as "Malik" as early as 2500 BC in northern Syria. Later, as "Milcom," he became the national god of Ammon. "Malik"/"Milcom" was a title or epithet meaning "king," connecting his identity to the father-god of the Hurrians, Kumarbi. Milcom was actually El, creator-god of the Amorites and Canaanites who was believed to live on Mount Hermon.
- Shortly after David established Jerusalem as the capital of Israel, his son Solomon built high places for Milcom, Chemosh, and Astarte on the Mount of Olives, which led Jewish religious leaders to call it the "Mount of Corruption," or "Mountain of the Destroyer."

- To complete His mission, Jesus ascended Mount Hermon for the Transfiguration and then traveled to Jerusalem. He spent the final week of His life living and preaching on the Mount of Olives, when He wasn't in Jerusalem teaching at the Temple. His decision to live on the Mount of Olives, rather than in the city, was, like climbing Mount Hermon, a deliberate act that sent a clear message to the spirit realm.

- Jesus was betrayed, crucified, and buried on the Mount of Olives. He descended to the abyss to "proclaim" to the "prisoners," the sons of God who'd been led by Shemihazah, the entity later known as "Kumarbi," "El," "Enlil," "Dagan," "Assur," and "Milcom."

- Jesus rose from His tomb on the Mount of Olives and, after forty days of teaching His disciples, He ascended to heaven from the Mount of Olives.

One final note to close out this chapter. Jesus has promised to put an exclamation point on His message to Molech:

Behold, a day is coming for the LORD, when the spoil taken from you will be divided in your midst. For I will gather all the nations against Jerusalem to battle, and the city shall be taken and the houses plundered and the women raped. Half of the city shall go out into exile, but the rest of the people shall not be cut off from the city. Then the LORD will go out and fight against those nations as when he fights on a day of battle. On that day his feet shall stand on the Mount of Olives that lies before Jerusalem on the east, and the Mount of Olives shall be split in two from east to west by a very wide valley, so that one half of the Mount shall move northward, and the other half southward. (Zechariah 14:1–4)

The final battle of the ages, Armageddon, will end when Jesus lands on the Mount of Olives and splits it in two.

Could the message be any clearer?

Chapter Twenty-One

KRONOS

The Greeks and Romans shared a good deal of their religion. The names were different, with the notable exception of Apollo, but the gods were pretty much the same. Zeus of the Greeks was Jupiter of the Romans. Likewise, Aphrodite was Venus, Ares was Mars, Hera was Juno, Hephaestus was Vulcan, and so on.

Similarly, Kronos, king of the Titans, was the equivalent of the old god of the Romans, Saturn. In both Roman and Greek religion, this was the deity who ruled the earth during a long-ago Golden Age, when humanity lived like gods, free from toil and care. Both were overthrown by their son, the storm-god, and confined to the netherworld. To the Greeks, this was Tartarus, a place as far below Hades as the earth is below heaven; in Roman myth, Jupiter put Saturn in chains to ensure that he didn't overeat. It was believed that Saturn consumed the passing days, months, and years, and it would have been a problem if the old god had turned his voracious appetite to eating the present and future as well.

Kronos' family relations were strained, to say the least. You've probably heard the story: The primordial couple, Ouranos (Sky) and Gaia (Earth), gave birth to the first generation of gods, the Titans, and some monstrous siblings—Argus, a giant with a hundred eyes, the Cyclopes, giants with only one eye, and the Hecatoncheires, giants with a hundred arms and legs. However, the passion of Ouranos was such, the story goes, that the Titans were trapped inside Gaia, unable to escape her womb. With the encouragement of his mother, Kronos led his siblings in a rebellion and castrated his father with an adamantine sickle.

You remember that this is similar to the story of the Hurrian father-god, Kumarbi, who likewise rebelled against his sky-god father, Anu (although Kumarbi performed the castration with his teeth). Like Kumarbi, Kronos was also eventually consigned to the underworld by his son, the storm-god. The similarities between the stories are detailed in an earlier chapter, but it's worth repeating that they are too many and too close to be coincidence. In short, the Greeks got the story from the Hurrians and/or the Hittites they encountered, probably in western or southern Anatolia (Turkey). Since we know Hittites, Hurrians (Horites) and Greeks (Hivites) were also in Canaan together during the Old Testament period at least through the time of David and Solomon, there were plenty of opportunities for religious and cultural cross-pollination between Mesopotamia and the Aegean over the centuries.

The dysfunctional family relations of Kronos didn't end with his parents. Because of a warning from Ouranos and Gaia that he was doomed to be overthrown by one of his children, Kronos devised a cunning plan:

> But Rhea was subject in love to Cronos and bore splendid children, Hestia, Demeter, and gold-shod Hera and strong Hades, pitiless in heart, who dwells under the earth, and the loud-crashing Earth-Shaker [Poseidon], and wise Zeus, father of gods and men, by whose thunder the wide earth is shaken. These great Cronos swallowed as each came forth from the womb to his mother's knees with this intent, that no other of the proud sons of Heaven should hold the kingly office amongst the deathless gods. For he learned from Earth and starry Heaven that he was destined to be overcome by his own son, strong though he was, through the contriving of great Zeus. Therefore he kept no blind

outlook, but watched and swallowed down his children: and unceasing grief seized Rhea.[353]

You'd think Rhea would have noticed a pattern after Kronos swallowed their first two or three kids, but it wasn't until she was pregnant with their youngest, Zeus, that she tried to save one. With the help of Gaia, Zeus was born and hidden away in a cave on Mount Ida in Crete, where his existence was concealed by a group of *daimones* ("spirits") called the Kouretes who danced and raised a ruckus with clashing shields and spears to drown out the sound of the infant Zeus' cries. When he reached maturity, he tricked Kronos into vomiting up his siblings and then led them in a long and bitter war against the Titans, which eventually ended with Zeus supplanting his father as king of the pantheon. Kronos and the Titans were banished to Tartarus, precisely where the "sons of God" from Genesis 6 are confined, according to the Apostle Peter.

Jewish religious scholars understood the connection between the Titans and the Watchers—and, by extension, the demigods of the Greeks and the Nephilim. Seventy-two Jewish scholars in the fourth century BC produced a version of the Hebrew Scriptures in Koine Greek at the direction of Ptolemy II, the Greek king who inherited Egypt after the breakup of Alexander the Great's empire. Ptolemy apparently wanted to add the Torah to the famous library of Alexandria in a language his constituents could understand.

We've already showed the connection between the Titans and the sons of God of Genesis 6, the sinful angels mentioned by Peter and Jude. The references in the Septuagint, however, are more obvious.

---

353. Hesiod, *The Homeric Hymns and Homerica with an English Translation by Hugh G. Evelyn-White*: *Theogony* (Medford, MA: Cambridge, MA., Harvard University Press; London, William Heinemann Ltd., 1914).

And the foreigners heard that David had been anointed king
over Israel. And all the foreigners went up to seek David. And
David heard and went down to the stronghold. And the foreigners gathered and met in the Valley of the Rephaim [*Titânes*]....

And the foreigners still continued to go up and meet in the
Valley of the Rephaim [*Titânes*]. (2 Samuel 5:17–18; 22, Lexham English Septuagint [LES])

References to the Valley of Rephaim/Titans also occur in 2 Samuel 23:13 and 1 Chronicles 11:15. Then there are references that are
less obvious because the Hebrew word *rephaim* is usually translated as
"shades" or "the dead" in our English Bibles:

Proverbs 21:16	Proverbs 21:16, LES
One who wanders from the way of good sense will rest in the assembly of the dead [*rephaim*].	A man who is misled from the way of righteousness will sleep in the congregation of the giants [*gigánton*].
Job 26:5	Job 26:5, LES
The dead [*rephaim*] tremble under the waters and their inhabitants.	Are not giants [*gígantes*] brought forth from beneath the water and its neighbors?
Proverbs 2:18	Proverbs 2:18, LES
for her house sinks down to death, and her paths to the departed [*rephaim*].	for she has set her house close by death and her paths close by Hades with the shades [*gigenón*, "Earth-born" = Titans, children of Gaia].

Another mention of the Titans occurs in the apocryphal Book of Judith:

> For their mighty one did not fall by the hands of the young men,nor did the sons of the Titans strike him down, nor did tall gants set upon him; but Judith daughter of Merari with the beauty of her countenance undid him. (Judith 16:3–6, NRSV)

The oldest text of Judith available to us today is from the Septuagint, so we don't know the book's original language for certain.[354] It may have been composed in Greek, since the earliest Hebrew copy is from the Middle Ages. The point is that by the time Greeks conquered the lands of the Bible more than three hundred years before the birth of Jesus, Jewish religious scholars and scribes had no problem directly linking the Titans to the Rephaim (i.e., the Nephilim) and describing them as giants. Jewish scholars recognized in Greek myths their own stories of the Watchers, the Nephilim, and the rebel gods who'd rejected the authority of the Creator, Yahweh. And the early church universally accepted these teachings as truth:

> But the angels transgressed this appointment. and were captivated by love of women, and begat children who are those that are called demons;
> —Justin Martyr, *Second Apology* V[355]

---

354. Deborah Levine Gera, "The Jewish Textual Traditions." In K. Brine, E. Ciletti & H. Lähnemann (Eds.), *The Sword of Judith: Judith Studies Across the Disciplines* (Cambridge: Open Book Publishers, 2010), pp. 23–39. Web. http://books.openedition.org/obp/986>, retrieved 4/5/21.

355. http://www.earlychristianwritings.com/text/justinmartyr-secondapology. html, retrieved 4/5/21.

...in the days of Noah He justly brought on the deluge for the purpose of extinguishing that most infamous race of men then existent, who could not bring forth fruit to God, since the angels that sinned had commingled with them.

  —Irenaeus, *Against Heresies* IV, 36.4[356]

...these [angels] fell into impure love of virgins, and were subjugated by the flesh, and he became negligent and wicked in the management of the things entrusted to him. Of these lovers of virgins, therefore, were begotten those who are called giants.

  —Athenagoras of Athens, *A Plea for the Christians* 24[357]

In my opinion, however, it is certain wicked demons, and, so to speak, of the race of Titans or Giants, who have been guilty of impiety towards the true God, and towards the angels in heaven, and who have fallen from it, and who haunt the denser parts of bodies, and frequent unclean places upon earth...

  —Origen, *Against Celsus* 4.92[358]

But from their unhallowed intercourse spurious men sprang, much greater in stature than ordinary men, whom they afterwards called giants; not those dragon-footed giants who waged war against God, as those blasphemous myths of the Greeks do sing, but wild in manners, and greater than men in size, inasmuch as they were sprung of angels; yet less than angels, as they were born of women.

  —Pseudo Clement, *Homily* 8:15[359]

---

356. https://www.newadvent.org/fathers/0103436.htm, retrieved 4/5/21.

357. https://www.newadvent.org/fathers/0205.htm, retrieved 4/5/21.

358. https://www.newadvent.org/fathers/04164.htm, retrieved 4/5/21.

359. https://www.newadvent.org/fathers/080808.htm, retrieved 4/5/21.

Plutarch…says that the mythical narratives told as concerning gods are certain tales about daemons, and the deeds of Giants and Titans celebrated in song among the Greeks are also stories about daemons, intended to suggest a new phase of thought.

Of this kind then perhaps were the statements in the Sacred Scripture concerning the giants before the Flood, and those concerning their progenitors, of whom it is said, "And when the angels of God saw the daughters of men that they were fair, they took unto them wives of all that they chose," and of these were born "the giants the men of renown which were of old."

For one might say that these daemons are those giants, and that their spirits have been deified by the subsequent generations of men, and that their battles, and their quarrels among themselves, and their wars are the subjects of these legends that are told as of gods.

—Eusebius, *Preparation for the Gospel* 5.4[360]

You get the idea. The preachers, teachers, and theologians of the early Christian church were nearly unanimous in the belief that the gods of the Greeks and Romans were not imaginary, as most of us modern Christians assume. They, like the Jewish scholars a few hundred years earlier, understood that the Olympians, Titans, Gigantes, heroes, and *daimones* of the pagans were supernatural beings called "angels," "Watchers," "sons of God," "Nephilim," "Rephaim," and "demons." In fact, the second-century theologian Irenaeus of Lyon, a student of Polycarp (who was a disciple of the Apostle John), connected the old gods of the Greeks to end-times prophecy:

Although certain as to the number of the name of Antichrist, yet we should come to no rash conclusions as to the name itself,

---

360. http://www.tertullian.org/fathers/eusebius_pe_05_book5.htm, retrieved 4/5/21.

because this number [666] is capable of being fitted to many names.... Teitan too, (TEITAN, the first syllable being written with the two Greek vowels ε and ι), among all the names which are found among us, is rather worthy of credit. For it has in itself the predicted number, and is composed of six letters, each syllable containing three letters; and [the word itself] is ancient, and removed from ordinary use; for among our kings we find none bearing this name Titan, nor have any of the idols which are worshipped in public among the Greeks and barbarians this appellation. Among many persons, too, this name is accounted divine, so that even the sun is termed "Titan" by those who do now possess [the rule]. This word, too, contains a certain outward appearance of vengeance, and of one inflicting merited punishment because he (Antichrist) pretends that he vindicates the oppressed. And besides this, it is an ancient name, one worthy of credit, of royal dignity, and still further, a name belonging to a tyrant. Inasmuch, then, as this name "Titan" has so much to recommend it, there is a strong degree of probability, that from among the many [names suggested], we infer, that perchance he who is to come shall be called "Titan."[361]

To his credit, Irenaeus added a warning that we shouldn't obsess over deciphering the meaning of "666," because "if it were necessary that his name should be distinctly revealed in this present time, it would have been announced by him who beheld the apocalyptic vision."[362]

In other words, if we were supposed to know the identity of the Antichrist, God would have revealed it to John and told him to let us know.

---

361. Irenaeus, *Against Heresies* V.30. https://www.newadvent.org/fathers/0103530.htm, retrieved 4/6/21.
362. Ibid.

The Greeks believed that the blood of the castrated sky-god Oura-nos impregnated Mother Earth, Gaia, who gave birth to the Gigantes, a tribe of a hundred giants usually depicted with serpents' tails in place of legs. At Gaia's urging, the Gigantes waged war against the Olympi-ans and were destroyed. It's tempting to connect the war between the Olympians and the Titans, called the "Titanomachy," and the later the "Gigantomachy," with God's response to the sins of the Watchers (the Titans) and the Nephilim (the Gigantes). The Greeks and Romans remembered these conflicts as epic struggles between divine combatants that ended with the losing side buried deep below the surface of the earth. (Thrashing giants were believed to be the cause of active volcanoes like Etna and Vesuvius.)[363]

Likewise, the Watchers followed their time on the earth chained in the netherworld while the Nephilim were drowned in the Flood—inglorious endings for the king-god and his children, the mighty men who were of old.

---

363. "Gigantes." Theoi Project, https://www.theoi.com/Gigante/Gigantes.html, retrieved 4/5/21.

Chapter Twenty-Two

REMEMBER THE TITANS!

The most famous Roman religious festival honored the god whose best-remembered character trait was eating his children. But, like the god for which it was named, the Saturnalia was adapted from an older version known to the Greeks.

The Kronia is first recorded in Ionia, the central part of western Anatolia (modern Turkey) in the eighth century BC, a little before the time of the prophet Isaiah.[364] From there, the celebration spread to Athens and the island of Rhodes,[365] ultimately making its way westward to Rome, shifting over time from midsummer to the winter solstice. Both festivals were a time of merriment and abandoning social norms, with gambling, gift-giving, suspension of normal business, and the reversal of roles by slaves and their masters.[366]

---

364. Jan N. Bremmer, "Remember the Titans!" In C. Auffarth and L. Stuckenbruck (eds.), *The Fall of the Angels* (Leiden; Boston: Brill, 2004), pp. 43–44.

365. Ibid., p. 44.

366. John F. Miller, "Roman Festivals," in *The Oxford Encyclopedia of Ancient Greece and Rome* (Oxford University Press, 2010), p. 172.

But don't let the annual party fool you. The god has a dark side. It's well documented that both Saturn and Kronos accepted human sacrifices.

Condemned prisoners were sacrificed to Kronos at Rhodes;[367] children were offered to the god at Crete;[368] and, as Baal Hammon, the god was offered sacrifices of Phoenician children well into the Christian era.[369] Perhaps most horrifying of all is the description of the first-century philosopher Plutarch.

[Carthaginians] offered up their own children, and those who had no children would buy little ones from poor people and cut their throats as if they were so many lambs or young birds; meanwhile the mother stood by without a tear or moan; but should she utter a single moan or let fall a single tear, she had to forfeit the money, and her child was sacrificed nevertheless; and the whole area before the statue was filled with a loud noise of flutes and drums took the cries of wailing should not reach the ears of the people.[370]

---

367. Porphyry, *On Abstinence from Animal Food*, 2.54 (http://www.tertullian. org/fathers/porphyry_abstinence_02_book2.htm, retrieved 6/15/19).

368. Ibid., 2.56.

369. Diodorus Siculus, *Library of World History* 13.86.3; 20.14.6 (http:// penelope.uchicago.edu/Thayer/E/Roman/Texts/Diodorus_Siculus/ home.html, retrieved 6/15/19); also Tertullian, *Apologeticus* 9.22 (http://www.tertullian.org/articles/mayor_apologeticum/mayor_ apologeticum_07translation.htm, retrieved 6/15/19).

370. Plutarch, *On Superstition* 13.4 (http://penelope.uchicago.edu/Thayer/E/ Roman/Texts/Plutarch/Moralia/De_superstitione*.html, retrieved 4/7/21).

This reputation followed Kronos down the centuries. As late as the Roman Imperial period (27 BC to about AD 400), a Greek inscription called him Κρόνου Τεκνοφάγου: "Kronos Child-eater."[371]

But we can't lay the blame for the cult of Kronos entirely on the Greeks. As you've already learned, this god is much older than Greek civilization, and he originated farther east, in northern Mesopotamia. Evidence suggests that the Kronia was ancient by the time the Greeks established themselves as a world power.

A text discovered in 1983 at the site of the capital city of the Hittite kingdom, Hattuša, dated to about 1400 BC, the time of the Israelite conquest of Canaan, describes a myth in which the king of the gods, the storm-god Teshub (Baal/Zeus/Jupiter by a different name) celebrates a ritual meal with the sun-goddess, Allani, and the "primeval gods" who'd been banished to the netherworld. These old gods were not just at the table; they sat in the place of honor at Teshub's right hand.

> The celebration of the temporary suspension of the cosmic order surely accompanied the temporary suspension of the social order on earth. In other words, the myth with the "primeval gods" will have been associated with a ritual of reversal between masters and slaves. Now the Titans were also called "the old gods," old and/or dumb people were insulted as Kronoi, and Attic comedy used expressions such as "older than Kronos" and "older than Kronos and the Titans." Evidently, the antiquity of this divine generation had become proverbial at a relatively early stage of the tradition. The Titans thus can be legitimately compared to the Hurrian "primeval" gods.[372]

---

371. Jan N. Bremmer, *Greek Religion and Culture, the Bible and the Ancient Near East* (Leiden; Boston: Brill, 2008), p. 84.

372. Bremmer, op. cit., p. 46.

The mention of the ancient Northern Syrian city of Ebla in the Hurrian tale suggests that the origin of the Kronia/Saturnalia is to be found there, in Syria.[373] This is consistent with a growing body of evidence that the cults of the Greek and Roman gods originated in Syria, Canaan, and Mesopotamia:

> [Martin L.] West drew attention to the conceptual similarity of the (Hittite) "former gods" (*karuilies siunes*) with the Titans, called Προτεροι Θεοι in *Theogony* 424, 486. Both groups were confined to the underworld (with the apparent exceptions of Atlas and Prometheus), and as Zeus banished the Titans thither, so Tešup [Teshub] banished the *karuilies siunes*, commonly twelve in number, like the Titans. They were in turn identified with the Mesopotamian Anunnaki. These were confined by Marduk to the underworld, or at least some of them were (half the six hundred, Enuma Elish vi 39–47, see 41–44), where they were ruled over variously by Dagan or Shamash.[374]

So, the earliest traces of Kronos are found in Mesopotamia, not Greece. Specifically, the trail leads to northwest Mesopotamia, in the area of the Mediterranean coast along the border between modern Syria and Turkey—precisely where we find the cults of El and the old god of the Hurrians, Kumarbi.

Scholar Amar Annus, who has done brilliant work tracing the Watchers back from Hebrew texts to older Mesopotamian sources, came to an astonishing conclusion when he dug into the origin of the name of the Titans. Annus notes first the existence of an ancient, and by the time of the judges in Israel, almost mythical Amorite tribe called the "Tidanu" or "Ditanu." (I told you we'd come back to these guys.) They had a bad reputation in Mesopotamia. There were considered uncivilized, warlike,

---

373. Ibid., p. 47.
374. Wyatt (2010), op. cit., p. 56.

and dangerous.[375] In fact, they were so threatening to the last Sumerian kings of Mesopotamia, the Third Dynasty of Ur, that around 2037 BC they began building a wall 175 miles long north of modern Baghdad specifically to keep the Tidanu away. We know this because the Sumerians named it *bàd martu muriq tidnim*,[376] which literally means "Amorite Wall Which Keeps the Tidnum [Tidanu] at a Distance."[377]

Annus notes that the name "*Ti/Di-ta/da-nu(m)*—most possibly 'large animal; aurochs; strong, wild bovide'—is the name of the eponymic tribe."[378] Now, if you were going to pick a totem animal to represent your tribe back in the day, the aurochs was a great choice. It's an extinct form of cattle from which modern domesticated breeds descend, and they were *huge*. Bulls stood about six feet at the shoulder, weighed about a ton, and had nasty horns that put a chill in a hunter's spine. Based on medieval art, a recommended tactic for hunting aurochs involved keeping a stout tree between the hunter and the animal. Aurochs were the largest land mammals in Europe until the last one died in 1627.[379]

The point is that the Ditanu/Tidanu, which apparently took the

375. Michael Heltzer, *The Suteans* (Naples: Instituto Universitario Orientale, 1981), p. 99.

376. Thorkild Jacobsen, *Cuneiform Texts in the National Museum, Copenhagen, Chiefly of Economical Contents* (Leiden: Brill, 1939), p. 7.

377. Walther Sallaberger, "From Urban Culture to Nomadism: A History of Upper Mesopotamia in the Late Third Millennium." In C. Kuzucuoğlu and C. Marro (eds.), *Sociétés humaines et changement climatique à la fin du troisième millénaire: une crise a-t-elle eu lieu en Haute Mésopotamie?* (Istanbul: Institut Français d'Études Anatoliennes-Georges Dumézil, 2007), pp. 444–445.

378. Annus (1999), op. cit., p. 19.

379. There's an active program to create a new breed similar to the aurochs to be released into the wild in Europe. Breeders hope to have a close match for the aurochs by 2025. Kieron Monks, "The Wild, Extinct Supercow Returning to Europe." CNN, Jan. 9, 2017. https://www.cnn.com/2017/01/09/world/auroch-rewilding/index.html, retrieved 4/6/21.

tribal name from *didānu or ditānu*, the Akkadian word for "aurochs," was linked to the Rephaim in ritual texts at Ugarit:

> Greatly exalted be Keret
> In the midst of the *rpum* [Rephaim] of the earth
> In the gathering of the assembly of the Ditanu.[380]

So, the Ditanu/Tidanu were connected to the Rephaim in mind and ritual among the ancient Amorites, who believed the Rephaim were the divinized ancestors of their kings. What's more, this assembly was summoned in a necromancy ritual for the coronation of Ugarit's last king, Ammurapi III.

> You are summoned, O Rephaim of the earth,
> You are invoked, O council of the Didanu!
> Ulkn, the Raphi', is summoned,
> Trmn, the Raphi', is summoned,
> Sdn-w-rdn is summoned,
> Ṭr 'llmn is summoned,
> the Rephaim of old are summoned!
> You are summoned, O Rephaim of the earth,
> You are invoked, O council of the Didanu![381]

This council or assembly was more than a group of honored forefathers, like the framers of the Constitution. One text from Ugarit makes reference to ritual offerings for the temple of Didanu,[382] and temples owed sacrifices are typically devoted to gods. Between the time of Abra-

---

380. Ugaritic text KTU 1.15. III, 13–15, cited by Annus, op. cit.

381. KTU 1.161, in Wyatt (2002), op. cit., p. 210.

382. Jordi Vidal, "The Origins of the Last Ugaritic Dynasty." *Altorientalishce Forschungen* 33 (2006), p. 168.

ham, around 2000 BC, and the time of the judges, circa 1200 BC, the Tidanu/Ditanu were transformed from a scary tribe of Amorites named for a giant wild bull into divine beings connected to the Rephaim, who likewise disappeared from the earth (in physical form) during that period.[383]

And—here's the interesting bit—the Tidanu/Ditanu are the origin of the name of the bad old gods of the Greeks:

> Then it may not be overbold to assume that the Greek *Titanes* originates from the name of the semi-mythical warrior-tribe (in Ugarit) *tdn*—mythically related to the *Rpum* in the Ugarit, and once actually tied together with Biblical Rephaim in II Samuel 5:18–22, where we have in some manuscripts Hebrew *rpʾm* rendered into LXX as *Titanes*.[384]

At the risk of sounding like a TV pitchman: But wait—there's more! The name of the Titan king, Kronos, probably has a similar origin:

> The bovid sense of the form Ditanu/Didanu is particularly intriguing in view of other tauromorph elements in the tradition. Thus, the prominent Titan Kronos was later identified with El, who is given the epithet *tr*, "Bull", in Ugaritic and biblical literature. Apart from this explicit allusion, we may well ask whether the name El, (Akkadian and Ugaritic ilu) does not already itself have a bovine sense.... Does it perhaps mean "Bull", (perhaps more generically "male animal"), so that the epithetal title *tr* is in effect a redundant gloss on it?...

383. Og of Bashan, defeated by the Israelites around 1406 BC, was described in the Bible as the last of the remnant of the Rephaim (Deuteronomy 3:11).
384. Annus (1999), op. cit., p. 20.

Furthermore, the name Kronos may well carry the same nuance, since it may be construed as referring to bovine horns (Akkadian, Ugaritic *qarnu*, Hebrew *qeren*), which feature prominently in divine iconography in the Near East.[385]

In other words, the name "Kronos" may derive from a Semitic word that essentially means "Horned One." And in this name, we may have discovered a basis for the artistic depictions of devils and demons through the ages as horned entities at home in the underworld.

This fits with the depiction of deities in Mesopotamia. The gods of Sumer were always shown wearing helmets with multiple sets of horns. The *lamassu* of Assyria looked like winged bulls with human heads and lion's feet. And when we compare the descriptions of the cherubim in Ezekiel 1 and Ezekiel 10, we realize that the face of the cherub is, in fact, the face of an ox—or an aurochs.

The veneration of the Tidanu/Ditanu/Titans and their demonic offspring, the Rephaim, stretches at least as far back as the time of Isaac and Jacob. A bone talisman dated to about 1750 BC, found in a royal tomb at Ebla in northern Syria, depicts a scene that suggests three ranks in the hierarchy of the afterlife: A lower level for the human dead, a top level inhabited by the gods, and a middle level occupied by entities that probably represent Rephaim or the Eblaite equivalent.[386] It's been suggested by scholars who have tried to interpret the symbols on the artifact that the item was a guide to the spirit of the dead king on how to attain status as one of the venerated dead.

But why would the Greeks choose the name of an Amorite tribe for the old gods imprisoned in Tartarus? Was that tribe literally descended

---

385. Wyatt (2010), op. cit., pp. 54–55.

386. Andrea Polcaro, "The Bone Talisman and the Ideology of Ancestors in Old Syrian Ebla: Tradition and Innovation in the Royal Funerary Ritual Iconography." In P. Matthiae (ed.), *Studia Eblaitica* (Wiesbaden: Harrassowitz Verlag, 2015), pp. 179–204.

from the rebellious "sons of God" in Genesis 6? In other words, were the Tidanu/Ditanu literally Nephilim?

Probably not. The Nephilim were destroyed in the Flood. Their spirits survived to become demons, but we don't believe there is Nephilim DNA floating around inside humans today. (Thank God. Their demonic spirits cause enough trouble as it is.)

What's clear are the connections between the religions of the ancient Amorites, the Hurrians and Hittites who lived to the north of Mesopotamia, and the Greeks of the classical era. It's not surprising that scholars are shifting away from the consensus view of a hundred years ago that Greco-Roman religion developed from prehistoric Indo-Europeans. Modern archaeology makes it more obvious with each passing year that the religion of Greece and Rome originated with the people of the Near East.

The biggest change regarding the relationship between humanity and the "former gods" was that, by the time the Greeks emerged onto the world stage, Kronos was the only one of the old gods who received any kind of worship. His brothers and sisters had small roles in the Greek cosmology, but Kronos was the only one with official rites.

This is a little odd, since the assembly, or council, of the Ditanu had its own temple at Ugarit as late as the time of the judges. It seems that as the centuries rolled by, the only one of the spirits in the abyss who still commanded any respect was their leader.

Since the Titans can be identified as the Watchers who defied their Creator in the distant past on Mount Hermon, then the Amorites worshiped those beings long after the Flood had destroyed their children, the Nephilim. Under the influence of the demon spirits of the Nephilim, these descendants of Canaan, son of Ham,[387] terrorized the ancient Near East from before the time of Abraham until the time of David, when the soldiers of Israel finally wiped out the Philistine "Sons of the Rapha."

---

387. Genesis 10:16.

Identifying the Titans as the Watchers who swore an oath on Mount Hermon is consistent with evidence from the myths of later civilizations. Textual evidence from ancient Mesopotamia identifies Kronos as the Phoenician Baal Hammon, and the earlier Mesopotamian deities Kumarbi (Hurrians), El (Canaan), Dagan (Amorites and Philistines), Assur (Assyria), and Enlil (Akkad and Sumer). All of them, from Kumarbi to Enlil, have their origins in northwest Syria or southeast Turkey, in an area generally bounded on the south by Jebel Bishri in northeast Syria and the Amanus mountains in southern Turkey. And that's precisely the region that eventually produced the Amorites and the tribe from which the Amorite kings of Babylon claimed descent, the Tidanu/Ditanu, which apparently took the name of the old gods called "Titans" by the later Greeks. In fact, one of the mountain peaks in the Bishri range northeast of Palmyra is called "Jebel Diddi," which may preserve the name of the ancient Amorite tribe.[388]

After the Flood, spirits in the vicinity of modern-day Aleppo led a group of Amorites to believe a twisted version of history—that the ancestors of this tribe had been demigods, "mighty men who were of old," and that the old gods were still available to serve if only the Amorites pledged their worship and made regular sacrifices to them. Over time, as the influence of these old gods spread westward through the lands of the Hurrians and Hittites, they were adopted into the religion of the Greeks as the Titans, a name that reflects the bull-like appearance of these entities, who may be, like the divine rebel from Eden, rebellious cherubim who thought they could overthrow their Creator.

In fact, this may be additional evidence that the "horned one," Kronos/Shemihazah, was the guardian cherub in Eden before he dared to try establishing his own kingdom on earth.

---

388. Daniel Bodi, "Is There a Connection Between the Amorites and the Arameans?" *Aram* 26:1 & 2 (Oxford: Aram Publishing, 2014), p. 385.

Even after his ejection from the mountain of God, Kronos has continued to influence the world. To this day, one can make the case that child sacrifice, which has become an industry, is a sanitized version of the ancient worship of a dark god who sits in Tartarus, waiting for the time to emerge and claim what he believes is rightfully his—the very throne of God.

Chapter Twenty-Three

BAAL HAMMON

The Phoenicians are remembered as the sailors *par excellence* of late antiquity, descendants of the Amorites who spread out from the city of Tyre to establish colonies all around the Mediterranean. Their ships circumnavigated Africa, reached Britain, and may even have traveled as far as the Americas. Less well known to us today, however, is that the Phoenicians, in the service of their chief god Baal Hammon, continued the horrific practice of child sacrifice into the Christian era.

According to Diodorus Siculus, a Greek historian of the first century, there was even a black-market trade in children to sacrifice to the god:

> In former times they (the Carthaginians) had been accustomed to sacrifice to this god the noblest of their sons, but more recently, secretly buying and nurturing children, they had sent these to the sacrifice.[389]

Diodorus identified the god of Carthage as "Kronos," king of the Titans. The Romans knew him as "Saturn," but the Carthaginians

---

389. Diodorus Siculus, *The Library of History* XX:xiv.

called him "Baal Hammon." Given that you've made it this far into this book, you won't be surprised to learn that this entity was also known as the Canaanite creator-god, "El."

> There is now overwhelming evidence identifying *B'l Hmn* of Zincirli and *B'l Hmn* of the western Punic colonies with Canaanite 'El. As a matter of fact, both the epithets *B'l Hmn* and *Tnt* (his consort) survived only on the peripheries of the spread of Canaanite culture, a mark of archaism comparable to the survival of linguistic archaism at the frontiers of the spread of a family of languages.
>
> Philo Byblius, and other classical sources, and inscriptions in Greek and Latin all establish the formula that *B'l Hmn* on the one hand, and *'El* on the other, are Greek *Kronos*, Latin *Saturnus*. These equations have long been known, and all new data confirm the ancient. Moreover, we now perceive the significance of the epithets *gerontis* used of the Kronos of Gadir (Cadiz), *senex* used of Saturnus of New Carthage, and, indeed, of the epithet *saeculo [frugifero]* used of the African Saturnus. They reproduce 'El's appellation *'ôlām*, "the Ancient One."[390]

It's no coincidence that this epithet of El is similar to one you've heard for Yahweh, "Ancient of Days." Skeptics take this as evidence that Yahweh *was* El, and the Hebrews simply changed his name and adopted his cult. We disagree; Yahweh and El are separate and distinct.

The connection between the epithets of Kronos, Saturn, and El, all variations on "old," "aged," or "the Ancient One," may lead us to another connection with an entity we mentioned in an earlier chapter:

---

390. Frank Moore Cross, *Canaanite Myth and Hebrew Epic: Essays in the History of the Religion of Israel* (London; Cambridge: Harvard University Press, 1973), pp. 24–25.

[A] mine inscription, owing to a poor facsimile, had been misread and hence remained undeciphered. It reads 'ld'lm, 'if ḏū 'ôlami, "El, the Ancient One" or "El, lord of Eternity."[391]

Could this link El—and thus Baal Hammon, Kronos, and his other manifestations—to Rapi'u, the underworld god who reigned at Ashtaroth and Edrei? Some think so. Respected scholar Frank Moore Cross, for example, translated the phrase *rapi'u malk 'ôlami* from Ugaritic text KTU 1.108 as an epithet of El ("the Hale One, eternal king") rather than "Rapi'u, King of Eternity."

It is probable that the name "Baal Hammon" means "Lord of the Amanus,"[392] which refers to a mountain range in southern Turkey just northeast of Mount Zaphon, the mountain sacred to Baal. The Amanus, today's Nur Mountains (from the Turkish *Nur Dağları*, "Mountains of Holy Light"), run alongside the Gulf of Iskenderun at the northeastern corner of the Mediterranean Sea, just north of Antakya (ancient Antioch). Zincirli, mentioned above, is the site of ancient Sam'al, about seventy miles north of Antakya. It controlled the northern pass through the Amanus mountains, while Kinalua, capital city of the kingdom of Palistin, about fifteen miles southeast of Antakya, guarded the southern pass.

To be clear, Baal Hammon is not the Baal of the Bible. That was the storm-god, whose proper name was Hadad or Adad, depending on where it was written. "Baal" simply means "lord," and it was used by the Canaanites and Phoenicians the same way we Christians call our God "Lord" instead of "Yahweh." But Baal Hammon's mountains, the Amanus, are only about seventy miles north of Mount Zaphon, home of the storm-god's palace—a mountain that, you remember, was likely dedicated to El (Baal Hammon) before it became sacred to Baal (Hadad).

---

391. Ibid., p. 19.
392. Ibid., pp. 26–27.

The worship of Baal Hammon continued until rather late in history. The Phoenicians built a maritime trading empire unrivaled in the ancient world that lasted from about the time of Ahab and Jezebel in the ninth century BC until the end of the Third Punic War in 146 BC, when Carthage was finally destroyed by Rome. The colony at Carthage was founded by Phoenicians from Tyre in what is modern-day Tunisia. As the Phoenicians extended their influence across the Mediterranean through settlements and trading outposts on the North African coast, southern Spain, and islands like Sicily and Sardinia, the worship of Baal Hammon spread as well. It appears the god and his consort, Tanit, became the supernatural power couple of Carthage around 480 BC, when a disastrous military defeat on the island of Sicily led to the colony's break with its home city, Tyre.[393]

Tanit, sometimes rendered "Tannit" or "Tinnit," was the Carthaginian version of the goddess Asherah,[394] although some scholars connect Tanit to the other great goddesses of the Canaanite pantheon, Astarte and Anat.[395] But since most scholars accept that Baal Hammon and El are one and the same, identifying Tanit as Asherah is probably correct. The etymology of her name is interesting, to say the least. "Tanit" is a feminine form of the Canaanite/Phoenician *tannin*, which means "serpent" or "dragon." Thus, "Tanit" is literally "Serpent Lady" or "Dragon Lady."[396] This supports her identification as Asherah, whose epithets *rabbat 'atiratu yammi* ("Lady Who Treads on the Sea[-dragon]")[397] and *dt btn* ("Serpent Lady")[398] are virtually identical.

---

393. Sergio Ribichini, "Beliefs and Religious Life." In: S. Moscati, (Ed.), *The Phoenicians* (London; New York: I.B. Tauris, 2001) p. 132.

394. Cross (1973), op. cit., p. 29.

395. John Day, "Asherah in the Hebrew Bible and Northwest Semitic Literature." *Journal of Biblical Literature*, Vol. 105, No. 3 (1986), p. 396.

396. Cross (1973), op. cit., p. 32.

397. Ibid.

398. Ibid., p. 19.

Tanit was sometimes called *Qudšu* ("the Holy One"),[399] and she was known by this name in Egypt as well as the Levant from about the time of Jacob through the time of the judges (about 1700–1200 BC). In Egyptian art, she's usually shown holding snakes in one or both hands.[400]

Now, it's probably not a coincidence that *bṯn* is the Ugaritic form of "Bashan," the land at the foot of Mount Hermon ruled by Og in the days of Moses. The epithet *ḏt bṯn* could therefore be read, "Lady of Bashan." (It also means that Bashan literally translates as "Place of the Serpent.")

While scholars don't completely agree on the identities and origins of Baal Hammon and Tanit, it is clear that the two, like Kronos, Saturn, and Molech, required a most precious sacrifice from worshipers—their children. In recent years, some scholars have tried to downplay the biblical accounts of child sacrifice, suggesting that they were invented by the Hebrew prophets to justify the conquest of Canaan and rationalize the destruction of Jerusalem and the Temple by Babylon. And God, speaking through the prophets, was very clear about His opinion of child sacrifice:

> You shall not give any of your children to offer them [literally, "to make them pass through (the fire)"] to Molech, and so profane the name of your God: I am the Lord. [...] Do not make yourselves unclean by any of these things, for by all these the nations I am driving out before you have become unclean, and the land became unclean, so that I punished its iniquity, and the land vomited out its inhabitants. (Leviticus 18:21, 24–25)

---

399. Nicolas Wyatt, "Asherah." In K. van der Toorn, B. Becking, & P. W. van der Horst (Eds.), *Dictionary of Deities and Demons in the Bible* (Leiden; Boston; Köln; Grand Rapids, MI; Cambridge: Brill; Eerdmans, 1999), p. 100.

400. Day (1986), op. cit., p. 389.

[Manasseh] burned his son as an offering and used fortune-telling and omens and dealt with mediums and with necromancers. He did much evil in the sight of the LORD, provoking him to anger.[...] And the LORD said by his servants the prophets, "Because Manasseh king of Judah has committed these abominations and has done things more evil than all that the Amorites did, who were before him, and has made Judah also to sin with his idols, therefore thus says the LORD, the God of Israel: Behold, I am bringing upon Jerusalem and Judah such disaster that the ears of everyone who hears of it will tingle." (2 Kings 21:6, 10–12)

For the sons of Judah have done evil in my sight, declares the LORD. They have set their detestable things in the house that is called by my name, to defile it. And they have built the high places of Topheth, which is in the Valley of the Son of Hinnom, to burn their sons and their daughters in the fire, which I did not command, nor did it come into my mind. Therefore, behold, the days are coming, declares the LORD, when it will no more be called Topheth, or the Valley of the Son of Hinnom, but the Valley of Slaughter; for they will bury in Topheth, because there is no room elsewhere. (Jeremiah 7:30–32)

But the prophets weren't alone in their condemnation of the Amorite-Canaanite-Phoenician practice of child sacrifice. Greeks and Romans were appalled by it as well. We've already shared the nightmarish account of Plutarch, who described how the poor of Carthage sold their children to be sacrificed by those with no children of their own. But the wealthy were not exempt from burning their children; according to Diodorus Siculus, the citizens of Carthage responded to a disastrous military defeat in 310 BC to Agathocles, ruler of the Sicilian city-state of Syracuse, by slaughtering hundreds of their children:

Therefore the Carthaginians, believing that the misfortune had come to them from the gods, betook themselves to every manner of supplication of the divine powers.... They also alleged that Kronos [Baal Hammon] had turned against them inasmuch as in former times they had been accustomed to sacrifice to this god the noblest of their sons, but more recently, secretly buying and nurturing children, they had sent these to the sacrifice; and when an investigation was made, some of those who had been sacrificed were discovered to have been supposititious [substitutions].... In their zeal to make amends for their omission, they selected two hundred of the noblest children and sacrificed them publicly; and others who were under suspicion sacrificed themselves voluntarily, in number not less than three hundred.[401]

Diodorus also provides the most graphic description of how this sacrifice was performed:

There was in their city a bronze image of Kronos, extending its hands, palms up and sloping toward the ground, so that each of the children when placed thereon rolled down and fell into a sort of gaping pit filled with fire.[402]

This is probably the inspiration for fanciful renderings you may have seen of an idol called "Moloch," an alternate spelling of "Molech," "Molek," and "Malik."[403] The truth is we don't know what the bronze idol of Baal Hammon looked like. It's possible that the artist's depiction

---

401. Diodorus Siculus, *The Library of History*, XX:14.

402. Ibid.

403. George Foot Moore, "The Image of Moloch," *Journal of Biblical Literature* 16 (1897), pp. 162–163.

Fanciful image of "Molech" by Charles Foster, published in the 1897 book *Bible Pictures and What They Teach Us*

Terra cotta figurine of the Phoenician god Baal Hammon

of Moloch was inspired by the Greek myth of the Minotaur, the can-nibalistic half-bull, half-man who was confined to the labyrinth on the island of Crete.[404] The images of Baal Hammon that have survived the last two thousand years depict a bearded man—although, as noted in a previous chapter, the name of his alter ego Kronos probably derives from the Semitic word for "horns."

If we've learned only one thing from the political situation in the United States since 2016, it's that the media promotes a narrative, and stories are shaped to fit that narrative. This was also true two thousand years ago. So, some modern archaeologists prefer to believe that the Hebrew, Greek, and Roman commentators who offered their opinions of Canaanite and Punic religion were biased against a rival culture, and the claims of infanticide were essentially political propaganda. It's claimed that the high rate of infant mortality in the ancient world would have made regular child sacrifices impossible. Any society engaging in such a practice, it's argued, would collapse by elevating its death rate above the birth rate.[405] They argue that the children buried at Phoenician settle-ments around the Mediterranean simply died of natural causes, and for some as yet undiscovered reason the Phoenicians set aside special burial grounds for deceased children. For lack of better, archaeologists have borrowed the biblical word "tophet" to describe these sites.

It's an imprecise use of the term. The Hebrew word *topheth* literally means "place of fire," a reference to the practice of burning children as offerings to Molech. The horror of the Topheth led Jews to use the Val-ley of the Son of Hinnom, where these sacrifices took place, as a symbol for the place of eternal torment for the wicked. The name in shortened

---

404. John S. Rundin, "Pozo Moro, Child Sacrifice, and the Greek Literary Tradition." *Journal of Biblical Literature*, Vol. 123, No. 3 (2004), p. 430.

405. Garnand, Stager & Greene, "Infants as Offerings: Palaeodemographic Patterns and Tophet Burial." *Studi Epigrafici e Linguistici* 29–30 (2012–13), p. 194.

form, *gei hinnom* ("Valley of Hinnom"), became *Gehenna* in Greek, and it's usually translated "hell" in the New Testament.

However, the revisionist arguments just don't hold up. Analysis shows that the Phoenicians could have sacrificed as many as *all* of their firstborn children, or up to one-third of their baby girls, without affecting their society in a significant way.[406]

The physical evidence that has so far escaped archaeologists in Israel has turned up in numerous places around the Mediterranean. Tophets similar to the one described in the Bible have been found at Carthage and nearby Phoenician sites in modern Tunisia and Algeria, at Motya on Sicily, and at Monte Sirai, Nora, Tharros, and Sulcis on Sardinia.[407]

But one of the most disturbing pieces of evidence comes from Spain, carved into a stone relief on a Punic funerary monument constructed around 500 BC:

> The relief depicts a banquet prepared for a monster that sits, facing the left part of the image. The monster has a human body and two heads, one above the other. The heads have open mouths with lolling tongues. In its left hand it holds the rear leg of a supine pig lying on a banquet table in front of it. In its right hand, it holds a bowl. Just over the rim of the bowl can be seen the head and feet of a small person. In the background, a figure in a long garment raises a bowl in a gesture of offering. Opposite the monster is the mutilated image of a third figure. It is standing and raising in its right hand a sword with a curved blade. Its head is in the shape of a bull or horse. Its left hand is touching the head of a second small person in a bowl on a second table or a tripod near the banquet table. The funerary tower on which this relief is carved comes from an area that, in the period

---

406. Ibid., p. 215.
407. Cross (1973), op. cit., p. 25.

of its construction, was clearly subject to Punic or Phoenician influence and resembles monuments from Achaemenid western Asia. The relief itself resembles eastern Mediterranean depictions of offerings or sacrifices, and the sword with the curved blade, associated with sacrifice, supports the resemblance. It appears that the small figures, most likely children, are being offered in bowls to the two-headed monster. Accordingly, it is reasonable to believe that the relief, however imaginatively, represents Northwest Semitic child sacrifice.[408]

Monument of Pozo Moro. Credit: Miguel Hermoso Cuesta – Own work, CC BY-SA 4.0, https://commons.wikimedia.org/w/index. php?curid=37278887

While it's unquestionably frightening, it's difficult to interpret exactly what the relief represents. It's not exactly the type of funerary monument we're accustomed to in the modern world. Charles Kennedy, who studied the monument not long after its discovery in 1971,

408. Rundin, op. cit., p. 426.

believes it represents the offering of infants to Death; that is, Molech.[409]
George Heider, in his groundbreaking book on Molech, agrees: "The
Pozo Moro tower relief is as close as we are ever apt to come to a pho-
tograph of the ancient cult in action, and it shows child sacrifice clearly
enough, if nothing else."[410]

Even so, the debate continues. Some scholars see nothing unusual
in the special burial sites the Phoenicians set aside for infants and young
children.[411] Others argue that the Pozo Moro mausoleum depicts neither children nor sacrifice.[412] However, a recent analysis of teeth retrieved
from 342 burial urns at Carthage, where the largest tophet contains
more than twenty thousand such urns,[413] revealed that infants under the
age of three months were significantly over-represented, meaning—to
put this nicely—they did not die of natural causes.[414]

The question is not whether the Phoenicians sacrificed their children, or even if they could have done it the way the prophets, Greeks,
and Romans said they did. They did. The question is *why*.

---

409. Charles Kennedy, "Tartessos, Tarshish and Tartarus: The Tower of Pozo
Moro and the Bible" (unpublished essay presented to the First International
Meeting of the Society of Biblical Literature, Salamanca, Spain, 1983), pp.
8–12.

410. Heiser, op. cit., p. 191.

411. Adriano Orsingher, "Understanding Tophets: A Short Introduction."
The Ancient Near East Today, http://www.asor.org/anetoday/2018/02/
Understanding-Tophets-Short, retrieved 4/14/18.

412. Joseph Azize, "'Child Sacrifice' without Children or Sacrifice: The Pozo
Moro Relief." *Ancient Near Eastern Studies* 51 (2014), pp. 263–277.

413. Maria E. Aubet, *The Phoenicians and the West* (Cambridge: Cambridge
University Press, 1987). p. 252.

414. Smith, Avishai, Greene & Stager, "Aging Cremated Infants: The
Problem of Sacrifice at the Tophet of Carthage." *Antiquity* 85:329 (2011),
pp. 859–874.

Generally speaking, Phoenician parents couldn't have been heartless, unfeeling monsters. Even an unfriendly witness like Plutarch noted that poor mothers who sold their children as substitute offerings for the children of the wealthy were compelled to keep from showing grief during the sacrifice by the threat of losing their fee. No, there was something more at work here—something spiritual.

As Diodorus noted, the Carthaginians believed their loss to the tyrant of Syracuse, Agathocles, was punishment for failing to provide the required sacrifices to their chief god, Baal Hammon. To atone, the city slaughtered some five hundred of its children. Why? Why would a Watcher-class angel demand child sacrifice from his human followers? There are a couple of possible reasons, but because the Bible doesn't tell us specifically, they are both speculative.

First, we know from Genesis 9 that "the blood is the life." God forbade consuming blood; further, He declared that for the shedding of human blood—even by animals—a reckoning would be required. Maybe the shedding of blood produces something the Fallen uses for supernatural power.

Second, this may be simple revenge. The Watchers witnessed the deaths of their children, the Nephilim, in the Flood of Noah. Maybe convincing humans that sacrificing children brings supernatural blessing from the gods was an act of retribution. Imagine how God the Father feels as He watches us willingly slaughter the most vulnerable and helpless among us, the children in *our* care, to win the favor of our older siblings, the angelic children of God who rebelled against Him.

We don't have to imagine. God told us *exactly* how He feels about it more than 2,500 years ago:

And you took your sons and your daughters, whom you had borne to me, and these you sacrificed to [the gods] to be devoured. Were your whorings so small a matter that you slaughtered my children and delivered them up as an offering by fire to them? (Ezekiel 16:20–21)

In short, because Israel and Judah worshiped other gods, which Yahweh compared to a faithless wife cheating on her husband, He declared that judgment was coming in the form of conquest by foreign invaders, both natural and supernatural. In this context, the pronouns "they" and "them" are just as likely to refer to the gods allotted to the nations as to the people of the pagan nations God would bring against Jerusalem.

Let's put this together: The references in 2 Peter and Jude suggest that the Watchers, the sinful angels of Genesis 6, were the Titans, supernatural entities banished to Tartarus for their sexual transgression that produced unholy children, the Nephilim. Thus, Shemihazah, chief of the rebellious Watchers, was Kronos, king of the Titans, who was called "Baal Hammon" by the Phoenicians. According to 1 Enoch, the Watchers were condemned by God to "see the destruction of their beloved ones" before being bound in the depths of the earth until the Judgment.[415]

The evidence of history leads to this conclusion: The Watchers and/ or the demon spirits of their dead children, the Rephaim/Nephilim, lured the pagan nations of the ancient world into burning their sons and daughters as sacrificial offerings to gods of the dead.

Now, consider this: God bought our freedom from the wages of sin—death—by sacrificing His Son for us. It was the ultimate reversal of the evil introduced to the world at Hermon.

---

415. George W. E. Nickelsburg & James C. VanderKam, *1 Enoch: The Hermeneia Translation* (Minneapolis: Fortress Press. Kindle Edition, 2012), p. 29.

Chapter Twenty-Four

SATURN

We finally arrive at the identity of this entity probably best known to us in the modern world. One of the days of the week in the English-speaking world, Saturday (Saturn's Day), and the second largest planet in the solar system are named for Saturn.

As with his older identities, Saturn was believed to be the former king of the cosmos, an old god whose rule had been ended by his son, the storm-god. In Saturn's case, this was Jupiter, the Roman name for the Greek Zeus, Hittite Tarhunz, Hurrian Teshub, Amorite Hadad (or Adad, but better known to us as Baal), and Akkadian and Babylonian Marduk. We also see echoes of this dysfunctional family relationship in the Norse gods Odin and Thor, and other places where the storm-god emerged as king of the pantheon—for example, Perun of the Slavs, Taranis of the Celts, and Indra of Vedic (ancient Hindu) religion.

As we've already noted, Saturn was the equivalent of Kronos, king of the Titans. In both Roman and Greek religion, he was the old god who ruled the earth during a long-ago Golden Age when humanity lived like gods, free from toil and care. Both were confined to the netherworld after they'd been dethroned.

Historians of the classical age made no distinction between Kronos, Saturn, and Baal Hammon. It was accepted that he was the same god worshiped under different names by Greeks, Romans, and Phoenicians. The parallel between child sacrifice and the myth of Saturn/Kronos devouring his own children is obvious. Diodorus Siculus, writing in the first century AD, drily noted that "the story passed down among the Greeks from ancient myth that Kronos did away with his own children appears to have been kept in mind among the Carthaginians through this observance."[416] Christian apologist Tertullian was less charitable:

> Since Saturn did not spare his own children, of course he stuck to his habit of not sparing those of other people, whom indeed their own parents offered of themselves, being pleased to answer the call, and fondled the infants, lest they should weep when being sacrificed. And yet a parent's murder of his child is far worse than simple homicide.[417]

Indeed. But in our civilized, modern world, we mostly avoid the guilt associated with infanticide by convincing ourselves that an unborn child is nothing more than a clump of cells inside a pregnant woman's body. Kronos and his minions have been very effective at selling this message—abortion was the world's leading cause of death in 2020, with roughly twice as many children terminated in the womb as deaths from cancer, HIV/AIDS, traffic fatalities, smoking, and alcohol combined.[418]

There are important differences, however, in the way the Romans saw Saturn and the Greek view of Kronos. Latin literature, especially in the works of the first century BC poet Virgil, tended to depict Saturn as a semi-historical character who'd found sanctuary in Italy, which Virgil

---

416. Diodorus Siculus, op. cit., 20.14.7.

417. Tertullian, op. cit.

418. Nearly 42.7 million, according to Worldometer. "Abortion No. 1 Cause of Death Worldwide in 2020." *Decision*, Jan. 5, 2021. https://decisionmagazine.com/abortion-no-1-cause-of-death-worldwide-in-2020/, retrieved 4/6/21.

described as *Saturnia tellus* ("Saturn's land").[419] In fact, Virgil was instrumental in the rehabilitation of Saturn. Unlike Hesiod's Kronos, who never interacted with humanity, in Virgil's work, Saturn evolved from a former ruler of the cosmos confined to Tartarus into an earthly sovereign ruling over an age of peace and plenty.[420]

While the accounts of Saturn's fall from power are similar to the tale of Kronos written by Hesiod centuries earlier, Romans believed that Saturn had been compelled to eliminate his male children so that the sons of his brother, Titan, would inherit the throne. Saturn's wife, Ops, hid the infant Jupiter, who was raised by his aunt, Vesta. When Jupiter reached maturity, he returned with an army and freed Saturn, who'd been imprisoned by Titan. Instead of showing a little gratitude, however, Saturn plotted an ambush to prevent Jupiter from claiming the kingship of the gods. When that failed, Saturn fled to Italy, where he lived as a farmer and ruled over an age of peace and prosperity. The main difference between Kronos and Saturn is that while both were reprehensible, Saturn was also weak and cowardly.

It begs the question: Why did anybody ever worship this god?

Still, the character of Saturn described by Virgil in the *Aeneid* became the semi-official version of the deity in the Roman Empire. It looks like a sort of supernatural whitewash, a rebranding of the old god to soften his image with the people. It began in the archaic Greek period; where Hesiod had left Kronos and the Titans imprisoned in Tartarus in his *Theogony*, the poet wrote in *Works and Days* that Zeus eventually relented and released his father from the underworld:

> But when earth had covered this generation also, Zeus the
> son of Cronos made yet another, the fourth, upon the fruitful
> earth, which was nobler and more righteous, a god-like race of

419. Patricia A. Johnston, "Vergil's Conception of Saturnus." *California Studies in Classical Antiquity*, Vol. 10 (1977), pp. 57–70.
420. Ibid., p. 57.

hero-men who are called demi-gods, the race before our own, throughout the boundless earth. Grim war and dread battle destroyed a part of them, [...] But to the others father Zeus the son of Cronos gave a living and an abode apart from men, and made them dwell at the ends of earth. And they live untouched by sorrow in the islands of the blessed along the shore of deep-swirling Ocean, happy heroes for whom the grain-giving earth bears honey-sweet fruit flourishing thrice a year, far from the deathless gods, and Cronos rules over them; for the father of men and gods released him from his bonds.[421]

To reiterate, we identify Saturn/Kronos as the Watcher chief Shemi-hazah, and he, like the rest of the angels who sinned, is still in chains in Tartarus. I mention these Greek and Roman stories only to show what the pagans of the biblical era believed about this entity.

We need to debunk one bit of fake news about Saturn before we go any further. The festival of Saturnalia, held between December 17 and 23, was undoubtedly the most popular of the year for Romans. As stated in an earlier chapter, it was marked by a reversal of societal norms, which apparently hearkened back to better days:

The first inhabitants of Italy were the Aborigines, whose king, Saturnus, is said to have been a man of such extraordinary justice, that no one was a slave in his reign, or had any private property, but all things were common to all, and undivided, as one estate for the use of every one; in memory of which way of life, it has been ordered that at the Saturnalia slaves should everywhere sit down with their masters at the entertainments, the rank of all

---

421. Hesiod, *The Homeric Hymns and Homerica with an English Translation by Hugh G. Evelyn-White. Works and Days* 156–169a. (Medford, MA: Cambridge, MA., Harvard University Press; London, William Heinemann Ltd., 1914).

being made equal. Italy was accordingly called, from the name of that king, Saturnia; and the hill on which he dwelt Saturnius, on which now stands the Capitol, as if Saturnus had been dislodged from his seat by Jupiter.[422]

It's widely believed by skeptics, and some well-meaning but misinformed Christians, that the date for celebrating Christmas was chosen by the early church to "Christianize" Saturnalia. The story goes that the festival was so popular that even Christians in the Roman Empire wouldn't give it up, so church leaders declared December 25 the birth day of Jesus, established a feast, and stole Saturnalia from the pagans.

That happens not to be the case.

The earliest record of the observance of Christmas is from Clement of Alexandria around AD 200.[423] But the first suggestion that Christmas might be linked to pagan worship didn't come until the twelfth century, about nine hundred years later.[424] In other words, as far as historians can tell, no Christians between the third through twelfth centuries thought they were accidentally worshiping a pagan god at Christmas. While some noted the proximity of December 25 to the winter solstice, which falls on December 21 or 22, early Christian writers did not believe the church chose the date. Rather, they saw it as a sign that God was the true sun, superior to the false gods of the pagans.[425]

The Donatist sect in North Africa celebrated Jesus' birth on December 25 in the early fourth century,[426] before Constantine became emperor

---

422. Justinus, *Epitome of Pompeius Trogus' 'Philippic Histories'* 43.1.3–5. http://www.attalus.org/translate/justin7.html#43.1, retrieved 4/13/21.

423. Clement of Alexandria, *The Stromata* 1.21.145. https://www. newadvent.org/fathers/02101.htm, retrieved 4/13/21.

424. Clement of Alexandria, *The Stromata* 1.21.145. https://www. newadvent.org/fathers/02101.htm, retrieved 4/13/21.

425. Ibid.

426. Ibid.

of Rome (so we can't blame him for setting the date, either). And while it's true that the emperor Aurelian made veneration of Sol Invictus the law throughout the Roman Empire in AD 274, a collection of ancient writings called *Inscriptiones Latinae Selectae* puts the feast day during the reign of Licinius (AD 308–324) on November 18.[427] There is little evidence that a feast for Sol Invictus was held on December 25 before the middle of the fourth century AD, and Christians were celebrating the birth of Christ on that date about half a century earlier.

So, given that nobody in the first century recorded the actual date of Jesus' birth, how did the early church arrive at December 25? It's a little complex, but it illustrates the motives of the Church Fathers, which did not include sneaking pagan worship into the faith.

Second-century Latin Christians in Rome and North Africa made an effort to calculate the exact date of Jesus' death. For reasons that escape us, they settled on March 25, AD 29.[428] (The reasons escape us because March 25 was not a Friday that year, nor was it Passover Eve, nor did Passover Eve fall on a Friday in AD 29, or even in the month of March.)[429] The March 25 date was also noted by early church theologians Tertullian and Augustine.[430]

There was a widespread belief among Jews of the day in the "integral age" of great prophets, which means it was thought that the prophets of Israel died on the same day they were conceived. It's not biblical, but that's not the point. What matters is the early church believed it, and that's how it was decided that Jesus was born in late December:

---

427. Hermann Dessau, *Inscriptiones latinae selectee, Vol 3* (Berlin: Weidmann, 1916), p. 24.

428. William J. Tighe, "Calculating Christmas: The Story Behind December 25." *Touchstone,* Dec. 2003, https://www.touchstonemag.com/archives/article.php?id=16-10-012-v, retrieved 4/13/21.

429. Ibid.

430. McGowan, op. cit.

Adding nine months to March 25 brings you to—you guessed it—December 25.

It's that simple. Saturn and Saturnalia had nothing to do with it.

The effort to claim the credit, however, is the work of the dark god and his minions. The recent pushback against celebrating Christmas has been so intense that some Christians are careful to avoid mentioning the holiday, except with trusted friends, lest they be accused of accidentally worshiping Saturn, Baal, Sol Invictus, or Nimrod—by other Christians. The Christmas season used to be the one time of year when Christ was openly proclaimed in our society. Sadly, zealous but misinformed believers have unwittingly helped the Fallen reclaim the holiday.

It's almost certain that Jesus was not born on December 25.[431] It's also true that the Christmas holiday has attracted a lot of baggage—pagan traditions, hyper-commercialization, and awful renditions of Christmas carols by pop divas. It doesn't matter. The important point is this: The early church did not establish December 25 as a feast day celebrating the birth of Jesus to copy or co-opt a pagan holiday.

That said, Saturn successfully rebranded the seventh day of the week, the Sabbath, as *Sāturni diēs*, Saturn's Day, in the second century AD when Rome replaced its eight-day cycle with a seven-day week. And there is biblical evidence that some Jews adopted the worship of Saturn during the Babylonian captivity:

> "You shall take up Sikkuth your king, and Kiyyun your star-god—your images that you made for yourselves, and I will send you into exile beyond Damascus," says the Lord, whose name is the God of hosts. (Amos 5:26–27)

---

431. It's far more likely that His birthdate was September 11, 3 BC. See Ernest L. Martin, *The Star That Astonished the World*, available to read online at www.askelm.com/star/.

Sikkuth appears to be a reference to a minor Babylonian god named Sakkud, or Sakkut.[432] However, the pronunciation was close enough to the Hebrew word *sukkat* ("hut") that the Jewish scholars who translated the Septuagint rendered the first line, "And you took along the tent of Molech." The consonants of Molech and *melek* ("king") are identical, but it's interesting that the translators were comfortable bringing the "king-god" into this passage. This is exactly how Stephen quoted Amos during his speech to the Sanhedrin.[433]

It's especially interesting since "Kiyyun" refers to the Babylonian name for Saturn, *Kajjamānu,* "the Steady One."[434] *Kajjamānu* was unimportant in the Mesopotamian pantheon, but it's indicative of the hubris of the king-god: Under his influence, most of the Western world now calls God's divinely ordained day of rest "Saturn's Day." And because that isn't enough, even Christians have been convinced that Saturn, not Jesus, is the reason we celebrate Christmas.

432. M. Stol, "Sakkuth." In Karel van der Toorn, Bob Becking, and Pieter W. van der Horst (Eds.), *Dictionary of Deities and Demons in the Bible* (Leiden; Boston; Köln; Grand Rapids, MI; Cambridge: Brill; Eerdmans, 1999), p. 722.

433. Acts 7:43.

434. M. Stol, "Kaiwan." In Karel van der Toorn, Bob Becking, and Pieter W. van der Horst (Eds.), *Dictionary of Deities and Demons in the Bible* (Leiden; Boston; Köln; Grand Rapids, MI; Cambridge: Brill; Eerdmans, 1999), p. 478.

Chapter Twenty-Five

SATURN'S REIGN

During the transition from the Roman Republic to the Roman Empire in the first century BC, the Roman poet Virgil invoked the Golden Age of Saturn to recall the "good old days" when life was easier, people were nobler, and everyone was happy. Virgil used that imagery in his poetry to suggest that Julius Caesar's nephew, Octavian, who emerged from a power struggle with Mark Antony to become Caesar Augustus, would usher in a return to that blessed time.

But the language Virgil used should cause you, as an alert reader, to sit up and take notice:

Now the last age by Cumae's Sibyl sung
Has come and gone, and the majestic roll
Of circling centuries begins anew:
Justice returns, returns old Saturn's reign,
With a new breed of men sent down from heaven.
Only do thou, at the boy's birth in whom
The iron shall cease, the golden race arise,
Befriend him, chaste Lucina; 'tis thine own
Apollo reigns. And in thy consulate,
This glorious age, O Pollio, shall begin,

And the months enter on their mighty march.
Under thy guidance, whatso tracks remain
Of our old wickedness, once done away,
Shall free the earth from never-ceasing fear.
He shall receive the life of gods, and see
Heroes with gods commingling, and himself
Be seen of them, and with his father's worth
Reign o'er a world at peace.
[…]
Assume thy greatness, for the time draws nigh,
Dear child of gods, great progeny of Jove! (Emphasis added)[435]

Virgil's *Eclogue IV* undoubtedly served a political purpose. Artists and poets need patrons to pay their bills, and the Pollio named in Virgil's poem was Gaius Asinius Pollio, a politician, orator, poet, playwright, literary critic, historian, and soldier. In 40 BC, Pollio began a term as consul, the highest elected official in Rome after helping arrange the Treaty of Brundisium. The pact cooled a growing rivalry between Octavian and Antony, two of the three members of the Second Triumvirate, the men who held the real power of the Roman state. On the surface, Virgil's poem was propaganda for the incoming administration, hailing a new age of peace and prosperity after decades of turmoil and civil war that peaked with the rise and fall of Julius Caesar.

On a deeper level, however, Virgil's poem refers to a lost prophecy from the oracle of Apollo at Cumae, a Greek colony near Naples, of a return to an age that ended when Jupiter dethroned Saturn—or, in biblical terms, when God sent the Flood. The new Golden Age would be ushered in by a messianic figure, a child who would become divine and rule over a world at peace.

---

435. Virgil, *Eclogue IV. The Internet Classics Archive*, http://classics.mit.edu/Virgil/eclogue.4.iv.html, retrieved 4/12/21.

But the earth had lived through that story once before and suffered intensely under the "new breed of men sent down from heaven" before the deluge. They were the mighty men of old called "Nephilim" in the Hebrew Scriptures, and "Rephaim" by the ancient Hebrews and their neighbors—demigods, semi-divine heroes, venerated in the religions of Greece and Rome.

To those familiar with the Genesis 6 backstory, the influence of the Watchers/Titans and Nephilim/"heroes" on later Greek and Roman religion and the role of the dark god Saturn/Shemihazah in leading the Watchers' rebellion, Virgil's poem is startling. Did pagans of the classical era really look back on the pre-Flood world with longing and nostalgia? Apparently so. And this desire to return to the Golden Age is still alive today.

Eclogue IV is the source of a phrase you're probably carrying in your wallet or purse right now. Charles Thomson, secretary of the Continental Congress from 1774 to 1789, designer of the Great Seal of the United States, placed the Latin phrase *novus ordo seclorum* ("new order of the ages") below the unfinished pyramid on the reverse side of the seal. That's a loose adaptation of line 5 of Virgil's poem: *Magnus ab integro seclorum nascitur ordo* ("the majestic roll of circling centuries begins anew").[436]

Reverse of the Great Seal of the United States

Thomson adapted the other Latin phrase on the reverse of the seal from Virgil, too. *Annuit cœptus*, taken from *The Georgics* Book I, line 40, essentially means, "Providence favors our undertakings."[437]

436. John D. MacArthur, "Original Source of Novus Ordo Seclorum." *Great Seal*, https://www.greatseal.com/mottoes/seclorumvirgil.html, retrieved 5/28/21.

437. John D. MacArthur, "Original Source of Annuit Coeptus." *Great Seal*, https://www.greatseal.com/mottoes/coeptisvirgil.html, retrieved 5/28/21.

The question, of course, is who was meant by "Providence." I don't know Thomson's heart, so it's possible he meant the God of the Bible. The other, more important, question is what meaning others ascribe to that symbol. Although Freemasons deny that the Eye of Providence is one of their symbols, and there is no evidence that Thomson was a Freemason, the All-Seeing Eye was recognized as a masonic symbol in 1797,[438] some fifteen years after the Great Seal was adopted—although the two eyes "are parallel uses of a shared icon."[439]

Tom Horn dissected the occult symbolism of the Great Seal in *Zenith 2016*, so I'll direct you there for a thorough examination of its hidden meaning. The reverse side, definitely the more relevant of the two, gained new importance when it was added to the back of the dollar bill in 1935. This was initiated by Vice President Henry Wallace, 32nd-Degree Scottish Rite Freemason, whose fellow 32nd-Degree Mason, President Franklin Roosevelt, directed that the reverse side of the Great Seal be added to the left back of the dollar and the obverse side be placed on the right, creating the impression that the mysterious pyramid and Eye of Providence were the principal symbols of the United States.[440]

However others may have interpreted the symbols, to Wallace and other adepts, the meaning was clear:

> Wallace viewed the unfinished pyramid with the all-seeing eye hovering above it on the Great Seal as a prophecy about the dawn of a new world with America at its head. Whenever the United States assumed its position as the new capital of the world, Wallace wrote, the Grand Architect would return and metaphorically the all-seeing eye would be fitted atop the Great

---

438. S. Brent Morris, "The Eye in the Pyramid." *A Page About Freemasonry*, http://web.mit.edu/dryfoo/Masons/Essays/eyepyr.html, retrieved 5/28/21.
439. Ibid.
440. Thomas R. Horn, *Zenith 2016* (Crane, Mo.: Defender, 2013), p. 133.

Seal pyramid as the finished "apex stone." For that to happen, Wallace penned in 1934, "It will take a more definite recognition of the Grand Architect of the Universe before the apex stone [capstone of the pyramid] is finally fitted into place and this nation in the full strength of its power is in position to assume leadership among the nations in inaugurating 'the New Order of the Ages.'"[441]

While it's understandable that a New Ager like Henry Wallace would look to Virgil's poetry and the symbolism it inspired as prophecy to be fulfilled, even Christians began interpreting Virgil's fourth *Eclogue* as prophecy in the early fourth century, seeing in it a foretelling of the imminent birth of Christ.[442] Lactantius, an early Christian writer and religious advisor to the Roman emperor Constantine, may be the one who first proposed this reading of the poem.[443] In his *Divinae Institutiones* (*The Divine Institutes*), Lactantius described Virgil's poem as a prophecy of the return of Jesus prior to His millennial reign.[444] About a century later, Augustine of Hippo argued that it was apparent that Virgil had repeated an authentic prophecy uttered by the Cumaean Sibyl.[445] This belief was widespread as late as medieval times, with many scholars across the centuries convinced that Virgil was a legitimate pre-Christian prophet.

It appears that his reputation carried over from the pagan world. The writings of Virgil were used as oracles in a practice called the *Sortes*

---

441. Ibid., p. 134.

442. Craig Kallendorf, *The Protean Virgil: Material Form and the Reception of the Classics* (Oxford, UK: Oxford University Press, 2015), p. 51.

443. Ibid.

444. Lactantius, *Divinae Institutiones* VII.24. https://www.newadvent.org/fathers/07017.htm, retrieved 4/16/21.

445. Ella Bourne, "The Messianic Prophecy in Vergil's Fourth Eclogue." *The Classical Journal*, Apr., 1916, Vol. 11, No. 7 (Apr., 1916), pp. 392–393.

Vergilianae ("Virgilian Lots"). That was a form of divination by interpreting passages selected at random from the works of the poet, in the same way that some Christians read meaning into Scriptures selected by opening the Bible and reading the first verses that come to hand. It's known that at least four Roman emperors (and at least one usurper) tried to divine the future through the poetry of Virgil. Even as late as the seventeenth century, England's King Charles I, at the suggestion of the poet Abraham Cowley, consulted the *Aeneid* in December of 1648 while he was held captive by forces loyal to Oliver Cromwell.[446] The verses Charles chose did not bode well, and sure enough, the deposed king was dead within a year.

The issue here is not whether Virgil accurately foretold the future (and if so, about what), but that learned men and women have believed that his words were supernaturally inspired for more than two thousand years. The belief that Virgil's words in *Eclogue IV* came from the Cumaean Sibyl gave them more credibility. In the early sixteenth century, Michelangelo included depictions of five of the Sibyls on the ceiling of the Vatican's Sistine Chapel alongside the Hebrew prophets Jonah, Jeremiah, Ezekiel, Joel, Zechariah, Isaiah, and Daniel. The pagan women were apparently included to represent the fact that the Messiah had come for all people and not just the Jews. During our tour of the Vatican in 2018, it was obvious even to my untrained eye that Michelangelo preferred painting the muscular male form; all of the Sibyls are powerfully built, and to quote one art critic, his painting of the Sibyl of Cumae is "intended to be a rendition of an aged old woman but she looks like an Olympic hammer thrower!"[447]

---

446. John Aubrey, *Remaines of Gentilisme and Judaisme*, J. Britten (ed.) (London: W. Satchell, Peyton, and Co., 1881), pp. 90–91.
447. "The Prophets and Sibyls of the Sistine Chapel." *Italian Renaissance Art.com*, https://www.italian-renaissance-art.com/Prophets. html#gallery[pageGallery]/6/, retrieved 4/19/21.

Her muscular physique may reflect the profound influence of the Cumaean Sibyl on Rome's collective identity. (On the other hand, it may simply reveal something about the personality of Michelangelo.) It's undeniable that the Cumaean Sibyl played a key role in the early history of Rome, or at least in the stories Romans told about their history. According to legend, the books of oracles that guided Roman government had been sold to Lucius Tarquinius Superbus, the semi-legendary last king of Rome who reigned between 535 and 509 BC (just after the conquest of Babylon by Cyrus the Great), but King Tarquin required some convincing:

> It is said that during the reign of Tarquinius another very wonderful piece of good luck also came to the Roman state, conferred upon it by the favour of some god or other divinity; and this good fortune was not of short duration, but throughout the whole existence of the country it has often saved it from great calamities.
>
> A certain woman who was not a native of the country came to the tyrant wishing to sell him nine books filled with Sibylline oracles; but when Tarquinius refused to purchase the books at the price she asked, she went away and burned three of them. And not long afterwards, bringing the remaining six books, she offered to sell them for the same price.
>
> But when they thought her a fool and mocked at her for asking the same price for the smaller number of books that she had been unable to get for even the larger number, she again went away and burned half of those that were left; then, bringing the remaining books, she asked the same amount of money for these. Tarquinius, wondering at the woman's purpose, sent for the augurs and acquainting them with the matter, asked them what he should do. These, knowing by certain signs that he had rejected a god-sent blessing, and declaring it to be a great misfortune that he had not purchased all the books, directed him to pay

the woman all the money she asked and to get the oracles that were left. The woman, after delivering the books and bidding him take great care of them, disappeared from among men.[448]

The Sibylline Books were kept in the temple of Jupiter on Capitoline Hill in the care of men chosen by the Roman Senate. The number of men with charge over the oracles grew over time from two to ten to fifteen, but their mission was unchanged: They consulted the books at the direction of the Senate to learn what religious rites were required to ward off disaster and offset ominous portents such as comets, shooting stars, and earthquakes.

Since it was believed the first collection of oracles had been compiled on Mount Ida in western Anatolia (Turkey), about twenty miles southeast of Troy, we can see a path by which rites and deities from the East might have been brought to Italy. In an earlier chapter, we mentioned a late Bronze Age treaty between the Hittite king Muwatalli II and Alaksandu of Wilusa (Troy) that referenced a "divine watercourse," a ritual feature for contacting the gods of the netherworld. This links the religious practices of the Aegean world to the ancient Hurrian cult center at Urkesh and suggests that the Hurrians, through contact with the neighboring Indo-European Luwian people to the west, had some influence over the religion of the Trojans. The Luwians settled a wide area of southern and western Asia Minor during the Bronze Age, including the area around Troy.[449] The Trojan hero Aeneas was claimed as an ancestor by Caesar Augustus and the four Roman emperors who followed him. So, while we don't have specific evidence to confirm the transmission of Hurrian religion to Rome, there are confirmed contacts between

---

448. Dionysus of Halicarnassus, *Roman Antiquities* IV.62.1–4. https://penelope.uchicago.edu/Thayer/E/Roman/Texts/Dionysius_of_Halicarnassus/4C*.html, retrieved 4/16/21.

449. "Petty States in Western Asia Minor." *Luwian Studies*. https://luwianstudies.org/petty-states-in-western-asia-minor/, retrieved 4/18/21.

the Hurrians, Hittites, Luwians, Amorites/Phoenicians, Greeks, and Romans. And each of those cultures had a pantheon headed up by a storm-god who'd replaced his father as king of the gods, who in turn had replaced or deposed the sky-god.

Culture	Sumer/Akkad	Hurrians	Syria	Canaan	Phoenicia	Hittites/Luwians	Greece	Rome
Sky-god	Anu	Anu	Anu	Ilib (?)	Baal Shamem	Anu	Ouranos	Caelus
Creator-god	Enlil	Kumarbi	Dagan	El	Baal Hammon	Kumarbi	Kronos	Saturn
Storm-god	Marduk	Teshub	Hadad	Baal	Baal	Tarhunz	Zeus	Jupiter

Now, this is where things get weird. We noted above that the Sibylline Books were kept in the temple of Jupiter Optimus Maximus on the Capitoline Hill. The hill, one of the seven for which Rome is famous, got its name from another one of the founding myths of Rome: When the foundation for the temple was excavated during the reign of Tarquinius Superbus, or possibly his ancestor Tarquinius Priscus, workers discovered a perfectly preserved decapitated head.[450] Oddly, this was interpreted as a *good* omen, a sign of Rome's future greatness. Latin for "head" is *caput*, hence *Capitolium*, the name of Jupiter's temple, and Capitoline Hill. Since Tarquinius Superbus was run out of Rome before construction was completed, the temple was dedicated by the first consul of the new Roman republic, Horatius Pulvillus, on September 13, 509 BC.[451]

Tarquinius Superbus began construction on a temple for Saturn at the base of the hill that formerly bore his name, with the dedication traditionally dated to 497 BC.[452] Since Saturn was believed to be the

---

450. Lukáš Surý, *The Temple of Jupiter Optimus Maximus in the Archaic Age* (Bachelor's thesis: Masaryk University. Brno, Czechia, 2012), p. 10.

451. Ibid., p. 5.

452. Robert E. A. Palmer, *Rome and Carthage at Peace* (Stuttgart: Franz Steiner, 1997), p. 63.

ruler of the long-ago Golden Age, he was associated with wealth, so
the treasury, Rome's reserve of gold and silver, was kept inside Saturn's
temple. It would seem that by the time the Jewish return to Zion was
well underway in the late sixth century BC, the image of Saturn had
been rehabilitated enough to earn a prominent place in the city, even if
he had been "dislodged from his seat by Jupiter."

There are a couple of interesting and relevant points to make here.
First, as you've probably guessed already, the word "capitol," designating
a building where a legislative body meets, derives from Capitoline Hill
in Rome. Contrary to what you might assume, the building in which
the US Congress meets was not called the Capitol because that's what
such buildings were called. When it was designed, calling a meeting
place for a legislature "the Capitol" was not the norm in the American
colonies—or anywhere else for that matter:

> When the Capitol in Washington was planned and named, Vir-
> ginia was the only American State (and presumably the only
> political unit anywhere) which was currently using that name
> for the headquarters of its legislature and of such other govern-
> mental affairs as might be conveniently housed with it. Else-
> where in this country State House was the prevailing name, and
> it had been customary from quite early times in the English
> colonies (including Virginia when Jamestown was its seat of
> colonial government.)[453]

The design submitted by Pierre Charles L'Enfant for the new American federal city named the building for the legislative branch of government "Congress House." Thomas Jefferson insisted on following the

---

453. George W. Hodgkins, "Naming the Capitol and the Capital." *Records
of the Columbia Historical Society, Washington, D.C.*, 1960/1962, Vol. 60/62
(1960/62), p. 37.

example of his home state of Virginia, which had named its legislative building "the Capitoll" (sic) in 1699.

> A final legacy of Jefferson's vision of the city is found in correspondence between him and L'Enfant. Jefferson consistently called the building to house Congress, the "Capitol," whereas L'Enfant just as consistently referred to it as "Congress House." The Roman allusion born in Williamsburg ninety-two years before would be preserved.[454]

So, through the influence of Thomas Jefferson, the building that housed the new legislative body of the American republic was named for the temple of the storm-god, Jupiter, which in turn was named for a severed head found during the temple's construction that augured good fortune for the growing city-state of Rome.

If you're a Christian, doesn't that bother you just a little bit?

454. James D. Kornwolf and Georgiana Wallis Kornwolf, "The Creation of the Federal City: Washington." *Architecture and Town Planning in Colonial North America: Vol. 3* (Baltimore: The Johns Hopkins University Press, 2002), p. 1552.

Chapter Twenty-Six

AMERICA'S TEMPLE

Fast-forward from ancient Rome about twenty-five hundred years. If you followed the tumultuous battle over the results of the 2020 American presidential election, you're aware that a group of protesters forced their way inside the Capitol on January 6, 2021, resulting in some property damage and the death of Ashli Babbitt, a thirty-five-year-old Air Force veteran who was fatally shot by a Capitol Police officer when she tried to vault over a barricade into a restricted area inside the building.

The media has consistently described the events of January 6, 2021, as insurrection, an attempted coup by "domestic terrorists." It was not. The Capitol rioters were a disorganized, ragtag mob that had no agenda other than venting frustration at America's political class as Congress convened to certify the results of the contentious presidential election. But, as my wife Sharon K. Gilbert noted in a chapter she contributed to the recent Tom Horn anthology, *Zeitgeist 2025*, the responses by our elected officials were eye-opening:

Very shortly after the so-called coup failed, Senator Chuck Schumer described the January 6, 2021 incursion into the House of Representatives this way:

It is very, very difficult to put into words what has transpired today. I have never lived through or even imagined an experience like the one we have just witnessed in this Capitol. President Franklin Roosevelt set aside Dec. 7, 1941, as a day that will live in infamy. Unfortunately, we can now add Jan. 6, 2021, to that very short list of dates in American history that will live forever in infamy.

This temple to democracy was desecrated, its windows smashed, our offices vandalized. […]

And Senator Schumer's alarmist battle cry was taken up two weeks later at the inauguration by Senator Amy Klobuchar:

Two weeks ago, when an angry, violent mob staged an insurrection and **desecrated this temple of our democracy**, it awakened us to our responsibilities as Americans. [Emphasis added][455]

Senators Schumer and Klobuchar were not alone in depicting the Capitol as hallowed ground:

This is a special place. This is a sacred place. This sacred place was desecrated by a mob today on our watch. This temple to democracy was defiled by was defiled by thugs, who roamed the halls—sat in this chair, Mr. Vice President—one that you vacated at 2:15 this afternoon. —Sen. Dick Durbin (D-IL)[456]

---

455. Sharon K. Gilbert, "A Long Ritual, a Dark Winter, and the Age of Aquarius." In Tom Horn, *Zeitgeist 2025* (Crane, MO: Defender, 2021), in press.

456. CBS 2 Chicago Staff, "Sen. Durbin On Senate Floor: 'This Sacred Place Was Desecrated' During Capitol Storming." *CBS 2 Chicago*, Jan. 6,

Members of the U.S. Capitol Police and across law enforcement are heroes. We saw their heroism in action on January 6 when they defended the most sacred space in our Republic against violent insurrectionists who attempted to prevent Congress from carrying out its constitutional duty. —Rep. Liz Cheney (R-WY)[457]

On Sunday, it was a great—my great honor to be sworn in as Speaker and to preside over a sacred ritual of renewal, as we gathered under this dome of this temple of democracy to open the 117th Congress. —House Speaker Nancy Pelosi (D-CA)[458]

Now, it's easy to dismiss these remarks as rhetoric to score political points against Donald Trump, who was not only blamed for the riot but impeached for allegedly inciting it, despite the fact that barricades around the Capitol were breached while the former president was still speaking to a crowd a mile away. But this characterization of the Capitol as "a temple" and "sacred space" was echoed by political commentators and religious leaders across the country after January 6. Those who wrote and spoke about the Capitol in religious terms may not even realize that they're very close to what the Fallen would have us believe about the nature and purpose of America's "Congress House."

Tom Horn has written at length about the occult world's purpose for

2021. https://chicago.cbslocal.com/2021/01/06/sen-durbin-on-senate-floor-this-sacred-place-was-desecrated-during-capitol-storming/, retrieved 4/24/21.

457. "Cheney: The Capitol Police Are Heroes & We Saw Their Heroism in Action on 1/6." Press release, Mar. 17, 2021. https://cheney.house.gov/2021/03/17/cheney-the-capitol-police-are-heroes-we-saw-their-heroism-in-action-on-1-6/, retrieved 4/24/21.

458. "Pelosi Remarks Upon Reconvening of the House of Representatives." Press release, Jan. 6, 2021. https://www.speaker.gov/newsroom/1621-1, retrieved 4/24/21.

the Capitol in *Apollyon Rising 2012* and its revised and expanded edition *Zenith 2016*. In short, occult adepts believe that a future world leader, the Antichrist, will be engendered in America's "temple to democracy." At the risk of being indelicate, the Washington Monument, the world's tallest obelisk at just over 555 feet, 5 inches (6,665 inches),[459] represents the missing male member of the Egyptian god of the dead, Osiris. The dome of the Capitol, at the other end of the National Mall, represents the womb of his sister-wife, Isis. The spatial relationship between the monument and the Capitol echoes the layout of St. Peter's Square in Rome, where an ancient Egyptian obelisk was erected by Pope Sixtus V in 1586 opposite St. Peter's Basilica, which, like the Capitol, is topped by a dome. The obvious difference between the two is that the obelisk in Rome is only eighty-four feet high.

The obelisk and dome of the Washington Monument and the US Capitol represent more than just classical architecture.

---

459. "Washington Monument: Frequently Asked Questions." *National Park Service*, https://www.nps.gov/wamo/faqs.htm, retrieved 5/24/21.

Tom Horn suggested in *Apollyon Rising 2012* and *Zenith 2016* that the occult purpose of the Capitol is to facilitate the return of Osiris, the Egyptian form of Apollo. This reincarnate entity would be the Antichrist—a resurrected Nimrod. I humbly suggest that there is another piece to this puzzle.

Sharon and I argued in *Giants, Gods & Dragons* that Apollo has been with us for millennia, riding the earth as the first horseman of the Apocalypse.[460] The god was well known in the ancient world, considered the ideal of Greek youth, and adopted as a personal god by Caesar Augustus, Nero, and other Roman emperors in the centuries that followed. Apollo, a plague-god, was worshiped more than two thousand years before John wrote the book of Revelation as Resheph in western Mesopotamia and as Nergal in Akkad and Sumer.[461] He was also adopted as the personal protector god by Amenhotep II,[462] convincingly identified by Dr. Douglas Petrovich as the Pharaoh of the Exodus.[463] This means two things: First, Resheph (Apollo) was well known in Egypt and considered distinct from Osiris; and second, the God of Israel convinced Pharaoh to let His people go by sending a series of plagues that the plague-god was powerless to stop.

Resheph is also mentioned in the Bible, most obviously by the prophet Habakkuk:

---

460. Gilbert & Gilbert (2020), op. cit., pp. 159–182.

461. Paolo Xella, "Resheph." In Karel van der Toorn, Bob Becking, and Pieter W. van der Horst (Eds.), *Dictionary of Deities and Demons in the Bible* (Leiden; Boston; Köln; Grand Rapids, MI; Cambridge: Brill; Eerdmans, 1999), p. 701.

462. Ibid.

463. Douglas N. Petrovich, "Amenhotep II and the Historicity of the Exodus-Pharaoh." *The Master's Seminary Journal* (2006). https://www.academia.edu/1049040/_2006_Amenhotep_II_and_the_Historicity_of_the_Exodus_Pharaoh, retrieved 4/30/21.

God came from Teman,
and the Holy One from Mount Paran. *Selah*
His splendor covered the heavens,
and the earth was full of his praise.
His brightness was like the light;
rays flashed from his hand;
and there he veiled his power.
Before him went pestilence [*Deber*],
and plague [*Resheph*] followed at his heels. (Habakkuk 3:3–5)

Deber, like Resheph, was a deity well known to the Semitic people of western Mesopotamia. Both were worshiped at Ebla at least a thousand years before the Exodus.[464] The point is that since Resheph/Apollo was following at God's heels as He led the Israelites from Mount Paran (an alternate name for Sinai) toward the Promised Land, then Resheph/Apollo is not among the group of rebels chained in the abyss for the rebellion at Mount Hermon. Not only was this an act of humiliation, since God had just demonstrated His superiority over Resheph/Apollo to the Pharaoh, this means Resheph/Apollo is not "the angel of the bottomless pit" of Revelation 9:11. The similarity of the name "Apollo" to "Apollyon" does not mean the two are one and the same.

While I think Tom has pointed us in the right direction with his analysis of the occult teachings and rituals he documents in *Apollyon Rising 2012* and *Zenith 2016*, I believe the Capitol symbolizes a purpose other than the incubation chamber for the Antichrist. As I argued in *Bad Moon Rising*, it's far more likely that the Son of Perdition will present himself to the world as a Jew, a deception far more devious and cruel than manifesting as the pope or the Muslim Mahdi (who will look very different to Sunnis and Shias anyway; one sect's Mahdi will be the

---

464. Ibid. Also see Giovanni Pettinato, *The Archives of Ebla: An Empire Inscribed in Clay.* (Garden City, NY: Doubleday & Company, Inc., 1981), p. 247.

other's Antichrist equivalent, the Dajjal—but I digress). Senators Chuck Schumer and Amy Klobuchar, Speaker Nancy Pelosi, Representative Liz Cheney, and others were far closer to the truth than they may even realize. The Capitol truly *is* America's temple, where principalities and powers, at the bidding of Jupiter/Zeus/Satan, have influenced this country for more than two hundred years.

To be clear, America is not the only nation under the influence of the Fallen. Remember, Satan offered to trade Jesus all the kingdoms of the world for His worship, and our Lord did not rebuke Satan for overstepping the limits of his authority. But we Christians, who tend to be among the most patriotic Americans, must remember that Jesus' kingdom is not of this world—and the Capitol is a temple to the god of this world. More than that, it reflects the model of the cosmos as embodied by the Capitoline Hill: Jupiter (Satan) above and Saturn (Shemihazah) below.

As Tom Horn noted in his groundbreaking books, the room at ground level in the Capitol, one floor below the rotunda, is called the crypt. No one is buried there, but the plan was to move the body of George Washington, who died in 1799, to a chamber in the crypt, which was to serve as the entry to Washington's tomb. Directly above the tomb, a ten-foot circular opening would have allowed visitors in the rotunda to look down on Washington's final resting place. However, after delays in construction, not least of which was the need to rebuild the Capitol after the British burned it during the War of 1812, Washington's descendants opted to honor the former president's will and left him interred at Mount Vernon.

The symbolism of birth and generation embodied by the Washington Monument and the Capitol is clear. And I believe Tom Horn is correct in identifying the Egyptian god of the dead, Osiris, as the object of this long occult ritual. However, the Roman Osiris is not Apollo—it's Saturn. Given the nature of the sin committed by Saturn/Shemihazah and his colleagues, commingling with human women, the symbolism of the obelisk is apt.

Why did Thomas Jefferson insist on calling our nation's legislative building the Capitol when the original *Capitolium* was not a domed building? In other words, if Jefferson was dead set on creating an American temple named for the house of Jupiter, why doesn't it look like the *Capitolium*? The Romans were the first to utilize domes for large buildings, but the dome didn't become popular in Roman architecture until the first century BC, almost five hundred years after the *Capitolium* was dedicated. Why, then, does the American Capitol feature such a prominent dome?

Here is the key: While the Capitol is named for the *Capitolium*, its design emulates another important religious structure in Rome, the Pantheon. While the Capitol dome as we see it today is much larger relative to the rest of the building than the dome atop the Pantheon, the Capitol's original dome was much closer to the Pantheon's in scale. The size and prominence of the Capitol dome grew as the structure was rebuilt and expanded in the nineteenth century. As the Capitol changed, the art and architecture of the building made its hidden purpose more obvious for those with eyes to see.

In *Giants, Gods & Dragons*, Sharon and I made the case that Apollo, as the first horseman of the Apocalypse and the symbol of Roman imperialism, went forth "conquering, and to conquer" by laying the foundation of Western civilization—Greek and Roman philosophy, law, art, literature, architecture, and systems of government. Little wonder that Jefferson insisted on calling the home of our nation's new legislative body the "Capitol," and that so much of our government architecture is inspired by, if not copied from, pagan temples of Greece and Rome. Indeed, the underside of the Capitol dome features the overtly pagan fresco titled *The Apotheosis of Washington*, a depiction of our nation's first president ascending to the heavens and becoming a god:

> Beside those pagan gods which accompany Washington inside the Capitol Dome, the scene is rich with symbols analogous with ancient and modern magic, including the powerful trident—

considered of the utmost importance for sorcery and indispens-able to the efficacy of infernal rites—and the caduceus, tied to Apollo and Freemasonic Gnosticism in which Jesus was a myth based on Apollo's son, Asclepius, the god of medicine and heal-ing whose snake-entwined staff remains a symbol of medicine today. Occult numerology associated with the legend of Isis and Osiris is also encoded throughout the painting, such as the thir-teen maidens, the six scenes of pagan gods around the perimeter forming a hexagram, and the entire scene bounded by the pow-erful Pythagorian/Freemasonic "binding" utility—seventy-two five-pointed stars within circles.[465]

The Apotheosis of Washington inside
the US Capitol

The fresco is viewed from the rotunda below through an oculus, a circular opening in the dome that creates the impression that Wash-ington is in the heavens among the gods, having become one himself.

465. Horn (2013), op. cit.

This is borrowed from the oculus in the dome of the Pantheon, which opened to the sky. This feature served a spiritual purpose:

> In topographical context, therefore, it would seem that the Pantheon operated as the focal point for an innovative religious system. It was a place of veneration of the principal Olympian divinities (probably including Romulus/Quirinus), along with the first divinized member of the gens Iulia, Julius Caesar.... The oculus in the dome presented that union of earth and sky that symbolized an apotheosis into the heavens.[466]

The Capitol not only features an oculus through which visitors can view the divinized Washington, but it includes a chamber at ground level intended to house the body of Washington, also visible from the rotunda above through an opening in the floor. It's as though the Capitol was constructed around a portal for George Washington's spirit to ascend into the heavens, just as the Pantheon in Rome was designed by Agrippa to symbolize the apotheosis of Julius Caesar and his successor, Caesar Augustus.

The seventy-two stars in the fresco represent the *elohim* placed by God over the nations after the Tower of Babel incident. There are seventy in the Bible, based on the number of people groups listed in the Table of Nations in Genesis 10, but the symbolic meaning of seventy is the same as seventy-two, which explains the seventy-two (or seventy, depending on the translation) disciples sent into Galilee by Jesus in Luke 10:1–20. Numerologically, seventy and seventy-two represent the same idea—the complete set, or "all of them." Seventy-two also happens to

---

466. Eugenio La Rocca, "Agrippa's Pantheon and Its Origin," in *The Pantheon: From Antiquity to the Present*, ed. by Tod A. Marder and Mark Wilson Jones (Cambridge: Cambridge University Press, 2015), pp. 49–78. https://erenow.net/ancient/the-pantheon-from-antiquity-to-the-present/2. php, retrieved 4/29/21.

be one-fifth of 360—the number of degrees in a circle, hence the five-pointed stars.

All of these symbols points to a deeper meaning to the fresco on the Capitol dome: Just as the Canaanite creator-god El lived on Mount Hermon with his consort and their seventy sons, the gods of the nations, the divinized Washington is surrounded by seventy-two stars that likewise represent the heavenly host.

It's also revealing that Washington is depicted with purple cloth draped over his legs, which hides them from view. Most interpret this as a sign of royalty, since purple was the color reserved for kings in the ancient world. As inconsistent as this is in a nation with no (official) royalty, the symbolism is disturbing on a deeper level: The legs of the statue of Saturn in his temple at Rome were bound with wool most of the year, representing his confinement in the netherworld. The wool was removed only during the annual Saturnalia festival. On the Capitol dome, Washington's legs are covered (with the color of royalty) but unbound, apparently symbolizing the return of the king(-god) to his place in the heavens.

In short, *The Apotheosis of Washington* depicts the man called the "father of our nation" as El/Saturn, who led America into a Golden Age represented by the scenes of commerce, agriculture, science, industry, transoceanic travel and communication, and victory over tyranny and kingly power.

The art and architecture of the Capitol make a clear statement: America is politically, militarily, and, most of all, spiritually Rome.

For American Christians, the implications are disturbing. Most of us have taken for granted that the pagan and occult symbols designed into our government buildings in general, and the Capitol, National Mall, and Washington Monument in particular, were simply artistic choices made for their aesthetic value. Our ignorance of those pagan symbols has led us to accept a false history that's much more comfortable than the truth.

Now consider how many state legislatures across the United States meet in buildings that are likewise inspired by the Pantheon. Thirty-nine of our fifty state capitol buildings are domed. At least half a dozen, including our home state of Missouri, are topped by statues of pagan deities. As many more are adorned by statues that, if not pagan, are most definitely not Christian.

It's worth noting that the same obelisk-and-dome imagery of the Capitol and Saint Peter's Square is found at most mosques. The minarets are explained as necessary for *muezzin* to sing the call to prayer, but why stand-alone towers that look like modified obelisks? Why not a bell tower? Or, given the military history of Islam, why not a ramparted wall around the mosque? Digging into the history of Islamic architecture and symbolism is beyond the scope of this book, but it's intriguing that symbols so closely linked to the centers of allegedly Christian religious and political power in Washington, DC, and Rome are also key elements of the imagery that defines Islam.

This is speculation, but is the worldwide distribution of obelisks and domes related to the return of old Saturn and his colleagues from the netherworld? (We'll address the biblical prophecy of that event in an upcoming chapter.) And what about the obelisks used as funerary markers all over the world—many of them for Christians?

Chapter Twenty-Seven

JUSTICE, BUT NOT AS WE KNOW IT

The Roman poet Virgil wrote in his *Eclogue IV* that the return of "old Saturn" was accompanied by the return of Justice. The poet wasn't using allegory to depict the return to an age of law and order; Justice was a goddess, Justitia, equivalent to the Greek goddess Dike.

Justitia was believed to be the daughter of Zeus and the Titaness Themis, the goddess of divine law and order, the rules of conduct established by the gods. Justice is the punisher of those who transgress the statutes of the gods. In that sense, she's like the ancient Mesopotamian goddess Inanna, who tricked her uncle Enki, the god who'd sent the *apkallu* (Watchers) to humanity with the gifts of civilization, into giving her the *mes* (pronounced "mezz"), which were the concepts that established the divine order of life. Inanna, better known as the Akkadian goddess Ishtar (and Astarte of the Bible), was the goddess associated with sex, war, justice and political power.[467] I discussed this entity in depth in my book *Bad Moon Rising*.

---

467. Sjur Cappelen Papazian, "Lady Justice (mother) and Lady Liberty (maiden)." *Cradle of Civilization*, Sept. 25, 2018. https://aratta.wordpress.com/2018/09/25/lady-justice-and-lady-liberty/, retrieved 5/1/21.

An Old Babylonian text first translated and published in 1997 seems to confirm at least some of the Bible's negative characterizations of Inanna's Canaanite counterpart, Astarte, including cult prostitution, "cross-gender activities…and the performance of sexual acts." […]

With all due respect to the learned scholars who have described this entity as "a complex, multifaceted goddess," the character of Inanna/Ishtar isn't as complicated as she's made out to be. Frankly, she's a bad screenwriter's idea of a fifteen-year-old boy's fantasy, interested mainly in sex and fighting and better than men at both. She was selfish and violent, ruled by her passions, and incredibly destructive when she didn't get her way.[468]

This is consistent with what we've seen of the riots for social justice that have spread around the world since the end of May, 2020. We shouldn't be surprised; myths of the pagan gods are propaganda to persuade humanity that they, not God, are the rightful rulers of earth. The divine order that "Justice" defends is opposed to the order decreed by God. The recent focus on "social justice" by activists around the world is a case in point. What rational person would conclude that civil disorder resulting in the most costly insurance claims since 1950 from "arson, vandalism, and looting" (the first year those figures were tracked)[469] is in any sense justified? It's not justice by any normal definition of the word. "Social justice" has been deployed by movements like Antifa and Black Lives Matter to rebrand hatred, bigotry, and discrimination.

---

468. Derek P. Gilbert, *Bad Moon Rising* (Crane, MO: Defender, 2018), pp. 116–120.

469. Jennifer A. Kingson, "Exclusive: $1 Billion-plus Riot Damage Is Most Expensive in Insurance History." *Axios*, Sept. 16, 2020. https://www.axios.com/riots-cost-property-damage-276c9bcc-a455-4067-b06a-66f9db4cea9c.html, retrieved 5/1/21.

"Anti-racism" in the form of Critical Race Theory is good, old-fashioned racism that's been weaponized to tear apart the fabric of Western civilization. As far back as 1934, Henry Wallace, later FDR's vice president during World War II, decried a failure to "bring the kingdom of heaven to earth in terms of social justice" that he blamed on racism, capitalism, and nationalism.[470] These are the very sins laid at the feet of Donald Trump and his supporters, typically identified by progressives in the media as white conservative Christians. As Sharon put it in *Zeitgeist 2025*:

> Welcome to the Age of Aquarius, my friends, when the gods of harmony and understanding define us all as bigots and haters. Social justice is being poured out like water from the NEW GODS of Capitol Hill, Saturn and Justitia, and we're expected to enjoy owning nothing.[471]

This and the draconian response to COVID-19 comprise the chaos that occult adepts believe will produce a New World Order, the manifestation of *Ordo ab Chao*—Order Out of Chaos. This is the return of Justice, who heralds the imminent arrival of old Saturn and his Golden Age. The Great Reset initiative of the World Economic Forum is one of the physical manifestations of the spiritual sea change that occult adepts are working to bring about.

There are additional identities by which old Saturn has shown himself to the world. Describing them in detail would fill a few extra chapters of this book. For example, Cernunnos, the horned god of the Celtic pantheon, possibly derives his name from Kronos (= Semitic *qeren*, "horned one").[472] Based on his representations in art, Cernunnos was one of the most important gods in Celtic cosmology, but because

---

470. Henry A. Wallace, *Statesmanship and Religion* (New York: Round Table Press, 1934), pp. 78–83.
471. S. Gilbert (2021), op. cit.
472. Wyatt (2010), op. cit., p. 55.

the Celts didn't leave a body of literature to explain their religion, we're left guessing as to his character and cult. However, there is a clear link between Cernunnos and the underworld, consistent with the character of this entity throughout history:

> [Cernunnos] is commonly represented squatting with crossed legs. Why? I think it is an allusion to his chthonian infernal nature. Macrobius tells us that Saturn was sometimes represented with tied legs, while Triton trumpeters with their tails thrust into the ground were sculpted on the fronton of his temple. Being assimilated to Kronos, Saturn, as well as the Titans and Giants, is son of Uran and Earth. Since the Giants were often represented with snake coils instead of legs, we may generically suggest that this feature alluded to supernatural beings which could live under ground. As Lampridius (*Comm.* 9) observes "to go with coils instead of legs and feet is like to move with the knees tied by bands, *quasi dracones* [as dragons]."[473]

This is an unexpected connection between Saturn and the divinized Washington on the Capitol dome, who's clearly sitting with his legs crossed beneath the purple cloak.

Now, let's go back to the riot at the Capitol. January 6 is the date celebrated each year by Western Christians as Epiphany, and Theophany by Christians in the Eastern churches. It's sometimes called Three Kings Day; the twelfth day of Christmas, when the three wise men from the East visited the Christ child. It marks the revelation of God incarnate in the form of Jesus. And what happened on Epiphany in 2021? America's temple was invaded by, as Sharon colorfully described them, the

---

473. Adolfo Zavaroni, "Remarks on Three Figures of Cernunnos." *Academia.edu.* https://www.academia.edu/13354523/Remarks_on_three_figures_of_Cernunnos, retrieved 5/1/21.

"'Q-Anon Shaman' in his crazy buffalo hat along with his selfie-taking hooligan buddies."[474]

Remember the very long association of bull imagery with this old entity—the horned helmets of ancient Sumer that indicated divine status, the name Kronos, derived from Semitic *qeren* ("horned one"), and the epithet of the god who held court on Mount Hermon, "Bull El." Isn't it odd that a man wearing a symbol of this old god should burst into the Capitol, and the national consciousness, on the day Christians celebrate the revelation of the One True God?

It would be a startling coincidence, if I believed in coincidences. Whether he knew it or not, the Q-Anon Shaman announced the return of the old horned god Saturn/Kronos/El in America's temple on the day marking the revelation of Christ's divinity.

There is one other strange convergence of symbols inside the United States Capitol. Several figures depicted inside the Capitol wear a Phrygian cap, a soft conical hat bent over at the top. According to the architect of the Capitol, this piece of headgear, also referred to as a liberty cap, was adopted as a symbol of freedom in the nineteenth century.[475] It's called a Phrygian cap because it was associated with Phrygia, an ancient kingdom in west central Anatolia (modern Turkey) that reached its peak in the eighth century BC under King Midas (yes, that one; he was real, although his "golden touch" was made up). A similar conical felt cap called a *pileus* was given to freed slaves in ancient Rome, and it made a comeback as a symbol during the American and French revolutions.[476]

Constantino Brumidi painted figures wearing the red Phrygian cap throughout the Capitol. They are generally female—for example, the goddess Liberty to Washington's right in *The Apotheosis of Washington* and

---

474. S. Gilbert (2021), op. cit.
475. AOC Curator, "The Liberty Cap in the Art of the U.S. Capitol."
Explore the Capitol Campus: Our Blog, Jan. 29, 2013. https://www.aoc.gov/explore-capitol-campus/blog/liberty-cap-art-us-capitol, retrieved 5/7/21.
476. Ibid.

the war-goddess Bellona in the Senate wing. However, Young America is depicted as a young man wearing a toga and a Phrygian cap in the section of *The Apotheosis of Washington* called "Agriculture," where America holds the reins of a horse while standing next to the grain-goddess Ceres, who's seated on a McCormick Reaper, a mechanical harvester that helped revolutionize American farming. The relevant bit here is that the depiction of America wearing a Phrygian cap is oddly similar to classical artwork featuring Ganymede, a minor figure in Greco-Roman religion.

Young America depicted as a youth wearing a Phrygian cap in the "Agriculture" section of *The Apotheosis of Washington*

Ganymede was believed to be the son of Tros, king of Troy, and "was comeliest of mortal men."[477] He was so comely, in fact, that he caught the fancy of the king of the gods, Jupiter/Zeus. By the late sixth century

---

477. Homer, *The Iliad of Homer. Rendered into English Prose for the Use of Those Who Cannot Read the Original,* ed. by Samuel Butler. Book XX, line 233 (Medford, MA: Longmans, Green and Co., 1898), digital edition.

BC, after the Persian conquest of Asia Minor, Phrygia had expanded to include northwestern Anatolia, the region around Troy—hence Ganymede's Phrygian cap. Zeus/Jupiter was so smitten with the young man that the storm-god transformed himself into an eagle and abducted Ganymede while he tended sheep on Mount Ida.

If you've heard the story, it was probably characterized as an honor for the young shepherd. After all, Ganymede was made the cupbearer of Zeus/Jupiter and allowed to live among the gods of Olympus. Who wouldn't want that?

There's more to the story. The original tale is darker.

First, we need to remember that the storm-god—Baal in Canaan, Zeus in Greece, and Jupiter in Rome—was identified by Jesus as Satan (see Matthew 12:22–26, and note that Beelzebul = "Baal the prince"). The Canaanites apparently believed that Baal was lord of the Rephaim, who were called "warriors of Baal." Recall the importance of the *kispum* among the ancient Amorites, a monthly ritual meal for the ancestral dead. The *kispum* featured a libation (drink offering), and the rite was so integral to Amorite society that the eldest son, the heir to the family estate responsible for performing the ritual, was called the "pourer of water" or "son of the cup." This custom was transmitted to the Greeks and Romans, who preserved the practice of preparing communal meals for the ancestral dead.

So, the story of Ganymede is essentially the tale of a beautiful boy abducted by the lord of the Rephaim to serve as his personal "pourer of water."

But the relationship went much farther than that. The Greek philosopher Plato, writing in the fourth century BC, attributed the story of Ganymede to the people of Crete:

Whether one makes the observation in earnest or in jest, one certainly should not fail to observe that when male unites with female for procreation the pleasure experienced is held to be due to nature, but contrary to nature when male mates with male or female with female, and that those first guilty of such enormities were impelled by their slavery to pleasure. And we all accuse the Cretans of concocting the story about Ganymede. Because it was the belief that they derived their laws from Zeus, they added on this story about Zeus in order that they might be following his example in enjoying this pleasure as well.[478]

In other words, Plato claimed the Cretans invented the myth to justify their practice of homosexuality.

Mosaic from second or third century AD depicting the abduction of Ganymede by Zeus in the guise of an eagle

However the story originated, the relationship between Ganymede and Zeus/Jupiter was well understood in the Greco-Roman world. The Latin form of Ganymede's name is Catamitus, from which we get the

478. Plato, Laws 1.636c—1.636d. https://www.perseus.tufts.edu/hopper/text?doc=Perseus%3Atext%3A1999.01.0166%3Abook%3D1%3Asection%3D636c, retrieved 5/7/21.

English word "catamite," which is a pubescent boy who's sexually inti-mate with an adult man. And the depiction of America on the Capi-tol dome as a young man wearing a Phrygian cap is similar to classical images of Ganymede, who was abducted to serve as the boy toy of Zeus/ Jupiter (Satan), whose temple in Rome is the source of the name of the Capitol.

But the significance of Young America as Ganymede doesn't end there. You see, as a reward for his, well, service, Zeus immortalized the young shepherd by placing him among the stars—as Aquarius, the Water Bearer.

Aquarius—the new age inaugurated by the Great Conjunction of December 21, 2020.

So, not only is Young America represented in the United States Cap-itol as the submissive sexual partner of Jupiter (Satan), he symbolizes the new Golden Age ruled by Saturn (Shemihazah).

Rather than exhausting the subject after the point has been made, we'll summarize: The chief god of the Roman pantheon, the deity worshiped in the *Capitolium*, was the storm-god, Jupiter. Under the names Zeus, the storm-god of the Greeks, and Baal, the West Semitic storm-god, he was unmasked by Jesus and identified as Satan. He is the god of this world, the spirit of this age. But Virgil, and others since, longed for a return of the Golden Age of Saturn that would replace the Age of Iron ruled by Jupiter and bring back a time of ease and prosperity.

The Capitol, America's "temple to democracy," was named for the temple of Jupiter Optimus Maximus but modeled on the Pantheon. That structure was designed by a friend of Caesar Augustus to repre-sent the apotheosis of Caesar and his predecessor, his uncle Julius, the founders of the Roman Empire. Likewise, the Capitol symbolizes the godhood of the man described as the father of our nation, George Wash-ington. Like Augustus, through whom Virgil believed the Golden Age of Saturn had returned, Washington was cast as the agent of this supernatural transfer of power—the return of the god who's been imprisoned in Tartarus to bring with him a new Golden Age.

The modern-day spiritual descendants of Virgil are trying to make the return of Saturn a reality. There are powerful, wealthy people who believe the stars signaled the advent of this new Golden Age, Saturn's return to his proper place in the Capitol, on December 21, 2020, with the conjunction of the planets that bear the names of the two great Roman gods.

Chapter Twenty-Eight

THE CULTS OF SATURN

This section of the book was originally intended to be longer. However, as research into the history and imagery connected to Saturn in his many forms revealed more information that's relevant to where we're going, it became obvious that documenting the work of a few deceived occultists in the present day isn't as important as it appeared at first. As Dr. Michael Heiser has observed about the 1946 Babalon (sic) Working of L. Ron Hubbard and Jack Parsons, if demons and fallen angels need the permission of a couple of deviants performing sex rites in the desert to enter our space-time, they're really lame.

I agree. Ceremonial magicians, sorcerers, witches, and practitioners of the occult believe they control the dark forces of the spirit realm. They've been duped. These entities are more powerful than the useful idiots who think they're protected inside a circle of salt. Shining a light on the work of the occultists is useful only to help us understand the growing number of deluded humans who welcome the influence of the old god on our world.

As mentioned in an earlier chapter, Saturn's demand that humans offer up our children continues to the present day. While we modern, enlightened Western Christians are rightly horrified by the ancient Amorite/Phoenician practice of sacrificing children, many of us personally know someone who has either had or facilitated an abortion.

It seems so clinical, especially since we've been so programmed to view a developing child as nothing more than a lifeless clump of cells that we no longer view the procedure for what it is—the termination of a human life. It's become so socially acceptable that not only was abortion the number-one cause of death worldwide in 2020,[479] but the nearly 42.7 million lives ended were more than triple the number of deaths from all communicable diseases, including COVID-19 (1.8 million) and HIV/AIDS (1.7 million).[480]

You don't likely need to be told that global spending on the coronavirus pandemic and the effort to eradicate HIV is far greater than on finding families for unwanted children. Of course, public policy directed at HIV/AIDS and unwanted pregnancies rarely includes promoting abstinence before marriage and monogamy, the only strategies proven to work. This speaks to the nature of the spirits at work behind the scenes. Slaughter of the innocents is one of the things for which Saturn/Kronos/ Baal Hammon/Shemihazah is best known. Maybe this is his revenge for watching his own children, the Nephilim, die in the Flood.

It's likely that most of those who are part of the abortion industry or who have accepted its dehumanizing propaganda don't recognize the influence of the dark god on what they do. There are those, however, who knowingly venerate this entity, even if they don't understand who he is and his ultimate goal.

In 1926, five German occultists led by Eugen Grosche founded a

---

479. Minnie Agdeppa, "Abortion Is the Leading Cause of Death Worldwide in 2020—Higher Than Cancer, Malaria, and Others Combined." *Christianity Daily*, Jan. 5, 2021. http://www.christianitydaily.com/ articles/10420/20210105/abortion-is-the-leading-cause-of-death-worldwide-in-2020—higher-than-cancer-malaria-and-others-combined.htm, retrieved 5/1/21.

480. Thomas D. Williams, "Abortion Leading Global Cause of Death in 2020 with 42.7 Million Killed." *Breitbart News*, Jan. 1, 2021, retrieved 5/1/21.

magical order called *Fraternitas Saturni*, or Brotherhood of Saturn. It describes itself as "a purely esoteric logic of knowledge that seeks to realize the impulse of the Aquarius age of spiritual clarity and freedom."[481] Outside observers have described it as "a unique blend of Scottish Freemasonry, Luciferianism, astrological mythology and Indian yoga systems, with an emphasis placed on the unique power that its adherents believed could be drawn from the dark side of Saturn."[482]

The group is set up along lines similar to Scottish Rite Freemasonry, at least in terms of its system of degrees as one progresses in the order.[483] Before 1960, members could ascend through a series of nine degrees, not including 0° (Novice), from Neophyte through *Magister Aquarii* ("Master of Aquarius"),[484] a reminder that the Age of Aquarius we fully entered on December 21, 2020, is, according to astrologers and occultists, ruled by Saturn. After 1960, the path to enlightenment was expanded to thirty-three degrees, from 0° (Neophyte) to 33°, the *Gradus Ordinis Templi Orientis Saturni*.[485]

Despite the fact that most of us have never heard of this group, likely because it's only been active in the German-speaking world, experts on the occult believe it's been profoundly influential:

---

481. "Welcome to the website of Fraternitas Saturni." *Fraternitas.de*, http://fraternitas.de/home.htm, retrieved 5/1/21.

482. Haley Ray, "Inside the Secret Society That Inspired the New Age Movement." *Narratively*, Dec. 12, 2018. https://narratively.com/inside-the-secret-society-that-inspired-the-new-age-movement/, retrieved 5/1/21.

483. Hans Thomas Hakl, "The Magical Order of the Fraternitas Saturni." In *Occultism in a Global Perspective*, ed. by Henrik Bogdan and Gordan Djurdjevic (Durham, UK: Acumen Publishing, 2013), p. 44.

484. Stephen Flowers, *Fire & Ice—The History, Structure and Rituals of Germany's Most Influential Modern Magical Order: The Brotherhood of Saturn* (St. Paul, Minn.: Llewellyn, 1994), pp. 77–88.

485. Ibid.

The Fraternitas Saturni (FS) is not only the most important secret magical lodge of twentieth-century Germany, but one of the most important of all modern magical lodges. The sheer volume of occult texts produced by its masters and leading members surpasses nearly everything written by other magical groups.... The only orders that can lay claim to more material are those associated with Aleister Crowley (1875–1947), notably the Ordo Templi Orientis (OTO) and Argenteum Astrum (A∴A∴) with their countless affiliations in various countries.[486]

As with other occult systems, the goal is "'divine' knowledge" to achieve "self-salvation," which can only be achieved through magic.[487]

The central feature of the Brotherhood of Saturn is the Égrégore, a non-physical entity created by the focused thought of the group. This is similar to a tulpa, a Theosophist concept through which a person or group, by focusing spiritual thought, creates a sort of imaginary friend who becomes sentient and autonomous. The term derives from the Greek *egregore*, which means "watcher." Yes, *that* kind of Watcher—the supernatural, "son of God" kind, of which Saturn/Shemihazah is one.

Its thirty-third degree is called "GOTOS," which derives from the term "Gradus O.T.O. Saturni," and somewhat resembles the office of Outer head of the Order (OHO) in the O.T.O. The OHO is the link between the Order and its "Secret Chiefs"—its Égrégore, or the Inner Head of the Order (IHO); the OHO is the IHO's mouthpiece. [...]

---

486. Hakl, op. cit., p. 37.
487. Ibid., p. 45.

The 24° FS has as it central "secret" the "knowledge" of the Beast's true nature; its name is supposed to be "Gregor," while it retains the number 666. But why Gregor? To explain this it is necessary to examine he founder of the FS, Eugen Grosche. He chose as his magical name Gregor A. Gregorius, or else Gregor E Gregor(ius). This suggests Grosche considered that he himself was the Great Beast of Revelation, and the Égrégore of the FS at one and the same time. At the precise moment that Grosche achieved the 33° (at Easter in 1960) Gotos became GOTOS, in the same way that Crowley became Baphomet, XI° in 1912.

This is the secret of both the O.T.O. and the FS—both orders exist for the sole purpose of empowering and exalting their founders, or their heirs in the office of OHO.[488] (Emphasis added)

This is why we're not spending more time on the current practitioners of Saturnian magic. Although the Brotherhood of Saturn is credited with inspiring the modern New Age movement,[489] which has deceived millions into believing that "ye shall be as gods," its members have been conned into believing that they understand and control Saturn.

A recent occult movement called the Order of Nine Angles (O9A) began attracting attention in the early 1980s for its neo-Nazi activism. Central to its ideology is the Tree of Wyrd, essentially a modified kabbalistic tree of life with only seven nodes instead of ten. At the top of the tree is the Norse all-father god, Odin, identified with Saturn.[490] While

---

488. Barbara Weiss, Ottmar Domainko, and Peter-Robert Koenig, "Saturn Gnosis: The Real Fraternitas Saturni." *Parareligion*, https://www.parareligion. ch/fs3.htm, retrieved 5/1/21.

489. Ray, op. cit.

490. William Ramsey, *Global Death Cult: The Order of Nine Angles, Atomwaffen, and the Slaughter of the Innocents* (California: William Ramsey Investigates, 2021), Kindle edition.

the O9A's alleged founder David Myatt has moved on from the group, converting to Islam and then abandoning it again in favor of his own home-brewed religion, the group considers itself truly Satanic, putting into practice what other sects such as the Church of Satan and Temple of Set only play at—creating a "new, more evolved human species."[491] The group embraces human sacrifice and jihadist terror as tactics toward the destruction of Western civilization, which, in the O9A's view, has been weakened by Magian (Jewish) and Nazarene (Christian) influences. This would clear the way for the rise of a new, superhuman civilization.[492] In that sense, the O9A is working toward the return of Saturn's reign and the fulfillment of Satan's promise that "ye shall be as gods."

Surprisingly, a young man who became the subject of a trio of HBO documentaries after his conviction for murder is now free and openly touting the power of summoning angels through the power of Enlil, one of the identities of the dark god.

On May 5, 1993, three eight-year-old boys went missing in West Memphis, Arkansas. They were found a day later, victims of what was characterized by prosecutors as "satanic sex ritual slayings."[493] Three teens, including then eighteen-year-old Damien Echols, were convicted in 1994 of the killings. In 2010, however, after the high-profile documentaries, the trio, dubbed the "West Memphis Three," were freed on

---

491. "Order of the Nine Angles," *Counter Extremism Project.* https://www. counterextremism.com/supremacy/order-nine-angles, retrieved 5/29/21.

492. Shanon Shah, "Order of Nine Angles." In James Crossley and Alastair Lockhart (eds.) *Critical Dictionary of Apocalyptic and Millenarian Movements.* Jan. 15, 2021. Retrieved from www.cdamm.org/articles/ona, 5/29/21.

493. The Associated Press, "Arguments Conclude in 'West Memphis Three' Appeals." *Arkansas Democrat-Gazette*, Oct. 2, 2009. https://www. arkansasonline.com/news/2009/oct/02/appeals-continue-slayings-ark-boys-93/, retrieved 5/4/21.

Alford pleas,[494] a legal tactic that allows defendants to plead guilty while maintaining their innocence.

It's not my intent to revisit the case. The HBO documentaries succeeded in mobilizing a legion of famous supporters behind Echols and his companions, including Hollywood A-listers Winona Ryder, Peter Jackson (director of *Lord of the Rings* and *The Hobbit*), and Johnny Depp, who's become a personal friend of Echols, and musicians like Eddie Vedder (Pearl Jam), Natalie Maines (Dixie Chicks), and the band Metallica,[495] which allowed their music to be used in the documentaries' soundtracks. Researcher William Ramsey let the investigators' case files speak for themselves in his book *Abomination: Devil Worship and Deception in the West Memphis Three Murders*. Ramsey told me in a 2014 interview that his interest in the case was prompted by Echols' references to the occultist Aleister Crowley in trial transcripts, which he found while researching the work of Crowley for his first book.[496] Contrary to the way the young man and the case were depicted by the HBO documentaries, the killings had the telltales of a satanic crime, and Echols, at least, had a very active interest in witchcraft and the occult.

---

494. Gavin Lesnick, "Plea Reached in West Memphis Murders." *Arkansas Democrat-Gazette*, Aug. 19, 2011. https://www.arkansasonline.com/ news/2011/aug/19/breaking-plea-reached-west-memphis-murders/?breaking, retrieved 5/4/21.

495. Clémence Michallon, "The West Memphis Three: How a Trilogy of HBO Documentaries Helped Free Three Men Convicted of Murder." *The Independent*, May 5, 2020. https://www.independent.co.uk/arts-entertainment/films/features/west-memphis-three-documentaries-damien-echols-jason-baldwin-jessie-misskelley-paradise-lost-hbo-a9498786.html, retrieved 5/4/21.

496. Derek P. Gilbert, "VFTB 170: Devil Worship, Deception and the West Memphis Three." *A View from the Bunker*, Feb. 2, 2014. https://www.vftb. net/?p=5007, retrieved 5/4/21.

His interest has only grown over time. Now that he's a free man, Damien Echols teaches "high magick" to subscribers through his Patreon page. What's of interest to us is that Echols believes he's discovered the key to unlocking the secrets of the paranormal and supernatural, and it's available from the entity we've been tracking throughout this book.

> One morning when I was in the middle of the angelic invocations involved in the Shem Operation, I experienced something that was initially disorienting and frightening. Suddenly it felt like the very earth dropped away beneath my feet. I was surrounded by an incredible amount of light—it was so bright that it felt like I was standing in the middle of the sun. Then it felt like something snapped, and I was surrounded by the darkness of an infinite void. [...]
>
> The closest I'll ever be able to come to articulating what happened is this: I saw the nighttime sky. It was crystal clear—truly beautiful. And then, across this vision of the sky, I saw a word spelled out, just as if the wind were gently rippling across the stars as if they were wheat. The word was *Enlil*. [...]
>
> So, of course, I began invoking him. Instead of calling upon all of the angelic intelligences I'd been using, I invoked Enlil in all directions—east, west, up, down, and everywhere in between. The resultant energy I experienced was unlike anything I'd ever felt, even after years of intense angel work. Enlil's presence was like feeling the unified power of a thousand archangels.[497]

Echols has been fooled. There is no doubt that he received something like power, and maybe he did feel the spiritual presence of the entity we've been studying—but I doubt it. Enlil/Saturn/Shemihazah and his colleagues are chained in a deep, dark hole and probably not

497. Damien Echols, *Angels and Archangels: The Western Path to Enlightenment* (Boulder, CO: Sounds True, 2020), pp. 261–263.

capable of direct contact with a power-seeking ceremonial magician like Echols. In all likelihood, however, the old god is still in touch with his demonic offspring, and it's a better guess that one or more of them gave Echols the thrill he described.

The point of this chapter is simply this: The old entity who led the rebellion that began on Mount Hermon hasn't been entirely forgotten. His human followers, however, aren't capable of summoning or weaponizing his supernatural power. To repeat, the denizens of the spirit realm don't need our permission to enter the natural world. Occultists like Echols, Hubbard, Parsons, and Crowley are truly pathetic. They are nothing more than useful idiots to entities like Saturn/Shemihazah—and their usefulness is limited to convincing *other* idiots to reject Jesus Christ by promoting an appealing false gospel.

The "king" god, who convinced his human followers, through his demonic minions, to call him "the" god, has little interest in helping humans fulfill their wishes and dreams. He has bigger plans—establishing his reign over God's prize jewel, earth.

But God has already told us how the end game plays out. Saturn's reign won't last half a year.

Chapter Twenty-Nine

ARMAGEDDON

The long war by the Fallen against their Creator is for control of God's *har mô'ēd*, His mount of assembly, Zion. That's His prize jewel, and that's why Saturn wants it:

> Great is the LORD and greatly to be praised
> in the city of our God!
> His holy mountain, beautiful in elevation,
> is the joy of all the earth,
> Mount Zion, in the far north,
> the city of the great King. (Psalm 48:1–2)

> So you shall know that I am the LORD your God,
> who dwells in Zion, my holy mountain.
> And Jerusalem shall be holy,
> and strangers shall never again pass through it. (Joel 3:17)

> For the LORD has chosen Zion;
> he has desired it for his dwelling place:
> "This is my resting place forever;
> here I will dwell, for I have desired it." (Psalm 132:13–14)

Plenty of other verses support this idea, but you get the point: God's holy mountain, His mount of assembly, is Zion—the Temple Mount in Jerusalem.

Yes, some believe Solomon's Temple was in the City of David, south of the Temple Mount. There are a number of reasons, including recent archaeological excavations in the City of David at the alternate location proposed for the Temple, that do not support this theory. The most obvious bit of evidence is the testimony of first-century Jewish historian Josephus, who wrote that the platform supporting the Temple measured five hundred cubits square. That's roughly a hundred feet wider than the City of David, which sits on a small, narrow hill south of the Temple Mount.[498] Had the platform been there, it would have hung out over the Kidron Valley, which is bad design to say the least.

Placing Armageddon at Jerusalem makes the most sense from a spiritual standpoint. It's the home of God's mount of assembly. Besides, other apocalyptic prophecies in the Old Testament point to Jerusalem at the site of the final showdown between good and evil.

> The oracle of the word of the LORD concerning Israel: Thus declares the LORD, who stretched out the heavens and founded the earth and formed the spirit of man within him: "Behold, I am about to make Jerusalem a cup of staggering to all the surrounding peoples. **The siege of Jerusalem will also be against Judah.** On that day I will make Jerusalem a heavy stone for all the peoples. All who lift it will surely hurt themselves. And all the nations of the earth will gather against it....
>
> And on that day I will seek to destroy all the nations that come against Jerusalem. (Zechariah 12:1–3, 9, emphasis added)

---

498. Gordon W. Franz, "Cornuke's *Temple* Book: 'The Greatest Archaeological Blunder of All Time.'" *Life and Land*, Nov. 1, 2015. https://www.lifeandland.org/2015/11/cornuke-temple/, retrieved 5/9/21.

For I will gather all the nations against Jerusalem to battle, and the city shall be taken and the houses plundered and the women raped. Half of the city shall go out into exile, but the rest of the people shall not be cut off from the city. Then the LORD will go out and fight against those nations as when he fights on a day of battle. **On that day his feet shall stand on the Mount of Olives that lies before Jerusalem on the east, and the Mount of Olives shall be split in two from east to west by a very wide valley,** so that one half of the Mount shall move northward, and the other half southward. And you shall flee to the valley of my mountains, for the valley of the mountains shall reach to Azal. And you shall flee as you fled from the earthquake in the days of Uzziah king of Judah. Then the LORD my God will come, and all the holy ones with him. (Zechariah 14:2–5, emphasis added)

For behold, in those days and at that time, when I restore the fortunes of Judah and Jerusalem, I will gather all the nations and bring them down to the Valley of Jehoshaphat. And I will enter into judgment with them there, on behalf of my people and my heritage Israel, because they have scattered them among the nations and have divided up my land. (Joel 3:1–2)

The phrase "on that day" refers to the Day of Yahweh, or Day of the Lord, the time of God's judgment against a rebellious and unbelieving world. Zechariah and Joel saw the same final battle as Ezekiel. God personally intervenes to destroy the army assembled against Israel. That's the Second Coming, the return of Messiah.

When He arrives, the Mount of Olives splits in two, creating "a very wide valley." This is probably the Valley of Jehoshaphat mentioned by Joel. This valley doesn't exist on any known map—at least it doesn't exist *today*. The name of the valley is not a reference to the king of Judah during the days of Ahab; Jehoshaphat's name means "Yahweh will judge," so the Valley of Jehoshaphat is literally the "Valley of Yahweh's Judgment."

That's where the Battle of Armageddon ends—between the west slope of the Mount of Olives and the eastern gate of Jerusalem, through which the Messiah will triumphantly enter His city once again.

The location is not random. This is where David probably buried the head of Goliath, thus turning the *rosh* ("head" or "summit") of the Mount of Olives into Golgotha ("Goliath's head"), the site of the Crucifixion. It's where an Ammonite princess convinced King Solomon to build a high place for the "king" god, Milcom, another name for El, one of the many identities worn by this entity over the centuries. Our Lord used the mount as His base of operations for the final week of His human life. Christ was buried on the Mount of Olives, descended from there to the abyss to declare His victory over the imprisoned rebels, and was taken from there up into heaven. And Zechariah has prophesied that when He returns, the Messiah will land there, at the Mount of Olives.

If you've studied end-times prophecy at all, you've probably been taught that Armageddon will be fought at Megiddo, not Jerusalem. It's a popular teaching, but it's based on the difficulty of transliterating from Hebrew to Greek to English. As famous as it is, the name "Armageddon" is found in only one verse in the entire Bible:

> The sixth angel poured out his bowl on the great river Euphrates, and its water was dried up, to prepare the way for the kings from the east. And I saw, coming out of the mouth of the dragon and out of the mouth of the beast and out of the mouth of the false prophet, three unclean spirits like frogs. For they are demonic spirits, performing signs, who go abroad to the kings of the whole world, to assemble them for battle on the great day of God the Almighty. ("Behold, I am coming like a thief! Blessed is the one who stays awake, keeping his garments on, that he may not go about naked and be seen exposed!") And they assembled them at the place that in Hebrew is called Armageddon. (Revelation 16:12–16)

John used slightly different terminology to describe the Day of the Lord, but "the great day of God the Almighty" clearly refers to the same event described by Zechariah and Amos. It's the same battle described by Ezekiel in chapters 38 and 39 of his book, about which we'll have more below.

English speakers trying to decipher the Hebrew words behind "Armageddon" concluded that it's a compound name based on the Hebrew *har magedōn* ("Mount Megiddo"), where the "-on" suffix indicates a place name. In fact, several English translations, such as the NASB, NRSV, and ASV, render the name either "Harmagedon" or "Har-Magedon." This has convinced respected prophecy teachers like Chuck Missler, Dwight Pentecost, John Walvoord, and Arnold Fruchtenbaum to place *har magedōn* near the city of Megiddo in the Valley of Jezreel.

To be fair, that is a logical conclusion from a military standpoint. Megiddo overlooks the valley, which connects the Jordan valley to the Mediterranean, and it guards a key pass through the Carmel mountain range. Several decisive battles were fought at or near Megiddo. In the fifteenth century BC, a little more than a decade before the Exodus, Pharaoh Thutmose III defeated a confederation of Canaanite city-states there. In 609 BC, Judah's King Josiah was killed in battle at Megiddo against Pharaoh Necho, who was leading an Egyptian force north to fight alongside the remnant of the Assyrian army against the rising power in the Near East, the Chaldean kingdom of Babylon. Things went badly for Josiah, who was killed by an Egyptian archer. Despite his efforts, less than twenty-five years later, Nebuchadnezzar's army sacked Jerusalem and destroyed the Temple. Some gratitude.

But with all due respect to the prophecy scholars named above, whose teachings I value highly, placing Armageddon at Megiddo just doesn't fit. First of all, there's no mountain at Megiddo. The ancient site of Megiddo is elevated above the plain, yes—but it's not a mountain. It's a tell, a mound created when people build and rebuild a settlement over centuries on the same spot. Second, it's unlikely that God would descend on the Mount of Olives when the armies of the world, led by the Antichrist, are fifty miles away at Megiddo. Most important, a battle at Megiddo doesn't fit the apocalyptic prophecies of Zechariah, Joel, Ezekiel,[499] and Jesus Himself,[500] all of whom pointed to Jerusalem as the site of the climactic battle.

The problem of identification comes from the difficulty in transliterating from Hebrew to Greek. In 1938, scholar Charles C. Torrey proposed a solution: Armageddon is based not on *har magedōn*, the name of a nonexistent mountain, but on a phrase we've used throughout this book, *har mô'ēd* ("mount of assembly"):

> How you are fallen from heaven,
> O Day Star, son of Dawn!
> How you are cut down to the ground,
> you who laid the nations low!
> You said in your heart,
> "I will ascend to heaven;
> above the stars of God
> I will set my throne on high;
> I will sit on the **mount of assembly** [*har mô'ēd*]
> in the **far reaches of the north**" [*yarkete tsaphon*—Mount Zaphon]. (Isaiah 14:12–13, emphasis added)

Torrey argued that scholars who weren't expert in Greek and Hebrew missed the fact that the Hebrew character *ayin*, transliterated

---

499. Ezekiel 39:11 locates the destruction of the army of Gog (the Antichrist) in "the Valley of the Travelers, east of the sea." I explained why that refers to the Plains of Moab, the Jordan valley between Mount Nebo and Jericho, in my book *Last Clash of the Titans* (pp. 164–178).

500. Luke 21:20–24. Jesus' prophecy of the destruction of Jerusalem is an example of an "already but not yet" prophecy fulfillment. The city was destroyed in AD 70 by the Romans, but it also refers to the Tribulation before His Second Coming.

into English with the character ' (sort of a reverse apostrophe), was usually represented in Greek by the letter *gamma*. This is only an approximation, because there is no letter or sound in Greek that corresponds to *ayin*. Likewise, there's no corresponding sound or letter in English for *ayin*, either. In modern Hebrew, *ayin* is vocalized as a glottal stop. So, when John wrote Revelation, he transliterated the Hebrew *mem-ayin-daleth* (M-'-D) into the closest Greek approximation, *mu-gamma-delta* (M-G-D).

Torrey's point was that those who were unaware of the difficulty of transliterating the *ayin* into Greek—and, more importantly, the critical role of the *har mô ʿēd* ("mount of assembly") in Hebrew theology—assumed that John's *gamma* represented the Hebrew *gimel*, and concluded the original Hebrew name must have been *mem-**gimel**-daleth* (M-G-D) instead of *mem-**ayin**-daleth* (M-'-D). Thus, *mô ʿēd* became *magedōn* and the battle of Armageddon was transplanted from Mount Zion in Jerusalem to Megiddo—a place of no supernatural significance where no mountain exists.

Make no mistake: Armageddon is the battle for control of the *har mô ʿēd*—Zion, God's mount of assembly. The final conflict of the age will be fought at Jerusalem.

Chapter Thirty

RETURN OF THE TITANS

The rebellion that's been leading to Armageddon for thousands of years began with entities created before mankind, the cherubim, seraphim, *malakim*, Watchers, and other supernatural creatures we may not even be aware of. Later came the hybrid progeny of the Watchers, the Nephilim—pre-Flood giants whose spirits were called "Rephaim" by the Hebrews of the Old Testament period. People who developed writing later, like the Greeks and Romans, called the old gods by different names, but their stories are so similar that we must conclude they've been passed from one culture to another over the centuries.

As a Christian, I accept the testimony of Jesus that the Old Testament is historically accurate. So, the account of this supernatural war in the Bible is the one we can trust. The prophecies of what will come are sure as well, although we won't see the pictures clearly until the events are right on top of us, assuming the Church is still here when these things come to pass.

The subject of the Nephilim/Rephaim has intrigued Christians for millennia. As we've noted, the early Church Fathers mainly agreed that Genesis 6:1–4 meant what it said: There were giants on the earth long ago, the offspring of angels and human women. Further, their spirits are the demons that still plague mankind. These spirits, and their fathers now imprisoned in Tartarus, will make up the army of the Antichrist at Armageddon.

There's no question that humans will be involved. Regardless of the timing of the Rapture, the "restrainer" of 2 Thessalonians 2:6 will be out of the way by the time of the showdown at Armageddon. There will be nothing to prevent these demonic spirits from possessing the armies of the unbelieving world. Why wouldn't the "warriors of Baal" volunteer for an assault on God's mount of assembly? Based on the low opinion of humans expressed by demons in the Bible, they consider us expendable at best. Evil spirits made their victims sick, blind, mute, and self-destructive, forcing their hosts to cut themselves and throw themselves into fire. If their human "meat suits" perish in the attack on Jerusalem, well, there are more where they came from.

Isn't it interesting that the greatest fear expressed by the demons Jesus cast out was being commanded "to depart into the abyss"?[501] That's where their supernatural parents are incarcerated. If anything, those rebel gods hate us even more than the demons do. Why? As Paul wrote, "Do you not know that we are to judge angels?"[502] Exactly how that works, I have no idea. But Paul had inside information, so count on it. Somehow, someday, you and I will be called upon to serve in what will be the most intriguing court cases in all of history. Do you think angels, especially the powerful Watcher-class entities who acted as gods of the nations, might be just a little upset about that?

Let's lay out a scenario here that might reflect the situation at the time of Armageddon. Some of this is necessarily speculative; remember, as Lord of Armies, God won't tell you and me everything in advance, because that would reveal His plans to the enemy. But here's what we can surmise from the evidence.

---

501. Luke 8:31.
502. 1 Corinthians 6:3.

An enemy from the north will arise in the last days and come against Israel. Their objective will be Zion, the *har mô'ēd*, God's mount of assembly. North in this case is not so much geographic north as it is spiritual north.

This is consistent with the Jewish tradition of evil descending upon Israel from the north. In the physical plane, the most fearsome enemies always attacked from the north. Assyria and Babylon were the two most feared, but the Syrians were always willing to ride down from Damascus to loot and pillage if they could get away with it. Invaders typically hit Israel from the north because crossing the Syrian desert to the east is foolish.

Supernatural threats to Israel likewise came from the north. Bashan, the entrance to the Canaanite underworld; Mount Hermon, El's mount of assembly and the site of the Watchers' rebellion; and Mount Zaphon, the home of Baal's palace, were all located north of Israel. This is the context for viewing the war of Gog and Magog in Ezekiel 38 and 39.

Gog is the Hebrew concept of Antichrist, the great supernatural, end-times enemy of God and Israel. Speculation linking the identity of Gog to any Russian leader is misguided. First, while there may be Russians in the coalition that comes to Jerusalem for the Battle of Armageddon, Russia as a nation is not part of Ezekiel's prophecy. With all due respect to Bible teachers who hold the Russia-is-Magog view, identifying *rosh* ("head") as Russia and Meshech as Moscow is folk etymology,[503] making connections simply because words sound the same. Language doesn't always work like that. For example, "dear" and "deer" sound the same, but please don't mistake your spouse for Bambi.

---

503. Meshech probably referred to the Mushki, people of ancient Anatolia known from Akkadian and Assyrian texts. See Derek P. Gilbert, *Last Clash of the Titans* (Crane, MO: Defender, 2018), pp. 153–154.

More importantly, the grisly sacrificial feasts of Ezekiel 39:17–20 and Revelation 19:17–21 confirm that the war of Gog ends at Armageddon. It's the same conflict. So, unless a plausible scenario includes a Russian Antichrist, and I'm not aware of one, we have to let that theory go.

We can agree, however, that the Beast that emerges from the sea in Revelation 13:1 is the Antichrist figure. A couple of things about the Beast: First, in the Bible, it's the cosmological location of the abyss. The sea represents chaos, and God subdued chaos in the first two verses of the Bible.

> In the beginning, God created the heavens and the earth. The earth was without form and void, and darkness was over the face of the deep. And the Spirit of God was hovering over the face of the waters. (Genesis 1:1–2)

The Hebrew word translated "deep" is *tehom*, which is a cognate—same word, different language—to the Akkadian *têmtum*. That, in turn, is a variant of Tiamat, the Sumerian chaos-dragon who was subdued by a warrior god, Marduk (or Enlil, in earlier versions of the story), to bring order to creation. Similar myths were common in the ancient Near East: Baal vs. Yamm, Teshub vs. Illuyanka, Zeus vs. Typhon, and the original, Yahweh vs. Leviathan.

The most obvious difference between the Bible's account and the others is that the conflict between God and chaos was over by the end of the second verse in the Bible. We see references to it later—for example, in Psalm 74:12–17—but there is no hint that God had any trouble bringing chaos to heel. Not so with the pagan stories. In every case, the warrior god needed outside help and more than one battle to subdue the sea-monster representing chaos. Chaos, being supernatural, is restrained, but not dead.

According to the Greek poet Hesiod, Zeus threw the serpentine chaos-monster Typhon into Tartarus to share a cellblock with Kronos and the Titans.[504] We're reasonably sure the Titans/Watchers are in Tartarus; Hesiod and Homer agreed on that point, and Peter confirmed it (2 Peter 2:4).

Two more data points: The Greeks believed the battle between Zeus and Typhon took place at Mount Kasios, which was their name for Baal's holy mountain, Zaphon. Scholars have long noted that Typhon's name resembles "Zaphon" so closely that they may be linked.[505] So, there is a clear connection between Zaphon, the mountain where the Antichrist/Gog will marshal his forces, and the chaos-god Typhon. And while this entity is called a "dragon" (with a hundred heads!) by Hesiod, Typhon is described elsewhere as "a hybrid between man and beast,"[506] with many wings, coils of vipers for legs, and a human head. In other words, the Greek chaos-god was a human-animal chimera, similar to the way ancient Mesopotamians described the *apkallu*, who were the Watchers/Titans.

And the Greeks remembered that this monstrous deity connected to Satan/Baal's mount of assembly was buried in Tartarus—the abyss, which is represented in the Bible by the sea. In Revelation, the Beast, which is described as a chimeric entity like the chaos-monster Typhon, emerges from the sea—the abyss—to become the Antichrist (Gog) and lead the war against God's holy mountain, Zion:

---

504. Hesiod, *The Homeric Hymns and Homerica with an English Translation by Hugh G. Evelyn-White. Theogony* (Medford, MA: Cambridge, MA, Harvard University Press; London, William Heinemann Ltd., 1914), line 869.

505. J. W. Van Henten, "Typhon." In K. van der Toorn, B. Becking, & P. W. van der Horst (Eds.), *Dictionary of Deities and Demons in the Bible* (Leiden; Boston; Köln; Grand Rapids, MI; Cambridge: Brill; Eerdmans, 1999), p. 879.

506. Apollodorus, *Library and Epitome (English)*. J. G. Frazer, Ed. (Medford, MA: Perseus Digital Library, 1921), Vol. 1, p. 47.

Then the dragon became furious with the woman and went off to make war on the rest of her offspring, on those who keep the commandments of God and hold to the testimony of Jesus. And he stood on the sand of the sea.

And I saw a beast rising out of the sea, with ten horns and seven heads, with ten diadems on its horns and blasphemous names on its heads. (Revelation 12:17–13:1)

These verses suggest that the dragon is standing on the shore when the Beast, the Antichrist/Gog, rises from the abyss. Please note that Satan/Baal's mount of assembly, Zaphon, today called Jebel al-Aqra, sits on the shore of the Mediterranean Sea.

So, could the Antichrist be the spirit of chaos, Leviathan? Yes, I think so. While the chaos-god Typhon wasn't one of the original Titans, he was believed to be their half-brother and is sometimes referred to as a Titan. And one of the great theologians of the early church, Irenaeus, thought that the best candidate for the Antichrist was "Teitan."

There is another connection: The "exceedingly terrifying" fourth beast of Daniel 7 is described as having "a mouth that spoke great things, and that seemed greater than its companions."[507] Scholars have long noted the similarities between the fourth beast and Typhon, the chaos-monster who dared challenge Zeus for control of the cosmos.[508]

It's worth asking whether an entity such as Typhon/Set/Leviathan could even be the Antichrist. The answer is yes. Satan is described as "a great red dragon, with seven heads and ten horns" in Revelation 12:3, and he entered Judas Iscariot, the betrayer of Jesus. Since Satan was able to possess or control Judas, then the Beast, whatever spirit it is, can and

---

507. See Daniel 7:7–8 and 19–22.

508. Jürg Eggler, *Influences and Traditions Underlying the Vision of Daniel 7:2–14* (Fribourg, Switzerland: University Press; Göttingen: Vandenhoeck and Ruprecht, 2000), pp. 8–9.

will do the same with another human host. What we perceive with our natural eyes is not the full picture. Remember, as Paul warned us, "even Satan disguises himself as an angel of light."

Now, what about the Titans? When the fifth of the trumpet-blowing angels sounds his horn, a star falls from heaven to earth with a key to the abyss—Tartarus. This is the return to earth of Shemihazah and the Watchers.

> He opened the shaft of the bottomless pit, and from the shaft rose smoke like the smoke of a great furnace, and the sun and the air were darkened with the smoke from the shaft. Then from the smoke came locusts on the earth, and they were given power like the power of scorpions of the earth. They were told not to harm the grass of the earth or any green plant or any tree, but only those people who do not have the seal of God on their foreheads. They were allowed to torment them for five months, but not to kill them, and their torment was like the torment of a scorpion when it stings someone. And in those days people will seek death and will not find it. They will long to die, but death will flee from them.
>
> In appearance the locusts were like horses prepared for battle: on their heads were what looked like crowns of gold; their faces were like human faces, their hair like women's hair, and their teeth like lions' teeth; they had breastplates like breastplates of iron, and the noise of their wings was like the noise of many chariots with horses rushing into battle. They have tails and stings like scorpions, and their power to hurt people for five months is in their tails. They have as king over them the angel of the bottomless pit. His name in Hebrew is Abaddon, and in Greek he is called Apollyon. (Revelation 9:2–11)

The supernatural entities known to the world thousands of years ago as Titans, Watchers, Anunnaki, and *apkallu* are the things that swarm out of the abyss in Revelation 9. That's where they are now, confined until the Judgment. They get a short time to torment humanity, taking revenge on God's prized creation for the punishment of watching their own children, the Nephilim/Rephaim, destroyed in the Flood of Noah.

Evidence: They'll be allowed to torment those without the seal of God on their foreheads for five months. Now, note the length of time the ark of Noah was on the water before it came to rest:

> The fountains of the deep and the windows of the heavens were closed, the rain from the heavens was restrained, and the waters receded from the earth continually. At the end of 150 days the waters had abated, and in the seventh month, on the seventeenth day of the month, the ark came to rest on the mountains of Ararat. (Genesis 8:2–4)

Measured in the thirty-day months of a lunar calendar, the standard in ancient Mesopotamia, 150 days is exactly five months. That's how long Shemihazah, Asael, and their colleagues watched helplessly while their children were destroyed with the rest of all flesh on the earth. In the end, they'll get 150 days to torment unrepentant humanity before Saturn's reign is brought to an end. The parallel is not coincidental, and it identifies the creatures from the abyss as the sinful angels mentioned in the epistles of Peter and Jude—the "sons of God" from Genesis 6, who were led by the entity who's at the heart of this study, Shemihazah/Saturn.

Granted, the description of the things from the pit doesn't match the Mesopotamian images of *apkallu* or Greek sculptures of the Titans. Remember, though, those entities were sent to the bottomless pit around the time of the Great Flood. Many years, perhaps a thousand or more, passed before the Sumerians began to create images of *apkallu* on cylinder seals and clay tablets. Those descriptions captured handed-down memories of supernatural human-animal hybrids, however, and that's basically what John described. The Titans, the Watchers of the Bible, return when the angel with the key opens the pit.

For those without the seal of God on their foreheads, it will literally be hell on earth.

Chapter Thirty-One

THE RISE OF APOLLYON

This leads to another piece of the end-times puzzle, and one of the reasons I decided to write this book: I believe the identity of Abaddon and Apollyon in Revelation 9:11, the angel of the bottomless pit, is Saturn—the Watcher chief Shemihazah. The opening of the bottomless pit marks his literal return to earth. It should be obvious by now that the return of old Saturn's reign will not bring the yearned-for Golden Age that's been dreamed of for more than two thousand years.

Now, there are many, including me prior to this study, who've identified Apollyon as Apollo. The similarity between the names "Apollo" and "Apollyon" is apparent, and respected Bible scholars generally agree that the similarity doesn't end there. The characteristics of Apollo as a warrior and plague-god, equated with the Semitic and Akkadian gods Resheph and Nergal, both of whom were believed to be gatekeepers to the underworld, are close enough to the meanings of the names "Abaddon" ("Destruction") and "Apollyon" ("Destroyer") that a case can be made for equating the two.

However, as we noted earlier, the prophet Habakkuk records that Resheph/Apollo followed behind God as He marched forth from Mount Sinai,[509] meaning that the plague-god was not in the abyss at least as late

---

509. Habakkuk 3:3–5.

as the time of the Exodus. Clues provided by John in Revelation 6:2 identify Apollo as the first horseman of the Apocalypse, and he's been riding the earth since Christ arrived on the throne room of God in the first century AD. It's safe to conclude that Apollo is not Apollyon.

A better fit is the entity who made Mount Hermon his *har mô'ēd* and persuaded Solomon to build a high place in his honor on the Mount of Olives, turning it into the *har ha-mašḥît*, the Mountain of the Destroyer—namely, Shemihazah, also known to history as "Saturn," "Kronos," "El," "Baal Hammon," "Dagan," "Enlil," "Assur," and "Kumarbi." Who would be king over the only entities that we know are in the abyss other than the chief of the Watchers confined there after the sin of Genesis 6? The connections between Shemihazah, El (Milcom/Molech), and Mount Hermon, the site of Shemihazah's rebellion and El's mount of assembly, point to this entity being the mysterious Abaddon/Apollyon of Revelation 9.

All of the identities worn by this rebellious Watcher are connected to the underworld: Kumarbi and the *abi*, Enlil the netherworld judge, Dagan the "Lord of the Corpse," the "two deeps" of El's abode, and the confinement of Kronos and Saturn in Tartarus. The last character in the Bible we can identify as this rebel from Genesis 6 is Abaddon/Apollyon.

Apollyon is mentioned only in Revelation 9:11. Abaddon is mentioned a few times in the Old Testament, usually in conjunction with Death (*māweth*, the Hebrew form of Mot, the Canaanite god of death) or Sheol, the Hebrew term for the underworld:

Sheol is naked before God,
and Abaddon has no covering. (Job 26:6)

Abaddon and Death say,
"We have heard a rumor of it with our ears." (Job 28:22)

Do you work wonders for the dead?
Do the departed [*rephaim*] rise up to praise you? *Selah*

Is your steadfast love declared in the grave,
or your faithfulness in Abaddon? (Psalm 88:10–11)

Sheol and Abaddon lie open before the LORD;
how much more the hearts of the children of man! (Proverbs 15:11)

Sheol and Abaddon are never satisfied,
and never satisfied are the eyes of man. (Proverbs 27:20)

The pairing of Abaddon with Sheol, the place of the dead, or Death—capitalized in Job 28 because it's a personal pronoun in that verse—is significant. In my view, Sheol/Death and Abaddon do not represent the same location or state of existence in the afterlife. I suggest that Sheol and Abaddon are roughly equivalent in Hebrew cosmology to Hades and Tartarus, respectively, in classical Greek religion. This would explain the parallels in Psalm 88:10–11. Verse 10 pairs "the dead" (Hebrew *metim*), deceased humans, with "the departed," which in Hebrew is *rephaim*—the *inhuman* dead, spirits of the semi-divine Nephilim created by the Watchers. Then verse 11 pairs "the grave," where human dead are laid to rest, with Abaddon ("Destruction"), where the Watchers are chained in darkness until the Judgment.

How can Abaddon be the name of both an entity and a place? Ask Hades. Or maybe it's similar to noble titles in the UK, where "Norfolk" can refer to a county in East Anglia or the Duke of Norfolk, depending on context.

The locust-like Titans/Watchers who emerge from the abyss in Revelation 9 are similar to the supernatural army in Joel chapter 2.[510] For some reason, a small group of Christians today aspires to join Joel's Army, mistakenly believing that they'd be serving as warriors for God. They're mistaken. Joel's Army isn't human, and it fights for the wrong team.

---

510. Compare Revelation 9:7–9 and Joel 2:4–5.

What Joel saw was the army of Gog marching to Armageddon. Bad things happen to Joel's Army. Read all the way down to verse 20:

I will remove the northerner far from you,
and drive him into a parched and desolate land,
his vanguard into the eastern sea,
and his rear guard into the western sea;
the stench and foul smell of him will rise,
for he has done great things. (Joel 2:20)

God *destroys* Joel's Army. This verse is Yahweh's prophecy of what happens on the Day of the Lord, the day when God judges the unbelieving nations of the world.

The timeline of these events is not entirely clear. The horde of Watchers swarms from the abyss when the fifth trumpet is sounded in heaven. This follows the unimaginable destruction caused by events of the first four trumpets described in Revelation 8:7–12.

The trumpet judgments begin shortly after the beginning of the seven-year period called the Great Tribulation, which is initiated by the opening of the sixth seal.[511] While it looks as though the earth is hit by a series of natural catastrophes, I suggest that all seven of the trumpet judgments refer to supernatural entities. We'll summarize them briefly:

The first trumpet (Revelation 8:7). Hail and fire follow the sounding of the first trumpet, echoing the plague against Egypt described in Exodus 9:22–25. "Hail" and "Fire" were known deities in the ancient world that are specifically described as angelic beings by the psalmist Asaph:

He gave over their cattle to the **hail**
and their flocks to **thunderbolts**.
He let loose on them his burning anger,

---

511. Revelation 6:12–17.

wrath, indignation, and distress,
a company of destroying angels.
(Psalm 78:48-49, emphasis added)

"Hail" was Barad, a god known from the northern Syrian city of Ebla as much as a thousand years before the Exodus whose names roughly translates as "(big) Chill."[512] The Hebrew word translated as "thunderbolts" is even more interesting: *reshephim* is derived from "Resheph" (Apollo), which suggests that *reshephim* was a class of supernatural being. This concept was known to the pagan neighbors of ancient Israel; in Sidon, a city on the Phoenician coast, an inscription from the fifth century BC mentions that an entire quarter of the town was named "land of the Reshephs."[513] So, it appears that the *reshephim* were sent out with Barad as a "company of destroying angels," wielding lightning and hail to execute God's judgment on Egypt. And it will happen again on a global scale when the first trumpet sounds.

The second trumpet (Revelation 8:8–9). A "great mountain, burning with fire," is thrown into the sea, destroying a third of the ships and a third of the life in the sea. Of course, you remember that "Great Mountain" was the main epithet of Enlil, one of the identities of Saturn/Shemihazah. The burning mountain of the second trumpet judgment is not this entity because he's chained up in the abyss. But John would have been familiar with 1 Enoch, which described angels as "burning mountains" in the netherworld,[514] and to Ezekiel's references to the "stones of fire" in Eden.[515]

---

512. Paolo Xella, "Barad." In K. van der Toorn, B. Becking, & P. W. van der Horst (Eds.), *Dictionary of Deities and Demons in the Bible 2nd extensively rev. ed.* (Leiden; Boston; Köln; Grand Rapids, MI; Cambridge: Brill; Eerdmans, 1999), 160.

513. Ibid.

514. 1 Enoch 21:1–10.

515. Ezekiel 28:14–16.

Whoever it is, the burning mountain of Revelation 8:8–9 is a destroying angel of great power, and he'll bring unprecedented destruction to those on the sea and in it.

The third trumpet (Revelation 8:10–11). As Tom Horn has written in *The Wormwood Prophecy* and its followup, *The Messenger*, the "great star" named Wormwood may be a physical object from space. However, it's just as likely that this is another supernatural entity tasked with carrying out God's judgment—perhaps by manipulating asteroid Apophis, which intersects earth's orbit on April 13, 2029.

The fourth trumpet (Revelation 8:12). A third of the sun, moon, and stars is "struck," or "smitten," so that "a third of their light might be darkened." Of all of the seven trumpet judgments, this one is least obviously connected to the angelic realm. Still, there is scriptural evidence to support the idea. Early in Israel's history, God gave Moses this warning:

> Beware lest you raise your eyes to heaven, and when you see the sun and the moon and the stars, all the host of heaven, you be drawn away and bow down to them and serve them, **things that the LORD your God has allotted to all the peoples under the whole heaven.** But the LORD has taken you and brought you out of the iron furnace, out of Egypt, to be a people of his own inheritance, as you are this day. (Deuteronomy 4:19-20, emphasis added)

With our modern bias, we tend to assume that God warned Moses to avoid the gods of the nations because they were imaginary deities. When you read the entire Bible, this passage gains context, and it becomes clear that He warned Moses to avoid the entities worshiped as the sun, moon, stars, and heavenly host, because God allotted them to the nations as their gods.

We dealt with the fifth trumpet, the opening of the abyss, in the previous chapter, so we'll skip it and go to the sixth:

The sixth trumpet (Revelation 9:13–21). After blowing his trumpet, the sixth angel is commanded to release the four angels bound in the Euphrates, who in turn lead an army of two hundred million that kills a third of humanity. A deep study of this section is beyond the scope of this book, but we can say with confidence that the army of two hundred million is not Chinese. Yes, China has a population of 1.7 billion, but it fields an army of under 2.2 million.[516] This trumpet, like the previous five, summons supernatural agents to carry out God's will. The description of this army is reminiscent of the descriptions of the Watchers released from the abyss and the supernatural army of Joel 2. In short, the sixth trumpet appears to summon the forces of the Antichrist to do battle at Jerusalem.

The seventh trumpet (Revelation 11:15). This triggers a series of events that culminates in the arrival of Antichrist, the Beast who emerges from the sea in Revelation 13:1. While Christian theologians have speculated on the identity of this character for nearly two thousand years, we're still searching for a consensus candidate. Many in the first-century church believed he was Nero, not just because he'd been an evil ruler who had persecuted the church, but because of a popular rumor that the emperor had not actually died in AD 68. The Nero Redivivus legend held that the disgraced ruler had staged his death and fled east to Rome's enemy, Parthia, from which he would lead a mighty army to reclaim his throne. As strange as it sounds today, this belief persisted into the fifth century![517]

Entire books have been written on this character, and we'll deal with him in a future book. Suffice it to say that the Antichrist, although he

---

516. S. Szmigiera, "The Biggest Armies in the World Ranked by Active Military Personnel in 2021." *Statista*, Mar. 30, 2021. https://www.statista.com/statistics/264443/the-worlds-largest-armies-based-on-active-force-level/, retrieved 5/25/21.

517. Augustine of Hippo, *City of God* XX.19.3. https://www.ccel.org/ccel/schaff/npnf102.iv.XX.19.html#iv.XX.19-p6, retrieved 5/25/21.

emerges from the abyss like the Watchers, is not Shemihazah/Saturn or one of the rebels from Mount Hermon.

The Watchers are given five months to vent their rage on humanity, probably toward the end of the seven-year Great Tribulation. It appears that the five-month reign of terror led by Abaddon/Apollyon, the Watcher chief Shemihazah, directly precedes the release of the four angels bound in the Euphrates and the demonic army of two hundred million that comes against Israel, slaughtering a third of humanity on the way.

Since there is no mention in Revelation of what happens at the end of the five months, we may assume that Abaddon/Apollyon (Saturn/Shemihazah) and his colleagues are part of the massive army arrayed against Israel that's destroyed at Armageddon.

Saturn's Golden Age may little more than five months—the time he and his colleagues are allowed to torment humanity followed by the time it takes the army of two hundred million to move into position. It's possible Saturn/Shemihazah knows this and doesn't care. Just as Adolf Hitler increased his efforts to exterminate the Jews within his reach in the closing days of World War II, even as his military commanders begged for resources to hold back the advancing Allied armies, the Titans/Watchers, facing their own imminent destruction, will be driven by an unimaginably intense hatred to kill as many humans as possible before the end.

Chapter Thirty-Two

THE ULTIMATE ZOMBIE APOCALYPSE

Many prophecy teachers focus on the unimaginable scale of the slaughter that takes place at Armageddon. This is often the reason the phrase "block the travelers" in Ezekiel 39:11 is taken to mean the valley is "choked with corpses." In my view, the Travelers are "blocked" because they are not resurrected at the last trump, as you will be, if you've accepted Jesus Christ as your Lord and Savior. Paul describes the evidence and the reasons for resurrection in 1 Corinthians 15:12–55. The long war between the Fallen and God revolves around whose children— the descendants of Adam and Eve or the Watchers' hybrid offspring, the Rephaim—will be resurrected into incorruptible bodies. But I digress.

What comes after the destruction of the army of Gog that confirms that this battle is one and the same as the battle of Armageddon. Ezekiel describes what can only be called a feast of the dead.

> As for you, son of man, thus says the Lord God: Speak to the birds of every sort and to all beasts of the field: "Assemble and come, gather from all around to the sacrificial feast that I am preparing for you, a great sacrificial feast on the mountains of Israel, and you shall eat flesh and drink blood. You shall eat the flesh of the mighty, and drink the blood of the princes of the earth—of rams, of lambs, and of he-goats, of bulls, all of them

fat beasts of Bashan. And you shall eat fat till you are filled, and drink blood till you are drunk, at the sacrificial feast that I am preparing for you. And you shall be filled at my table with horses and charioteers, with mighty men and all kinds of warriors," declares the Lord God. (Ezekiel 39:17–20)

It's unquestionably gory, but there are important clues in this passage. First, note the description of the army of Gog: "The mighty" is Hebrew *gibborim*, a word used in Genesis 6:4 to describe the Nephilim of the distant past. Nimrod, the would-be founder of the world's first empire who tried to build an artificial cosmic mountain at Babel, is described in Genesis 10:8 as "the first on earth to be a mighty man [*gibbôr*]." Second, the Lord's description of the "princes of the earth" as "fat beasts of Bashan" is not a literary device to describe the army of Gog as fattened animals being led to slaughter. Bashan's connection to the underworld is what's in view here.

Bashan was considered an evil place by the Hebrews, the literal entrance to the netherworld. It belonged to the Canaanite god Rapi'u, "King of Eternity." By linking the princes of the earth to Bashan, Ezekiel made a theological point: The warriors fighting for Gog will be sold out to the god of Bashan, whether his name is Rapi'u, El, Dagan, Kronos, Baal Hammon, or Saturn.

In Psalm 22:12–13, the prophesied Messiah is surrounded by "strong bulls of Bashan." Those bulls were not cattle; they were demonic warriors fighting in the army of Gog. They will fall in the Valley of the Travelers when God intervenes to save His people at a battle fought on the mountains of Israel. Even the reference to horses and charioteers in Ezekiel 39:20 recalls the description of the Rephaim in the Ugaritic texts KTU 1.20–22.

Let's refer back to the Rephaim Texts for another important detail:

To his sanctuary the saviours [Rephaim] hurried indeed,
to his sanctuary hurried indeed the divinities [*elohim*].

They harnessed the chariots;
the horses they hitched.
They mounted their chariots,
they came on their mounts.
They journeyed a day
and a second.
After sunrise on the third
the saviours arrived at the threshing-floors,
the divinities at the plantations....
Just as Anat hurries to the chase,
(and) sets the birds of heaven wheeling in flight,
(so) he slaughtered oxen and sheep,
he felled bulls
and the fattest of rams,
year-old calves,
skipping lambs,
kids.
Like silver to vagabonds [Travelers] were the olives,
(like) gold to vagabonds were the dates.
...a table (set) with fruit of the vine,
with fruit of the vine of royal quality.[518]

In this Amorite religious text written six hundred years before Ezekiel was born, the Rephaim travel until dawn of the third day to eat a
sacrificial meal on Mount Hermon, the sanctuary of El, a feast of slaughtered bulls, rams, lambs, and goats—where, as we noted in an earlier
chapter, the Rephaim were to be "revivified" by "the name of El." But
Ezekiel prophesied a day when these warriors of Baal would *become* the
bulls, rams, lambs, and goats offered up at a sacrificial feast for creation
served by Yahweh Himself.

---

518. KTU 1.22 ii 21–27, i 15–16. In Wyatt (2002), op. cit., pp. 320–322.

The imagery Ezekiel employed to describe the cataclysmic war of Gog and Magog is so intriguing that it's easy to overlook key details that the prophet salted throughout the preceding chapters. If we turn back to chapter 32, we find that the prophet offered some information about just who the *gibborim* are. This is a long section, but trust me—it's worth reading.

> In the twelfth year, in the twelfth month, on the fifteenth day of the month, the word of the Lord came to me: "Son of man, wail over the multitude of Egypt, and send them down, her and the daughters of majestic nations, to the world below, to those who have gone down to the pit:
>
> "Whom do you surpass in beauty?
> Go down and be laid to rest with the uncircumcised."
>
> They shall fall amid those who are slain by the sword. Egypt is delivered to the sword; drag her away, and all her multitudes. The mighty chiefs shall speak of them, with their helpers, out of the midst of Sheol: "They have come down, they lie still, the uncircumcised, slain by the sword....
>
> And they do not lie with the mighty, the fallen from among the uncircumcised, who went down to Sheol with their weapons of war, whose swords were laid under their heads, and whose iniquities are upon their bones; for the terror of the mighty men was in the land of the living." (Ezekiel 32:17–21, 27)

The phrase translated "mighty chiefs" in verse 21 is *'ēlê gibbôrîm*, literally, "rulers of the *gibborim*." The verse echoes Isaiah 14:9–11, where the "shades" (Rephaim) were "stirred up" to welcome the rebel from Eden when he was cast down. Remember, that's in the context of our new theory that Helel Ben Shachar of Isaiah 14, generally understood to be Lucifer/Satan, was actually the Watcher chief Shemihazah (Saturn/Kronos, et al), who led the rebellion that created the "shades."

Verse 27 deserves special attention. The Hebrew behind the words, "the mighty, the fallen," is *gibbôrîm nōphelîm*. While it's tempting to read Nephilim for "the fallen," that doesn't quite work. The same Hebrew word appears in verse 22, in the phrase "fallen by the sword."[519] Swapping "Nephilim" for *nōphelîm* there yields "Nephilim by the sword," and that makes no sense.

But Ezekiel doesn't need Nephilim in that verse to make his point. The English Standard Version is usually my preferred translation, but circumcision is not the point of this verse. A more accurate reading is, "And they do not lie with the fallen heroes [*gibbôrîm*] of ancient times."[520] The Jewish translators of the Septuagint, who produced a Greek version of the Old Testament from Hebrew texts around 200 BC, understood the passage the same way and rendered the phrase "the giants that fell of old."

According to Dr. Daniel Block, who has written an excellent scholarly commentary on the book of Ezekiel, argues that this passage is the prophet telling us that these "chiefs of the Gibborim" hold special status in the underworld:

> According to Ezekiel 32:21, these heroic personages speak from the midst of Sheol, which may suggest that they are located in the heart of the netherworld, perhaps a more honorable assignment than "the remotest recesses of the pit," where the uncircumcised and those who have fallen by the sword lie. The description in v. 27 indicates that these individuals have indeed been afforded

519. Michael S. Heiser, "Sheol: The OT 'Bad Place'?" Sept. 6, 2009, http://drmsh.com/sheol-the-ot-bad-place/, retrieved 5/20/21.

520. The technical explanation of the underlying Hebrew boils down to this: It appears the Masoretic text, on which most English translations are based, substituted (or miscopied) *mē 'ărēlîm* ("uncircumcised") for the original *mē 'ôlām* ("ancient times"). See Daniel Block, "Beyond the Grave: Ezekiel's Vision of Death and Afterlife." *Bulletin for Biblical Research* 2 (1992), p. 125, especially note #73.

noble burials. There they lie with their weapons of war, their swords laid under their heads and their shields placed upon their bones. Ancient burial customs in which personal items and symbols of status were buried with the corpses of the deceased provide the source of this image.

Ezekiel's use of the antediluvian heroic traditions at this point is shocking. How could the prophet possibly perceive these men as noble and hold them up as honorable residents of Sheol, when his own religious tradition presents them as the epitome of wickedness, corruption, and violence (Gen[esis] 6:5, 11–12)?[521]

Dr. Block may be reading into the text a more favorable depiction of the *gibborim* than Ezekiel intended. I believe the prophet meant only that the *gibborim*—the spirits of the Rephaim/Nephilim, who are the Travelers of Ezekiel 39:11—were fundamentally different in substance from the run-of-the-mill dead. The *gibborim* of Ezekiel 32 have status in the underworld because they are the spirits of human-angel hybrids, not because they're noble and honorable. And their prophesied end comes in the place that bears their name, the Valley of the Travelers, because Ezekiel knew very well what those entities are—the demonic spirits of the ancient Rephaim/Nephilim.

Now let's connect the war of Gog and Magog to Armageddon. The same gruesome feast described in Ezekiel 39:17–20 was prophesied by John:

Then I saw an angel standing in the sun, and with a loud voice he called to all the birds that fly directly overhead, "Come, gather for the great supper of God, to eat the flesh of kings, the flesh of captains, the flesh of mighty men, the flesh of horses and their riders, and the flesh of all men, both free and slave, both small and great." And I saw the beast and the kings of the earth with

521. Ibid.

their armies gathered to make war against him who was sitting on the horse and against his army. And the beast was captured, and with it the false prophet who in its presence had done the signs by which he deceived those who had received the mark of the beast and those who worshiped its image. These two were thrown alive into the lake of fire that burns with sulfur. And the rest were slain by the sword that came from the mouth of him who was sitting on the horse, and all the birds were gorged with their flesh. (Revelation 19:17–21)

The angel's invitation to the "great supper of God" is the same one issued by God in Ezekiel 39. The parallels between the two are too close to be coincidental. The similarities have been noted for centuries by Bible scholars like Matthew Henry,[522] E. W. Bullinger,[523] A. R. Fausset,[524] and others.

As a conscientious priest who lived according to the Law, Ezekiel must have been horrified by this repugnant feast! He protested mightily when God directed him to bake his bread over a fire built from human dung:

Then I said, "Ah, Lord GOD! Behold, I have never defiled myself. From my youth up till now I have never eaten what died of itself or was torn by beasts, nor has tainted meat come into my mouth." (Ezekiel 4:14)

522. Matthew Henry, *Matthew Henry Commentary on the Whole Bible*. https://www.biblestudytools.com/commentaries/matthew-henry-complete/ezekiel/39.html, retrieved 5/11/21.

523. E. W. Bullinger, *Commentary on Revelation* (1909). http://www.ccel.org/ccel/bullinger/apocalypse.xix.html?highlight=xxxix#highlight, retrieved 5/11/21.

524. Robert Jamieson, A. R. Fausset, & David Brown, *Commentary Critical and Explanatory on the Whole Bible* (1871). https://www.blueletterbible.org/Comm/jfb/Eze/Eze_039.cfm?a=841017, retrieved 5/11/21.

But at Armageddon, Yahweh Himself serves the ultimate taboo, human flesh and blood, as a sacrificial feast to unclean animals, scavengers. As Daniel Block notes, there is something unique about this for God to be so extreme:

> [The banquet] is designated a *zebaḥ*, which derives from a root meaning "to slaughter," and seems to have had reference to any sacrifices that were burned on an altar (*mizbēaḥ*). More than one kind of *zebaḥ* was celebrated in Israel, but it was generally assumed that this meal was eaten in the presence of Yahweh (*lipnê yhwh*), that is, as his guest.... Ezekiel's designation of this banquet as a *zebaḥ* classifies it as a ritual event. But by altering all the roles he grossly caricatures the normal image of a *zebaḥ*. In place of a human worshiper slaughtering animals in the presence of Yahweh, Yahweh slaughters humans for the sake of animals, who gather from all over the world (*missābîb*) for this gigantic celebration (*zebaḥ gādôl*) on the mountains of Israel. The battlefield has been transformed into a huge sacrificial table.
>
> Second, the invitation describes the menu. The last statement of v. 17 is thematic, calling on the participants to partake of flesh and blood, a merismic expression for carcasses as wholes. V. 18 specifies these as the flesh of heroic figures (*gibbôrîm*) and the blood of the princes of the earth (*něśî'ê hā'āreṣ*), which are to be devoured like fare normally served at a *zebaḥ* table: rams (*'êlîm*), lambs (*kārîm*), male goats (*'attûdîm*), bulls (*pārîm*), and the fatlings of Bashan (*měrî'ê bāšān*). **These terms are obviously not used literally, but as animal designations for nobility.**[525] (Emphasis added)

---

525. Daniel I. Block, *The Book of Ezekiel, Chapters 25–48* (Grand Rapids, MI: Wm. B. Eerdmans Publishing Co., 1997), pp. 475–476.

Ezekiel highlighted the nobility of the *gibborim* who will be slaughtered to provide this grisly ritual feast for the same reason he noted the special status of the *gibborim* of the underworld—they're fundamentally different from ordinary human soldiers. Gog's army is made up of demonic "warriors of Baal," the Rephaim.

Put another way, Ezekiel's prophecy describes an army that's possessed by the spirits of the Nephilim destroyed in the Flood, the semi-divine children of Shemihazah/Saturn and his co-conspirators. The forces of the Antichrist at Armageddon will literally be an army of the evil dead, and the battle will be, in a real sense, the ultimate zombie apocalypse.

As Dr. Block notes, "The literary image sketched here must have been shocking for a person as sensitive to cultic matters as Ezekiel."[526] But the conflict leading up to this repulsive feast is not just one more battle in a long list of battles fought through the ages. In this war, a supernaturally empowered army led by a creature from the abyss lays siege to God's holy mountain.

John's account of the aftermath of Armageddon follows Ezekiel's description of the Gog-Magog war because they describe the same event. As Bullinger wrote, "It is absurd to talk about 'John borrowing from Ezekiel,' as so many say. There is no 'borrowing' in the matter. Both prophecies are 'given by inspiration of God.'"[527] The war of Gog and Magog is Armageddon, and it will be fought at Jerusalem for control of Zion, God's mount of assembly, and it results in the reversal of an ancient Amorite ritual. Instead of arriving at the *har mô'ēd* for a ritual meal in their honor, the Rephaim become a sacrificial feast for all of creation.

And once again, Saturn/Shemihazah will see his children fall before the power of Yahweh.

---

526. Ibid., p. 477.
527. Bullinger, op. cit.

Chapter Thirty-Three

CONCLUSION

Saturn has escaped notice by most Christians. Most of us don't believe the small-*g* gods of the pagans even exist, and Saturn isn't even mentioned by that name in the Bible.

I hope that by this point in the book, you recognize that this character not only exists, but also that he's played a much larger role in human history than you imagined. Since prehistoric times, he's been called:

- **Shemihazah:** Chief of the Watchers who rebelled and made a mutual pact on Mount Hermon to corrupt humanity genetically and through the introduction of forbidden knowledge; the archangel Michael was tasked with binding Shemihazah and his colleagues "in the valleys of the earth" until the day of Judgment.
- **Kumarbi:** Father of the gods of the Hurrian pantheon who overthrew his father, the sky-god Anu, and was overthrown in turn by the storm-god Teshub and confined to the netherworld; contact with Kumarbi and other netherworld spirits was made through a ritual pit called the *abi*, first documented around 3500 BC and still used by the Hebrews, who called it an ôb, 2,500 years later.

- **El:** Creator-god of the Canaanites who held court on Mount Hermon with his consort and seventy sons; his epithet, "Milcom" ("king"), was twisted by the Hebrews into "Molech," connecting El to the underworld and child sacrifice.
- **Enlil:** Name derives from *il-ilû* ("god of gods"); became chief god of Mesopotamia around the middle of the third millennium BC, probably due to the influence of the Akkadians and Amorites; he was later replaced by Marduk, who consigned Enlil to the netherworld.
- **Dagan:** Later called "Dagon," chief god of the Amorites along the Euphrates and the Philistines from the time of the Judges through the time of David and Solomon; epithet *bēl pagrê* ("lord of the corpse" or "lord of the dead") connects Dagan to the netherworld.
- **Kronos:** King of the Titans who overthrew his father, the sky-god Ouranos, castrating him with a sickle, and later overthrown by his son, the storm-god Zeus, and confined to Tartarus; swallowed his children to try to prevent their rebellion; name probably derives from Semitic *qeren* ("horned one").
- **Baal Hammon:** Chief god of the Phoenicians best remembered for accepting child sacrifice; name means "lord of the Amanus," a mountain range in southeast Turkey near Mount Zaphon, the mountain sacred to the storm-god Baal.
- **Saturn:** The Roman name for "Kronos" and "Baal Hammon"; like Kronos and Kumarbi, rebelled against his father, the sky-god Caelus, and was deposed by his son, the storm-god Jupiter; later released from Tartarus and settled in Italy to rule over a Golden Age that later Romans thought had returned with the rise to power of Caesar Augustus in the first century BC.

After the Flood, the cult inspired by Shemihazah, probably through the influence of his demonic offspring, spread from the Ararat Plain nearly six thousand years ago. It reached northern Mesopotamia by

3500 BC, where he was worshiped by the Hurrians as Kumarbi. By the middle of the next millennium, the cult of the Watcher chief, under the name "El," had entered the Levant and penetrated as far south as Akkad. By 2300 BC, the Akkadians brought Enlil (*il-ilû*) to Sumer as "the" god, while the great king Sargon of Akkad paid homage to another of the god's identities, Dagan, at Tuttul on the Euphrates.

When the Israelites established themselves in what had been Canaan, they were confronted by multiple aspects of the fallen Watcher: El of the Canaanites, Milcom/Molech ("king") of the Ammonites, and probably Baal-Peor in Moab. When Assyria emerged as the dominant power in Mesopotamia, their chief god Assur was yet one more face worn by Shemihazah.

In the second half of the first millennium BC, the cult of this god moved west across the Mediterranean as Kronos of the Greeks, Baal Hammon of the Phoenicians, and Saturn of the Romans.

The Roman poet Virgil wrote a piece around 40 BC that foretold a new Golden Age with the return of "old Saturn's reign." This imagery was drawn from the work of the Greek poet Hesiod, who lived between about 750 BC and 650 BC, around the same time as the prophet Isaiah. Hesiod described an era when life was good and easy, when Kronos ruled in heaven. The Golden Age was followed by periods of increasing strife and difficulty called the silver, bronze, and iron ages.

The Greek poets Homer and Hesiod called the men of the Golden Age *meropes anthrôpoi*, a term derived from the Semitic root *rp'*, which is behind the word "Rephaim." In other words, the men of the Golden Age were demigods—by definition, Nephilim. Like the Hebrews and early Christian church, the Greeks knew that the spirits of the demigod heroes of old became *daimones* upon their death, but the *daimones* of Greece were very different from the demons of Jewish and Christian cosmology.

But this is the world that some modern secret societies and occultists want to recreate. They dream of bringing ushering in a new Golden Age. Prominent astrologers point to the conjunction of Saturn and Jupiter on

December 21, 2020 as marking the beginning of this new era, bringing us fully into the Age of Aquarius, an astrological sign ruled by Saturn. As they see it, the conjunction was a spiritual transfer of power—the return of Saturn to his rightful place atop the Capitoline Hill, and with it, the dawn of a new age of ease and plenty.

Virgil has been credited with oracular ability since very soon after he wrote *Eclogue IV*. Some believed that he transcribed genuine oracles from the Cumaean Sibyl; others, including many Christians, have considered Virgil an authentic, albeit pagan, prophet.

This entity has been playing a very long game, and not entirely by choice; it's a safe guess that Saturn/Shemihazah didn't expect to be thrown into the abyss, a story that I believe is described in parallel Scriptures found in Ezekiel 28:11–19 and Isaiah 14:3–23. These have traditionally been understood as polemics against Satan for his deception that lured Adam and Eve into sin. While that's possible, nothing in Ezekiel 28 or Isaiah 14 explicitly connect the story of the rebel's ejection from Eden to the sin of Adam and Eve. Identifying the divine rebel in Ezekiel and Isaiah as Shemihazah resolves the question of how Satan could be both a *nachash* ("serpent"), used elsewhere in the Old Testament interchangeably with *saraph*, and a "guardian cherub." Seraphim and cherubim are described very differently by Isaiah and Ezekiel,[528] and none of the mentions of the cherubim in the Bible hint at anything serpentine.

If I am correct in identifying the rebel of Ezekiel 28 and Isaiah 14 as Shemihazah, the characterization of the Watcher chief by the prophets hints at the role he must have played in the early days of God's royal court. The nine precious stones of his covering are similar, though not identical, to the twelve stones of the high priest's ephod.[529] But it must be noted that the Septuagint translation does include the ephod stones

---

528. Compare Isaiah 6:2 for a description of the seraphim to Ezekiel 1:5–14 and 10:9–14 for a portrayal of the cherubim.

529. Leslie C. Allen, Ezekiel 20–48, *Word Biblical Commentary* (Dallas: Word, Inc., 1990), pp. xxix, 94.

described in Exodus 28:17–20, suggesting that the older Hebrew Scriptures drew an explicit connection between this rebel on the mountain of God and the high priest of God's people on earth.

Consider the possibility: Shemihazah, chief of the Watchers, the "signet" or "sealer of perfection," may have been the high priest in Eden before leading his followers to earth to establish his own kingdom.

Over the long centuries, using his demonic minions—spirits of the demigod children he watched die in the Flood—to influence humanity, his cult never died. Even as the followers of Christ spread the gospel throughout the Mediterranean world, Greece, Rome, and Phoenicia continued the celebrate the rites of Kronos, Saturn, and Baal Hammon. And, as I wrote in *Bad Moon Rising*, the gods of Mesopotamia banded together in a coalition to counter Christ's unexpected resurrection and formed a new religion headed by "the" god, *al-ilah*—Allah.

He's been worshiped by many names over the ages, but always as creator, father of the gods, or "the king." This is consistent with the pride and ambition described by Ezekiel and Isaiah of a being of unimaginable power, wisdom, and beauty who aspired to make himself greater than God.

A day is coming when this entity returns to the earth. Shemihazah will live up to the names he was given by John in Revelation 9: Abaddon and Apollyon, "the Destroyer." It will be a horrific day for those here to see it—the beginning of five months of unimaginable torment, a period that echoes the pivotal one hundred fifty days of Noah's Flood that cleansed the earth of Nephilim.

What are the relationships between Abaddon/Apollyon, the Antichrist, and Satan? I believe they are, respectively: the Watcher chief Shemihazah; the chaos-dragon Leviathan; and the entity who revealed himself to the world as the storm-god Baal, Zeus, and Jupiter. The book of Revelation depicts Satan as the superior officer of the three in the final war of the ages. Drawing on descriptions of the Antichrist figure in Daniel 7:23–26 and 11:36–45, it appears that Leviathan serves as Satan's commander-in-chief in the war that leads to Armageddon. But what about Apollyon—Shemihazah/Saturn?

The Bible tells us nothing about the end of Saturn's reign. The torture that he and the Watchers/Titans inflict on humanity stops after five months, but we're not told how or why. John simply moves on to describing the release of the four angels bound in the Euphrates and the terrifying supernatural army of two hundred million that slaughters a third of humanity. It's possible that the Shemihazah and the rebel Watchers are part of this army of evil spirits that comes to do battle at Jerusalem.

And it's probable that the reason we don't know how Shemihazah and the Watchers meet their end is because God hasn't shown all His cards. He's not called LORD of Hosts ("Yahweh of Armies") for nothing. We shouldn't expect the greatest General in history to reveal His military strategy to the Enemy.

What we do know for certain is this: He has not only planned the defeat of these rebels, but He'll do it in a way that shows to one and all the futility of their schemes.

> He who sits in the heavens laughs;
> the LORD holds them in derision.
> Then he will speak to them in his wrath,
> and terrify them in his fury, saying,
> "As for me, I have set my King
> on Zion, my holy hill." (Psalm 2:4–6)

This war is for control of God's mount of assembly, Zion. Shemihazah, old Saturn, wanted to create his own mount of assembly, his *har môʿēd*, in the "heights of the north." When that failed, the aging Solomon was persuaded by Shemihazah/Milcom to erect a high place on the Mount of Olives, looking down on the Temple.

It's no coincidence that the pivotal events of the final weeks of Jesus' time on earth took place on three key mountains: Hermon, the site of Shemihazah's rebellion, where Jesus declared His divinity and was transfigured into a being of light; the Mount of Olives, called the Mount of the Destroyer because of Solomon's desecration, where Jesus delivered the Olivet Discourse and was arrested, crucified, buried, resurrected, and caught up to heaven forty days later; and the Temple Mount, the ultimate prize in this long war, where Jesus spent much of His final week preaching, teaching, and healing.

The Watchers are in Tartarus now, but they are loosed for five months at the end. With their demonic offspring and the rest of the rebel gods who still walk the earth, the kings of the earth will be drawn into the greatest, most terrible battle the world has ever known: Armageddon.

It is then that the prophesied judgment of the gods begins:

On that day the Lord will punish
the host of heaven, in heaven,
and the kings of the earth, on the earth.
They will be gathered together
as prisoners in a pit;
they will be shut up in a prison,
and after many days they will be punished.
Then the moon will be confounded
and the sun ashamed,
for the LORD of hosts reigns
on Mount Zion and in Jerusalem,
and his glory will be before his elders. (Isaiah 24:21–23)

Saturn's reign will be short, and it will be bloody. The Golden Age hoped for by occultists, secret societies, and New Agers will last at least five months, and perhaps a little longer. It ends at Armageddon if not before. And it will be hell on earth.

You don't need to be here to witness the death and destruction. Your ticket out is the gospel of Jesus Christ:

Now I would remind you, brothers, of the gospel I preached
to you, which you received, in which you stand, and by which

you are being saved, if you hold fast to the word I preached to
you—unless you believed in vain.

For I delivered to you as of first importance what I also
received: that **Christ died for our sins in accordance with the
Scriptures, that he was buried, that he was raised on the third
day in accordance with the Scriptures...** (1 Corinthians 15:1–
4, emphasis added)

That's it. That is the gospel by which we are saved. Just accept the
historic fact of the death and resurrection of Jesus Christ, through which
He bought you back from Saturn, Satan, and the rest of their co-conspirators in the long war to bring down the throne of God.

Salvation is that simple, and that profound. Christ's resurrection on
the third day, a reversal of the pagan ritual for the Rephaim, is the template for all of us who have accepted Him as our Lord:

Just as we have borne the image of the man of dust [Adam], we
shall also bear the image of the man of heaven [Jesus].

I tell you this, brothers: flesh and blood cannot inherit the
kingdom of God, nor does the perishable inherit the imperishable. Behold! I tell you a mystery. We shall not all sleep, but we
shall all be changed, in a moment, in the twinkling of an eye,
at the last trumpet. For the trumpet will sound, and the dead
will be raised imperishable, and we shall be changed. For this
perishable body must put on the imperishable, and this mortal
body must put on immortality. When the perishable puts on
the imperishable, and the mortal puts on immortality, then shall
come to pass the saying that is written:

"Death is swallowed up in victory."
"O death, where is your victory?
O death, where is your sting?" (1 Corinthians 15:49–55)

ABOUT THE AUTHOR

Derek P. Gilbert hosts the daily news analysis program *Five in Ten* for SkyWatchTV and co-hosts the weekly video programs *SciFriday* and *Unraveling Revelation* with his wife, author and analyst Sharon K. Gilbert. In 2021, they will launch a new weekly program for SkyWatchTV, *The Bible's Greatest Mysteries*.

Derek is the author of the groundbreaking books *Bad Moon Rising*, an analysis of the spiritual forces behind Islam; *The Great Inception*; and *Last Clash of the Titans*.

He's also the coauthor with Sharon K. Gilbert of *Giants, Gods & Dragons*, a fresh take on end-times prophecy that identifies the entities traditionally called the Four Horsemen of the Apocalypse, and *Veneration*, which exposes the influence of the pagan cult of the dead in ancient Israel (and on the prophecies of Isaiah and Ezekiel). Since 2014, the Gilberts produced a weekly audio series of Bible studies called *Gilbert House Fellowship*, available online at www.gilberthouse.org.

Derek has also coauthored with Josh Peck *The Day the Earth Stands Still*, a timely book on the modern UFO phenomenon that reveals, for the first time, the occult origins of the belief in "ancient aliens."

Made in the USA
Middletown, DE
05 October 2024

62034797R00210